Farev
Last (

Farewell to the Last Golden Era

The Yankees, the Pirates and the 1960 Baseball Season

BILL MORALES

GV863.A1 M626 2011
Morales, Rubil.
Farewell to the last golden era : the Yankees, the Pirates and the 1960 baseball season
Jefferson, N.C. : McFarland

McFarland & Company, Inc., Publishers
Jefferson, North Carolina, and London

All photographs are courtesy of the National Baseball Hall of Fame Library, Cooperstown, New York

LIBRARY OF CONGRESS ONLINE CATALOG DATA

Morales, Rubil.
Farewell to the last golden era : the Yankees, the Pirates and the 1960 baseball season / Bill Morales.
p. cm.
Includes bibliographical references and index.

ISBN 978-0-7864-6327-5
softcover : 50# alkaline paper ♾

1. New York Yankees (Baseball team) — History — 20th century. 2. Pittsburgh Pirates (Baseball team) — History — 20th century. 3. World Series (Baseball) (1960). 4. Baseball — United States — History — 20th century. I. Title.
2011021775

BRITISH LIBRARY CATALOGUING DATA ARE AVAILABLE

© 2011 Rubil Morales. All rights reserved

No part of this book may be reproduced or transmitted in any form or by any means, electronic or mechanical, including photocopying or recording, or by any information storage and retrieval system, without permission in writing from the publisher.

On the cover: Maris, Mazeroski and Mantle above a depiction of Pittsburgh's Forbes Field

Manufactured in the United States of America

McFarland & Company, Inc., Publishers
Box 611, Jefferson, North Carolina 28640
www.mcfarlandpub.com

In Memoriam

Tony La Perla (1917–1983)
Sal La Perla (1929–1993)

Table of Contents

Preface

The 1960 Major League Baseball season came to an abrupt end at precisely 3:36:30 P.M. Eastern Standard Time on Thursday, October 13, with Yogi Berra watching forlornly as a ball off the bat of Bill Mazeroski disappeared over the left field wall at Forbes Field. The underdog Pittsburgh Pirates had won in stunning fashion over the mighty New York Yankees, making Maz forever part of baseball lore. But with the hindsight of fifty years, it is clear that something more than another baseball season had come to a close. The 1960 season also marked the end of an era of the National Pastime.

Major League Baseball as a sixteen-team configuration — its Golden Age — lasted between 1901 and 1960. This Golden Age can be divided into three eras. The first began with the formation of the American League as a rival to the long-established National League in 1901, was sparked by the brilliant play of Ty Cobb and Honus Wagner, and ended with the infamous Black Sox scandal in 1919. The second, between 1920 and 1939, was bracketed by the emergence of Babe Ruth as the game's gate attraction par excellence and the retirement of fellow Yankee great Lou Gehrig. The third, between 1939 and 1960, began with the emergence of the Yankee Clipper, Joe DiMaggio, as the game's predominant name, ran through World War II, witnessed Jackie Robinson's breaking of the color barrier, and ended with the retirement of Boston's Splendid Splinter, Ted Williams. In this book, I tell the story of the final year of that third, and last, golden era.

History, it is said, is written from the point of view of the winners. This book is no exception. More than anything else, the following pages tell the story of the New York Yankees and the Pittsburgh Pirates, and the events that led to Bill Mazeroski's famous World Series home run. But there was more to the 1960 season than Pittsburgh and New York. Going on the road with the Yankees and Pirates, we can readily see the changes, large and small, that would characterize the sport in the coming decades: surnames on the backs of uniforms, exploding scoreboards, the increasing impact of international players, and, foremost of all, expansion.

The geography of Major League Baseball was a dominant topic of debate throughout 1960. As the Yankees and Pirates were battling their way toward their October clash, a third major league was struggling to be born. Branch Rickey's Continental League didn't survive, but out of this struggle came the first venture at expansion, and with it a new, albeit Gilded Age, of Major League Baseball. I say "Gilded" because by 1960 the ascendancy of professional football as the National Pastime was already underway. The past and future of American professional sports intersected in the year of Bill Mazeroski's home run.

In writing this book, I have tried to be as faithful to the period as possible. For example, the reader will notice that while I use the word "defense" and, occasionally, "offense," I avoid the more modern usage of "the offense" and "the defense"—what is more telling of football's hegemony than its co-opting of baseball's language with that of its own? I also refer to players of Hispanic descent as "Latins" and not "Latinos," again in an attempt to remain faithful to the times. I admit to one deviation: blacks are referred to as African Americans rather than as Negroes.

Chapter One

"As inevitable as tomorrow — but not as imminent"

When it opened on Miami Beach's famed Gold Coast in December 1954, the $13 million Fontainebleau was the latest in modern luxury hotels. Designed by the architect Morris Lapidus and built on the site of the old Firestone estate on Collins Avenue, the Fontainebleau was a modernist marriage of form and function, its semi-circular bulk made to capture the cool breezes blowing in from the Atlantic Ocean. Outside, on the fourteen-acre grounds, were other marvels: an Olympic size swimming pool, a smaller kids' pool, and an ice rink. The inside of the 565-room hotel was done in a French motif, with the furniture French provincial. Luxury suites went for $175 a night and featured built-in ironing boards as well as bidets. A fake fireplace was installed in the Presidential suite. A staff of 900 people serviced a clientele that ranged from foreign dignitaries and their entourages to the gaggle of tourists taking advantage of package deals. The economic recession of 1958 had put a damper on things, but by February 1959 the Fontainebleau was once again in full swing. Cadillac convertibles were rolling up to the entrance and pampered women were modeling mink stoles in every pastel shade. The management, regretfully, was turning away guests for lack of room.

The growing demand for space had inspired the Fontainebleau's owner, Ben Novack, to begin building a fourteen-story addition, featuring an auditorium and hotel annex. The annex would increase the total number of rooms to 1000, almost doubling the current capacity. There had been one big stumbling block to these plans. Sunshine was Miami Beach's most treasured commodity and the projected wing would have cast the Eden

Roc Hotel, located next to the Fontainebleau on Collins Avenue, in shadow by the early afternoon. The Miami City Council came to the Eden Roc's rescue, passing an ordinance requiring hotel wings to be set back so as to protect adjoining properties. The dispute eventually went all the way to the Florida Supreme Court, which overturned the Miami Beach ordinance. The Fontainebleau expansion continued forward.

The question of expansion was also very much on the minds of Major League Baseball executives as they arrived at the Fontainebleau for their annual Winter Meetings in the first week of December 1959. Where and when expansion would occur, however, were questions that neither Baseball Commissioner Ford Frick nor league presidents Warren Giles and Joe Cronin were quite prepared to answer. But it was not a topic they had the luxury of ignoring. You see, like the Eden Roc Hotel, they also had a shadow looming over them.

In 1960, Major League Baseball consisted of sixteen professional teams. The senior circuit, the National League of Professional Baseball Clubs (established in 1876), had franchises in Philadelphia, Pittsburgh, Cincinnati, Chicago, Milwaukee, St. Louis, Los Angles, and San Francisco. The junior circuit, the American League of Professional Baseball Clubs (established in 1901), operated in Boston, New York, Baltimore, Washington, Cleveland, Detroit, Chicago, and Kansas City. Each and every team was located near a major body of water: the Atlantic Coast (New York, Boston, and Baltimore); the Pacific Coast (San Francisco and Los Angeles); the Delaware and Potomac Rivers (Philadelphia and Washington); the Ohio River (Cincinnati and Pittsburgh); the Mississippi and Missouri Rivers (St. Louis and Kansas City); and the Great Lakes (Chicago, Detroit, Cleveland, and Milwaukee). Major League Baseball had yet to venture into the Arizona desert, the Texas plains, or the Rocky Mountains.

For the first fifty-two years of the modern era, which began in 1901, there had been no teams west of the Mississippi River, or south of the Potomac and Ohio Rivers. This reflected the growth of industrialization and urbanization that occurred in the United States during the second half of the nineteenth century. With the exception of the nation's capital, Washington, D.C., the original Major League cities were all, to some degree or another, industrial cities; the industries they supported (oil, steel, automobile manufacturing, textiles, etc.) were located in the Northeast, not in the South or West. So too were the major transportation, communication, and financial links. As the pace of industrialization progressed, increasing numbers of native-born Americans abandoned the farm for the city, knocking elbows with immigrants from Southern and Eastern Europe. Baseball provided a pastime for one and all, the ball field's green grasses a wistful reminder of an agrarian past no longer part of their daily existence. In America, the second Industrial Revolution, mass society, and professional baseball grew together, with all its accompanying prejudices.

After World War II, Major League Baseball finally broke out of its northeastern quadrant. In the National League, the Boston Braves moved to Milwaukee in 1953; in 1958 the Brooklyn Dodgers and New York Giants found new homes in Los Angeles and San Francisco, respectively. In the American League, the Philadelphia Athletics abandoned the City of Brotherly Love for Kansas City in 1955. The only exception to this western flight was the AL franchise in St. Louis, the Browns, which trekked in an easterly direction to become the Baltimore Orioles in 1954. These moves were all undertaken by teams located in cities which had traditionally supported two Major League teams. The internal emigration of Americans from cities to the new middle class suburbs in the late 1940s and 1950s, coupled with the advent of television, had resulted in decreased attendance at these urban ballparks. The weaker franchises in these cities (except for the Browns) decided to seek a new fan base, and consequently, greater fortunes in the West. The urban areas on the far side of the Mississippi River, wanting the status symbol of a big league team, eagerly embraced them.

Still, as the year 1960 beckoned, Major League Baseball had not quite caught up with the demographic facts of life. The nation's population had more than doubled since 1901 (from 76 million to 179 million) but the Majors still held at sixteen franchises. To be sure, ten of those teams were located in cities that ranked among the ten most populated urban areas of the United States: 1. New York, 2. Chicago, 3. Los Angeles, 4. Philadelphia, 5. Detroit, 6. Baltimore, 8. Cleveland, 9. Washington, D.C., 10. St. Louis. Milwaukee, San Francisco, and Boston were ranked eleventh, twelfth, and thirteenth, respectively. But Pittsburgh, the eleventh largest city in 1900, now ranked sixteenth. Trailing behind were Cincinnati (twenty-first) and Kansas City (twenty-seventh). Meanwhile, Houston, the seventh largest city in the country, had no big league team. Neither did Dallas (ranked number fourteen) or the Twin Cities of Minneapolis-St. Paul, which together would have comprised the ninth largest metropolis in the U.S. The biggest anomaly of all, however, was New York City. Despite a population of 7.8 million, it had only one franchise; Chicago, with less than half of New York's population, supported *two* Major League teams.[1]

But the Major League Baseball executives who gathered for the Winter Meetings had other things on their minds. They strolled through the Fontainebleau gardens, sunned themselves by the pool, and played a round or two of golf. On Sunday, December 6, they met with the major league player representatives, led by the NL's Robin Roberts and the AL's Harvey Kuenn, at the nearby Indian Creek Country Club. It was later described as being "one of the most amicable meetings on record."[2] The owners agreed to improve ballpark conditions in certain cities, reduce scheduling problems, and hike up the players' meal money allowance to $10 a day (the owners being fully appreciative of the rising cost of living). The players, for their part, endorsed Commissioner Frick's plans for a new television deal.

For some time now, Commissioner Frick had been urging NL president Warren Giles and AL chief Joe Cronin to come up with plans for adding new franchises. However, as the plenary meetings began at the Fontainbleau on Monday, December 7, expansion remained the object of strong resistance on the part of the Lords of Baseball. Giles declared that the NL had no plans whatsoever in that regard. Cronin refused to commit the AL without some reciprocal action on the part of the senior circuit. The unwillingness of the established leagues to take the initiative on expansion left the door open for other possibilities.

On the afternoon of December 7, a seventy-eight-year-old resident of Pittsburgh, Pennsylvania, checked into the Fontainebleau Hotel. He was the fabled Branch Wesley Rickey, nicknamed the Mahatma, Major League catcher, manager, and front office executive par excellence, who had invented the farm system with the St. Louis Cardinals in the early 1920s and had brought Jackie Robinson to the Brooklyn Dodgers in 1947. Rickey had been out of baseball since ceding his post as the general manager of the Pittsburgh Pirates, a club he ran between 1950 and 1955. Now he was back, his arrival in Miami coinciding with the annual Winter Meetings being held at the Fontainebleau. In truth, for the Lords of Baseball, the Mahatma's presence in the midst of this conference was about as welcome as Virgil Sollozzo attending a meeting of the New York five families. The reason for this uneasiness was Rickey's newest venture: a third major league.

Since his retirement, the Mahatma had been observing the progress of Major League Baseball with an increasing sense of doom. "Baseball may die in the 1960s," he warned. The short-sighted men who ran the game continued to alienate fans by allowing stadiums to deteriorate and refusing to furnish adequate parking facilities. But more than anything else, Rickey claimed, the problem was that the National Pastime was "no longer national." The nation's population had more than doubled since 1900 with no reciprocal expansion of Major League teams. At least 32 cities, he argued, "can and should play."[3] Therefore, he had put his considerable fame and prestige behind the new Continental League, projected to begin operations in 1961.

On Tuesday, December 8, the Continental League took center stage at the Fontainebleau. With Rickey at the press conference were the executives representing the new loop's five maiden entries: Jack Kent Cooke of Toronto, Bob Howsam of Denver, Craig Cullinan of Houston, Wheelock Whitney, Jr. of Minneapolis, and Dwight Davis of New York (the Davis Cup in tennis was donated by his family). Also present at the Fontainebleau was the CL's founder and legal counsel, William Shea of New York. But, as usual, it was the Mahatma who was the focus of the press cameras. The cane-thumping, cigar-chomping Rickey waxed forth in the tradition of Daniel Webster, Edmund Burke, and William Pitt. The subject of his oratorical artistry was the strained relations between the new league and the Lords of Baseball.

The Continental League, Rickey told the assembled audience, "is as inevitable as tomorrow—but not as imminent." It was inevitable in the sense that five of the eight cities required to begin operations had already signed on for a projected 1961 start. All had posted the $50,000 entrance fee (for operating expenses) and had committed themselves to either renovating old stadiums or building new ones, such as the one planned for the old World's Fair site at Flushing Meadows, Queens. At the end of the press conference, the Mahatma surprised the audience by announcing that Atlanta had been admitted as the CL's sixth entry. The league, he said, was considering other possible entries for the seventh and eighth spots, including Dallas, Montreal, and Buffalo. That it was not imminent was due to the machinations of Major League Baseball. The Continental League, Rickey charged, could not round out its full complement of eight cities until Joe Cronin made clear whether the American League was committed to expansion in 1961. Potential entrants, Rickey noted, were holding back in the hopes of securing a franchise in one of the two existing big leagues. The (purposeful) indecisiveness of Cronin had already caused the Dallas

Branch Rickey (left) and Bill Shea, founders of the Continental League, which Rickey said was "as inevitable as tomorrow but not as imminent." Baseball commissioner Ford Frick agreed with the second part of Rickey's statement.

group to waver. His thick eyebrows working at their indignant best beneath thick eyeglasses, the Mahatma blasted Major League Baseball as "a monopoly that calls itself the national pastime."[4]

With that salvo Branch Rickey struck the Lords of Baseball at their most vulnerable spot. Throughout 1959, and for several years previously, the U.S. Congress had been investigating monopolistic practices in professional sports. Baseball, being the oldest and most prominent, received the greatest scrutiny from Capitol Hill. Leading the charge was Senator Estes Kefauver. Mostly forgotten now, in the 1950s Kefauver was a familiar name to Americans as head of a Senate committee investigating organized crime and as the Democratic Party's vice-presidential candidate in Adlai Stevenson's failed campaign for the White House in 1956. In February 1959, Kefauver, in his capacity as chairman of the Senate Anti-Monopoly Sub-committee, introduced a bill that would have limited the number of players any one Major League team could control to 80, as opposed to the nearly 450 allegedly under direct, or indirect, jurisdiction. The effect of this action would be to provide a pool of players for Rickey's new Continental League, which Kefauver very much supported.

As it struggled to contain the congressional offensive, Major League Baseball was being assaulted on another flank. When the Dodgers and Giants owners, Walter O'Malley and Horace Stoneham, absconded for the West Coast after the 1957 season, New York Mayor Robert F. Wagner appointed Bill Shea, a corporation lawyer, to investigate the possibility of bringing a Major League franchise back to the Big Apple. William Alfred Shea was born in New York's Washington Heights (Giants territory) on June 21, 1907, and grew up the Ridgewood area of Brooklyn. Because his high school Spanish teacher was related to Yankee pitcher Herb Pennock, the young Shea received free passes to games at Yankee Stadium. Educated at Georgetown University, Shea had been associated for decades with the New York law firm of Gould Shea. Shea, however, was no ordinary lawyer. Some quipped that he had no idea where the courthouse was.[5] His métier was that of a power broker, someone who combined charm, street smarts, bluffs, and when necessary, threats, to advance the interest of the powerful and famous.

And so, at Wagner's request, Shea began to recruit a new Major League team for New York. He approached the Cincinnati Reds, Philadelphia Phillies, and Branch Rickey's former team, the Pittsburgh Pirates, but all declined to relocate. So, rebuffed by big leagues, Shea decided to form a third major loop. At New York's Hotel Biltmore on July 1, 1959, he announced the creation of the Continental League. The CL, he declared, would "operate within the structure of organized baseball." Two days later at a congressional hearing in Washington, Commissioner Frick and league presidents Giles and Cronin promised to cooperate with Shea in negotiating player rights, territorial jurisdictions, player pensions, and issues related to minor league farm systems. Major League Baseball had no choice but to cooperate, lest it feel the sting of congressional anti-trust legislation.

As talented as he was at the art of the deal, Shea was trained as a lawyer, not a baseball man. He needed an experienced hand to run the league, someone who could stand on equal par with Frick, Giles, and Cronin. In short, a man who knew where all the bodies were buried. A behind-the-scenes wire puller, he needed a front man in dealing with congressmen and senators in the full glare of the camera lights. Thus, at a news conference at the Warwick Hotel in New York on August 18, 1959, Shea announced that Branch Rickey had been hired as the president of the

Continental League. And so, at the Fontainebleau press conference in December 1959, it was the Mahatma who held Major League Baseball's feet to the fire.

By raising the specter of congressional investigation, the Mahatma was putting pressure on Major League Baseball to declare unequivocally whatever plans it had for future expansion. In truth, Warren Giles disliked the whole idea of expansion, while Joe Cronin had been Hamlet-like on the subject. It was Cronin, in fact, that Rickey was putting on the spot: fish or cut bait. An exasperated Cronin declared that the AL had no plans for expansion in 1961, 1962, 1963, 1964, 1965, etc. His guarded response was enough to put the CL back on track. Rickey went home to Pittsburgh, and from there flew to Dallas, where on December 22 he announced that Dallas–Ft. Worth would be the seventh member of the new loop. The eighth and final entry, the Mahatma promised, would be announced by January 1, 1960.

As Rickey was sparring with Frick, Giles, and Cronin at the Fontainebleau, a member of the New York Yankees was also making the news. Lawrence Peter Berra—"Lawdie" to his parents and siblings, "Mr. Berra" to Yankee manager Casey Stengel, and "Yogi" to everyone else—was 3,000 miles across the Atlantic testing the European interest in the National Pastime. Yogi, his wife Carmen, and their two older sons Larry (10) and Timmy (8) visited France and Spain before moving on to Italy, which the Yankee catcher had last seen as a Navy seaman during World War II. The visit to Milan was a homecoming of sorts; the Berra family traced its roots to this northern Italian city. In fact, Yogi had grown up speaking the Milanese dialect in The Hill section of St. Louis, but he recognized that it was not proper Italian, and so was reluctant to use it on his tour of Italy. Consuming Italian food, on the other hand, was no embarrassment at all. At one point on the journey when the bus tour stopped for lunch, Yogi put away a plate of macaroni, two helpings of tripe, a salad, ice cream, and half a bottle of Italian wine.

Italian customs officials did not know quite what to make of the assortment of bats, gloves, and balls that Yogi brought over on the Alitalia flight from New York. They promised to release the cargo—donated by an organization billing itself as Baseball for Italy, Inc.—as soon as they figured out what to assess it in custom duties. Not that it mattered much to the average Italian. They had no idea who Yogi was. Soccer (or football as it is called everywhere else in the world except in the United States) was the national sport, and Italians were not about to spoil their soccer fields to accommodate this strange game. Yogi, always a clever man with a dollar, concluded that professional baseball would have an uphill battle establishing a fan base in his land of origin. Italians, he noted, took a siesta everyday between one and four in the afternoon — not a good thing for the gate given the traditional 2:00 P.M. starting time for day games.

As Yogi and his family completed their tour of Italy, American-style football was on display at Yankee Stadium. On Sunday, December 6, a crowd of 68,496 was on hand as the New York Giants crushed the Cleveland Browns, 48–7, winning their second consecutive Eastern Division championship, and third in four years. The game almost ended in a forfeit. Delirious Giants fans spilled out on the field 113 seconds before the final gun sounded, tearing down one goal post before stadium security restored order. Returning to work on Monday at his office at 745 Fifth Avenue, Yankee general manager George Weiss was more concerned with a wreckage of a different sort at the "House That Ruth Built."

The proud Yankees, the team of Ruth, Gehrig, and DiMaggio, winners of seven pennants in nine years under Casey Stengel, had finished a disappointing 79–75 in 1959. Their record put them a distant third behind the pennant-winning Chicago White Sox and the second-place Cleveland Indians. Personnel changes obviously were in order. After weeks of fruitless trade talks with several National League teams, on December 11 Weiss concluded a deal with the Kansas City Athletics. He traded outfielders Hank Bauer and Norm Siebern, pitcher Don Larsen, and first baseman Marv Throneberry to the A's for outfielder Roger Maris, shortstop Joe DeMaestri, and first baseman Kent Hadley.

Weiss had now made fifteen deals with the Athletics, involving fifty-nine players, since the ballclub had moved from Philadelphia to Kansas City in 1955. All of these deals had vastly improved the Yankees at the expense of the A's and the rest of the league. Other American League club officials were outraged, especially Cleveland Indians general manager Frank Lane who had traded Maris to Kansas City for Puerto Rico–born first baseman Vic Power in 1958. But that mattered little to Weiss. Bauer, a mainstay in all of Manager Stengel's pennant-winning teams, was, at thirty-seven, clearly over the hill. Siebern was a left-handed hitter with some power, but he hit mostly to the opposite field. In Maris the Yankees were acquiring a consummately talented outfielder, who could run, throw, and hit with power. Moreover, with his pull-hitting left-handed stroke, Maris, unlike Siebern, was expected to take full advantage of Yankee Stadium's short right field porch.

For all of his protests, Lane — "Trader Frank" as he was called — wasn't exactly standing pat. A few days before the Maris deal, the Cleveland GM had negotiated a transaction with Chicago White Sox owner Bill Veeck. Lane packed off outfielder Minnie Minoso and three throw-ins to the White Sox in exchange for catcher John Romano and third baseman Bubba Phillips. Lane, who had acquired Minoso from Chicago two years earlier, was now sending him back to the Pale Hose in order to fill gaps behind the plate and in the infield in preparation for another pennant run in 1960. Minoso — *Orestes Miñoso* to Latin American fans — is perhaps best known today for being the only Major Leaguer to have played in six different decades. But that was basically a publicity stunt which hardly does him justice. In the black Cuban, Veeck was re-acquiring a power-hitting outfielder who hit .302 with 21 homers and 92 RBIs the previous season. The "Go Go Sox," who had won with speed and brilliant fielding in 1959, had now added hitting punch in their attempt to repeat as champions in 1960.

Six days after the Maris trade, "Trader Frank" was in action once again. He dispatched second baseman Billy Martin, pitcher Cal McLish, and first baseman Gordy Coleman to the Cincinnati Reds for second baseman Johnny Temple. The stocky Temple was a perennial National League all-star who had had his best season in 1959, hitting .311. He was expected to provide hitting and fielding artistry as well as fiery leadership; TV broadcaster Joe Garagiola selected Temple as the second sacker for his "Best Fighter in a Brawl" all-star team.[6] Martin, a famous brawler himself and former Yankee World Series hero at second base, was by this time a sad facsimile of his former self. The real catch for the pitching-starved Reds was Calvin Coolidge Julius Caesar Tuskahoma McLish, who was 19–8 with Cleveland in 1959. The thirty-four-year-old right hander had come up with the Dodgers in 1944 as one of Branch Rickey's "war babies." McLish, who hailed from Anadarko, Oklahoma, and was part Choctaw Indian, thus found himself traded from the Tribe (as the Cleveland club was affectionately known) to the Reds. For George Weiss, Lane's latest trade was sweet indeed: a player he hated (Martin) and one he feared (McLish beat the Yankees six times in 1959) had been banished to the National League.

At Pittsburgh, Pennsylvania, a walk-out by trolley and bus workers

Chapter Two

"The lowest form of cheesecake"

For Major League Baseball, the period between the beginning of the New Year and the first week of February was traditionally a time for ceremonies. Some of these ceremonies were lavish, much ballyhooed affairs, in which star players, managers, and front office executives comingled with the elites of the political and journalistic worlds. Others were smaller, long-standing rituals, which helped keep baseball in the headlines during the long wait for spring training. Still others were quite new, a byproduct of the political or economic needs of the moment. Taken together, these ceremonies tell the story of a major American institution at a crossroads in its history. Whither the National Pastime?

The first ceremony properly belongs to the previous year's calendar. But since it was (purposely) unannounced, most people first learned of it on New Year's Day 1960 in the pages of the *New York Times*. On December 31, 1959, Matt Burns and Seymour Goldsmith, two men living at opposite ends of Yonkers, New York, journeyed separately to Flatbush for a rendezvous at Ebbets Field, the now abandoned home of the Brooklyn Dodgers. Framed in front of the marbled entrance and the rotunda's grilled gates, Burns, the resident representative of the Los Angeles Dodgers, formally handed over the keys of Ebbets Field to Goldsmith, a vice-president in the Kratter Corporation, a New York construction firm. Apart from *Times* reporter Joe Sheehan and cameraman Ernie Sisto (dispatched to the scene at the last moment) the only other apparent witness to this ceremony was a three-year-old reddish mutt named Angel. Part collie and part chow,

Angel was the only fulltime tenant of Ebbets Field since the departure of the Dodgers for California after the 1957 season. The ceremony over, Burns took off with a packing case full of dusty files. Some would remain at the team offices at 130 Clinton Street; others were destined for the club's training camp at Vero Beach, Florida. Left behind was the locker of Roy Campanella, the great Dodger catcher of the 1940s and 50s who had been paralyzed from the waist down in a car accident two years earlier. Inside the locker was Campy's grey road uniform with the number "39." The locker would be delivered to him later along with the uniform. The fate of Angel remains unknown.[1]

The last major league game at Ebbets Field was played on September 24, 1957. A crowd of 6,702 fans saw the Brooklyn Dodgers defeat the Pittsburgh Pirates, 2–0. Team owner Walter O'Malley subsequently sold the property to the Kratter group for an undisclosed seven-digit price. O'Malley had leased back the park, utilizing it for international soccer matches, fraternal rallies, and other events. But, with work finally commencing on a new stadium in Los Angeles at Chavez Ravine, the Dodgers had let the option lapse on their old home. Two days after the surrender of the keys ceremony, it was announced that a 1,317-apartment complex for middle income residents, the largest in New York City, would be built on the site of Ebbets Field. Brooklyn fans had hoped against hope that the "Boys of Summer" would see the error of their ways and return to Flatbush to do battle once again with the hated Yankees in the World Series. But with physical possession passing to the Kratter Corporation, it was truly the end of the romance.

As the Brooklyn faithful raked over the ashes of past glories, Branch Rickey and Bill Shea were looking to lead the Continental League into a bright future. Although Commissioner Ford Frick had promised the cooperation of the major leagues, relations between the Lords of Baseball and the Continentals had not improved significantly since the baseball Winter Meetings at the Fontainebleau the previous month. Thus, Shea and Rickey resorted to what amounted to a new ritual, a pilgrimage to Washington to lobby the solons of the Senate on behalf of their new league. On January 4, they met with New York Senator Kenneth Keating in his Capitol Hill offices. No doubt charmed by the Mahatma — and like most politicians eager for a photo op — Senator Keating declared himself ready "day or night" to mediate between the Continental League and Major League Baseball.

The Lords of Baseball, keen to the danger, embarked on their own pilgrimage to Washington. On January 11, Frick emerged from a meeting with Senator Keating as the newspaper cameras clicked away. The commissioner certainly did not want to appear as if he were against the idea of a third baseball circuit. That would upset the heads of the congressional anti-trust committees, Senator Kefauver and Congressman Emmanuel Cellar, and roil the anti-trust waters yet again. Therefore, Frick struck an optimistic pose. The Continental League "can't miss," he declared. But Frick was not about to let Rickey and Shea entirely off the hook; the new loop had to "prove itself first." Its ultimate success was dependent on four basic conditions, he said. One, the new league could not expect a "giveaway program" by the majors; Rickey, Shea, and company would have to recruit players on their own. Two, compensation would have to be given to the minor league cities affected by the move of the Continentals into their territory, the so-called indemnities. Three, major league caliber ballparks, with adequate seating capacity, would have to be built. And four, a satisfactory player pension plan had to be put in place. Frick also hinted that, should the Continental League fail, the majors might be willing to absorb some of its teams.[2]

Bill Shea responded immediately to Commissioner Frick's comments: the Continental League would not fail. Each new franchise, he pointed out, was prepared to set aside $80,000 a year toward player pensions, the money to be supplemented by all-star games and TV receipts. New stadiums were being built or renovated. Shea had no interest in the Polo Grounds, the late home of the departed New York Giants. Nor did he want to share tenancy with the Yankees in the Bronx. He preferred to go forward with the construction of a $15 million ballpark at Flushing Meadows, Queens. This made sense since the CL entry wished to court the Long Island clientele, both in Brooklyn and Queens as well burgeoning Nassau County. Moreover, given the inevitable low caliber of play, otherwise reluctant fans might be lured by a state-of-the-art ballpark. The Flushing Meadows stadium would have all the modern conveniences, including elevators and movable stairs. There would be seating for 55,000 for baseball and ample parking available (a sore point at Yankee Stadium). Shea was also "fighting like hell for a retractable roof" in order to turn Flushing Meadows into an all-weather facility.[3] All that remained was for the New York City Board of Estimate to approve the selling of the municipal bonds needed to kick start the project.[4] To hear Rickey and

Shea tell it, time, money, and the U.S. Congress all seemed to be on the CL's side.

On January 29, 1960, Branch Rickey held a press conference at New York's Hotel Delmonico. With much fanfare he announced the admission of Buffalo as the eighth, and final, member of the Continental League. There were, of course, outstanding issues to be worked out. Parks were being built or renovated to ensure major league quality. In fact, Rickey would meet with New York Parks Commissioner Robert Moses "within a few days" regarding the Board of Estimate authorization of bonds to finance the Flushing Meadows stadium. Compensation to the International League for the Toronto and Buffalo franchises was a concern, but the CL was willing to pay "reasonable indemnities."[5] Sixty years ago, Rickey noted, the American League had begun operations in circumstances similar to those faced by his new circuit. There had been doubts then about a new league, but within two years American and National League teams were squaring off in the World Series. The Mahatma expected the Continental League to be no less successful.

As now constituted, the new loop would have teams in New York, Toronto, Atlanta, Minneapolis, Houston, Dallas, Denver, and Buffalo. The Continental League would not bring the Dodgers back to Brooklyn, but it would restore New York's status as a multi-team town. It would expand into the growing cities of the Sun Belt. It would bring big league ball to the Twin Cities. There were shortcomings, to be sure. While the league reached as far as Colorado (Denver was 1,620 miles from New York), it did not find fertile ground in California, the fastest growing state, and settled for the less populous (and colder) Buffalo and Toronto. Moreover, going to Atlanta would put the new league on a collision course with the Jim Crow South. Still, even as constituted, the CL would redress many of the anomalies regarding the geography of Major League Baseball.

That the Continental League could encompass such an expanse of territory at all was a function of dramatic improvements in air travel technology. Just five years earlier propeller-driven airplanes, with their wings at right angles to the fuselage, would have required nine to eleven hours to travel from coast to coast. By 1960 most commercial flights were now being made in the new swept-wing jets that spanned the same distance in a mere five hours. In 1959 big league ballplayers could travel to California in a new $5 million DC-8 Mainliner. The plane was 150' 6" long, 42' 4" high, and boasted a wing span of 142' 5". Equipped with 52 first class seats and 53 coach seats, it had a cargo capacity of 12,000 pounds. Holding 17,500 gallons of fuel, its cruising speed was 600 miles per hour.[6] As much as anything, it was the Jet Age that made California baseball possible, reducing Ebbets Field to one fulltime resident, the dog named Angel. These dramatic improvements in transportation now also made the CL a major headache for the Lords of Baseball.

But again, the Continental League was not the only shadow hovering over Major League Baseball. On January 18, 1960, the NFL owners and top executives arrived at the Kenilworth Hotel in Miami Beach for their annual winter meetings. Located about five miles north of the Fontainebleau Hotel at Bal Harbour, the Kenilworth was also the work of Morris Lapidus. It was Italianate rather than French, and smaller in size than the Fontainebleau—just as the NFL was a smaller operation than Major League Baseball. The Kenilworth was the venue for entertainer Arthur Godfrey's popular television show, *Talent Scouts*, and as it happened, the main item on the league's agenda was that of electing a new commissioner to replace the late Bert Bell. The result was a stalemate as ballot after ballot was taken at the Kenilworth without a clear-cut winner emerging. *Miami Herald* sports editor Jimmy Burns quipped, "Perhaps the NFL owners have been influenced by the Miami Chamber of Commerce slogan: 'Stay through May.'"[7]

Finally, a compromise candidate emerged: the Los Angeles Rams' thirty-three-year-old general manager, Alvin Ray (Pete) Rozelle. On January 26, on the twenty-third ballot, Rozelle received the required three-quarters vote and was hired at a salary of $50,000 per year. A former public relations man, the 6-feet-1½-inch Rozelle had never played organized football. His greatest claim to fame was having been on the same basketball team as Dodger center fielder Duke Snider during their days at Compton High School in Los Angeles. Some people did not think he was up to the job. *New York Herald-Tribune* sportswriter Stanley Woodward called him "a space cadet" and complained that he had let the NFL owners run wild at the first meeting he ran.[8]

The results of the meeting suggest otherwise. With Rozelle in the chair, the owners proceeded to amend the league's constitution, eliminating the unanimous vote required for expansion. From here on, only 10 of 12 votes would be needed to add new franchises. On January 28 Rozelle announced the admission of a new NFL franchise, the Dallas Rangers, which would begin operations in the fall of 1960. It would be coached by former New York Giant assistant Tom Landry. A second new franchise in Minneapolis-St. Paul (which had pulled out of the AFL earlier in the month) would begin play in 1961. Rozelle also announced that the league offices would be moved from Philadelphia to New York City. With this symbolic act, the young commissioner served notice that professional football was ready to compete on an equal par with the National Pastime.

One of those that sensed the danger posed by the rise of professional football was Branch Rickey. The major leagues, he insisted, had remained static for fifty years, refusing to expand beyond its sixteen franchises. The Continental League would stir up interest, create new fans, and pump up the entertainment dollar. But Frick, Giles, and Cronin stood in the way. "Baseball may die," intoned the Mahatma. "My only hope is that I die before it does." But, according to sportswriter Roger Kahn, it was more than just a reluctance to expand that was hurting baseball. In a *Sport Magazine* article titled "Football's Taking Over," Kahn argued that baseball had "bungled ceaselessly" in the last decade, while professional football had "progressed spectacularly." The key was the differing approaches by these two major sports organizations to the new medium of television.

By blacking out home games, Kahn noted, Bert Bell had carefully sheltered pro football from saturation on the air waves. The Major League Baseball club owners, on the other hand, had allowed the individual teams to beam home games indiscriminately into people's living rooms. The inevitable result was decreased attendance at the ballpark. There was another major difference as well: baseball might be a better "live" sport, said Kahn, but football "televised beautifully." The action was confined to a manageable space and came through vividly [and this was before the use of instant replay, which by eliminating the huddle, provides the illusion of continuous action]. Compare that with baseball. One could watch an entire baseball game without realizing that there were nine players on the field. Consequently, said Kahn, Major League Baseball was fast becoming "a game" rather than "The Game."[9]

As Rickey, Kahn, and others pondered the future of "the Game," on January 15 Major League Baseball settled into one of its time worn rituals: the mailing of player contracts for the upcoming season. What this meant, said Tommy Holmes of the *New York Herald Tribune*, was "that the local silly season of our so called national pastime is about to commence in our fair town." The Yankees, for whom contract terms were tantamount to a state secret, would now suddenly "welcome newspaper stories of individual signings as worthwhile off-season publicity calculated to keep fans talking."[10]

There was, in fact, a method to this "silliness." During the offseason, the New York Yankees had to compete for newsprint with not just the NFL, but with a myriad of other sports. In 1960 boxing was still a major attraction, drawing fans to the old Madison Square Garden at Eighth Avenue and 49th Street. Speculation was building over the re-match somewhere in the city between Ingemar Johanson of Sweden (the last undisputed white heavyweight champion of the world) and former title holder Floyd Patterson. "Ingo" had flattened Patterson in three rounds at Yankee Stadium the previous June. The New York Knickerbockers were not a good team, but fans flocked to the Garden to see the Goliath of basketball, Wilt (the Stilt) Chamberlain, who in his rookie year was erasing scoring and rebounding records. Like the Knicks, the New York Rangers were also a second division club in ice hockey. But fans followed the exploits of the Montreal Canadiens, with their "masked goalie" Jacques Plante and the legendary Maurice (the Rocket) Richard. That winter the equally legendary Gordie Howe was closing in on the Rocket's record of 544 career goals. The five major New York dailies carried items rarely, if ever, found in the metro area sports pages today, such as winter baseball in Latin America and high school and local college sports. The results of Vince McMahon, Sr.'s World Wide Wrestling Federation matches, featuring such ring stalwarts as Bruno Sammartino, Haystacks Calhoun, Antonino Rocca, and Killer Kowalski, were, believe it or not, "fit to print" in the sports section of the venerable *New York Times.*

As a result, the Bronx Bombers tried to create headlines out of the ritual of contract- signing. On January 20, Bill Skowron became the first Yankee to agree to terms for the upcoming season. Speaking to reporters at the Yankees' Fifth Avenue offices, he expressed satisfaction with a deal that would pay him $25,000 in 1960, a $2,000 raise. The Yankees "treated me very nicely," he told reporters.[11] The "Moose" posed in a hitting stance for the cameras, holding his folded contract as a bat.

William Joseph Skowron was born on December 18, 1930, at Chicago, Illinois, in a North Side neighborhood populated by immigrants from Eastern Europe (the name Skowron is Polish). He was a baseball and football star at Weber Catholic High School, before going on to further glory at Purdue University in Indiana. The Yankees signed him as an amateur

Yogi Berra (left) and Casey Stengel pose for the ritual contract signing ceremony at the Yankees' Fifth Avenue offices. After Berra signed a blank contract — three times —*New York Times* columnist Arthur Daley called the publicity stunt "the lowest form of cheesecake."

free agent in 1950, after the then White Sox GM Frank Lane declined to sign him, believing Skowron had a poor throwing arm. "It was the biggest mistake I ever made," Lane later said.[12] Meanwhile, Casey Stengel was soon touting the 5'11", 195 pounder as the "next Lou Gehrig." Skowron made the big club in 1955, the same year as Elston Howard, and proceeded to have four .300 seasons in a row. But he turned out to almost be as injury-plagued as that other wounded warrior, Mickey Mantle. In 1959, a bad back and broken wrist had limited Skowron to just 74 games. His absence from the lineup — he hit 15 homers and 59 RBIs before departing for good on July 27 — was a major factor in the Yankees descent to the rank of mere mortals. That off-season the Moose could be found swimming (or rather, paddling, since he was afraid of water) at the YMCA pool at Ridgewood, New Jersey, as doctors told him that a water cure would help create greater flexibility in his muscle-bound frame.

A week later, on January 27, the Yankees contract-signing ceremony featured left-handed pitching ace Whitey Ford. Driving in from his Lake Success, Long Island, home, Ford, with a 16–10 record and an ERA of 3.04 in 1959, signed for a reported $35,000. It was the same salary as the previous year. But Ford was so delighted at avoiding a cut that, he joked, he had looked immediately for a stamp to mail back his signed contract. A live ceremony, with the New York press on hand to witness it, suited the Yankee brass better. Ford joined Manager Casey Stengel at the team's Fifth Avenue offices for a photo op, with Casey jokingly placing the contract in Whitey's coat pocket, as Assistant GM Roy Hamey (Branch Rickey's predecessor at Pittsburgh) looked on.

The next day it was Yogi Berra's turn in the limelight. He received $50,000, also the same salary as the previous year. Yogi's signing ceremony digressed in several directions: his trip to Italy, his new home in Montclair, New Jersey, and the Yankee prospects for 1960. Unlike Bob Friend, Yogi missed out on an audience with the Pope. "I couldn't catch him," he told the assembled reporters. The Yankee catcher was more enthused with his new Essex County home (which was "full of rooms" and "full of trees") than he was with the artwork at St. Peter's ("They're all right — if you like painting"). Turning to the coming season, he declared that the team had improved itself greatly with the Maris trade. As with Whitey Ford's signing, Casey Stengel was on hand to provide color. The Old Perfessor interviewed Yogi for transmission on Armed Forces Radio, a rare treat for the thousands of GIs and their families stationed overseas in this era of the Cold War.

However, *New York Times* sports columnist Arthur Daley was not buying any of it, dismissing the whole ritual as pure fraud. Yogi, he noted, had signed a blank contract — three times, no less — for the benefit of the cameras. It was, scoffed Daley, "the lowest form of cheesecake."[13]

True, it was basically a publicity stunt. But, perhaps, there was a deeper meaning to this annual contract-signing ritual. At a time when free agency and guaranteed pacts did not exist, when players toiled under restrictions of the reserve clause, the contract-signing ceremony created the fiction that the player had signed at his own volition, with no undue pressure. One might even say that the paper — whether actually signed or not — provided a fig leaf of respectability for a system that grossly discriminated against players. Still, to George Weiss's chagrin, not every Yankee was willing to participate in the "cheesecake" pose. The team's premier slugger and main gate attraction, Mickey Mantle, had already rejected the contract offer made by the Yankees, which called for a salary of $60,000, reportedly down $15,000 from his 1959 salary. Also unhappy was one of the Yankees' newest — and most controversial — off-season acquisitions. Two days after Mantle, Roger Maris rejected the Yankee offer of $18,000.

Pittsburgh was not the sports town that New York was. True, it boasted one of the oldest NFL franchises in the Pittsburgh Steelers. But the Steelers, despite the presence of the great quarterback Bobby Layne, were not title contenders. The city had no NBA or NHL club to absorb attention during the winter of 1959–60. Instead, newspapers like the *Pittsburgh Press* and *Pittsburgh Post-Dispatch* devoted much of their coverage to NCAA basketball and University of West Virginia star Jerry West. High school basketball in the Pittsburgh-West Virginia area also received much attention. Readers could also follow the careers of local boys who had made good elsewhere. The favorite topic in this regard was St. Louis Cardinals star Stan Musial, a product of nearby Donora, Pennsylvania. The 38-year-old Musial, a seven-time batting champion, was reported to be engaged in a rigorous training program after hitting only .255 in 1959. Television viewers might tune into Winter Baseball League games from Cuba. There were no Pirate standouts in Cuba but much speculation regarding the identity of the Cuban beauty in charge of the scoreboard in Havana.

Like Weiss, Pirates GM Joe L. Brown also went about the business of contract-signing rituals. On January 7, 1960, first basemen Dick Stuart signed for a reported $18,000, up $6,000 from the previous year. A native

San Franciscan, Stuart was signed at the beginning of the Branch Rickey era in Pittsburgh. But despite awesome power numbers in the minors — he smashed 66 homers at Lincoln, Nebraska, in 1956 — his progress was retarded by his whimsical defensive ability. The 6-foot-3-inch strong boy was legendary for his bad fielding, as attested by his nicknames "Dr. Strangeglove" and "Old Stone Fingers." With the Pirates in 1959, he hit .297 in 1959 with 27 home runs and 78 RBIs in just 397 at-bats. Stuart was a quirky character who claimed he could not do without ten hours of sleep; otherwise he would get up with a belly ache. He had been playing winter ball in the Dominican Republic, but was cut after posting a .229 batting average. Stuart blamed his poor winter performance on his inability to eat the native food, which he claimed had caused him to lose twenty pounds. He must be the only man in history who lost weight by eating Latin cuisine. The *Pittsburgh Post Gazette* ran a picture of Stuart's signing. He and Brown were shown "strumming" their bats like banjos, the player and the executive evidently in perfect harmony with each other.[14] Reserve clause? What reserve clause?

On January 21 twenty-three-year-old second baseman Bill Mazeroski came to terms, receiving an undetermined cut in pay. Injured and overweight, Mazeroski hit only .241 in 1959 with seven home runs and 59 runs batted in (down from his 1958 numbers, when he hit .275, with 19 homers and 68 RBIs). He was also beaten out for the Gold Glove Award by Dodger second sacker Charlie Neal. On January 25 the Pirates signed pitcher Harvey Haddix . The left-hander was only 12–12 on the year, but on May 26 he had been the central figure in one of the most celebrated games in the history of baseball. Haddix threw twelve innings of no-hit ball against the Milwaukee Braves, only to lose both the no-hitter and the game in the top of the thirteenth inning. (The winning pitcher Lew Burdette hurled a 12-hit shutout in a game that took two hours and fifty-four minutes to play at Milwaukee's County Stadium). Haddix (nicknamed "the Kitten") could take some solace in the $5,000 raise in his salary.

The Sporting News, "the Bible of Baseball," devoted its first edition of the year to the dramatic rise in Major League salaries; $600,000 payrolls, it seemed, were now the norm. With few stars to go around, extravagant bids were being made. John W. Galbreath, the 62-year-old owner of the Pittsburgh Pirates, was said to have offered $400,000 for Detroit Tigers star Al Kaline.[15] No such offer materialized, but Galbreath must have been in a generous mood that winter. Despite the team's disappointing record, the Bucs payroll was reportedly at half a million dollars, an all-time high. No player made more than $40,000, but there were eleven men in the $25,000 to $35,000 range. Ace reliever Elroy Face, a spectacular 18–1 in 1959, was upped $10,000 to $35,000, becoming the highest paid player on the team. Also earning a healthy raise in pay was third baseman Don Hoak, a Branch Rickey discovery at Brooklyn. As with the Yankees, "cheesecake" had its limits, however. Shortstop and team captain Dick Groat, who had slumped to .275 in 1959, was reportedly bitter about the 25 percent pay cut. He did not leave his Swissvale, Pennsylvania, home (about ten miles from downtown Pittsburgh) for a photo op at the club's Forbes Field offices. Neither did right fielder Roberto Clemente, who remained planted at his Rio Piedras, Puerto Rico, home.

While the Mantles and Marises, and Clementes and Groats sulked in their tents, another annual ritual was underway in the winter of 1959–60: the sports banquet. There were hundreds of them spread throughout the country, mostly small gatherings lucky to attract a ballplayer or two. But a few were lavish affairs. Two such sports banquets, one in New York, the other at Pittsburgh, stood out in particular.

On January 30, 1960, the New York Chapter of the Baseball Writers' Association of America held their thirty-seventh annual dinner at the Astor Hotel in Manhattan. The 1,400 guests gathered in the grand ballroom, including New York governor Nelson A. Rockefeller and New York City mayor Robert F. Wagner. But aside from Rockefeller and Wagner, New Yorkers were conspicuously missing from the spotlight. The major awards of the night went to two members of the pennant-winning Chicago White Sox. Second baseman Nellie Fox received the Sid Mercer Player of the Year award. Manager Al López was honored with the Bill Slocum Award for his "long and meritorious service to baseball." To add insult to injury, the New York writers awarded the Ben Epstein "Good Guy" award to Hank Bauer. The vote had been taken before the popular Yankee was traded to Kansas City for Roger Maris.

The night's big winners came from very different backgrounds. Nelson Fox hailed from St. Thomas, Pennsylvania, a small town in the southernmost part of the state, about equidistant between Philadelphia and Pittsburgh. He started his Major League career with the Athletics, who gave up on him never thinking he would develop into the best American League second sacker of the 1950s. In 1959, Nellie hit .306 with 70 RBIs and won the league MVP honors. Alfonso Ramón López (nicknamed "El Señor) was born in the Ybor City section of Tampa, Florida, a cigar-making center that attracted scores of immigrants from Spain, Italy, and Cuba in the late nineteenth and early twentieth centuries. (This area would produce two other famous major league managers, Tony La Russa and Lou Piniella). Al López was the only AL manager other than Casey Stengel to win pennants in the 1950s.

The biggest hand of the night went to Ty Cobb, now 73 and recently released from Emory University Hospital in Atlanta Georgia, where he had been undergoing a series of tests. The "Georgia Peach" was given a belated Player of the Year award for the 1911 season, in which he hit .420. The White Sox were exactly the kind of team that delighted Cobb, built on speed and solid defense. López's "Go Go Sox" had managed to cop the AL pennant, despite hitting only 73 home runs. Cobb was especially thrilled by the return of the stolen base as offensive weapon in the person of Luis Aparicio, the Pale Hose shortstop, and San Francisco Giants center fielder Willie Mays. The Venezuelan-born Aparicio had stolen 56 bases, and along with Mays, was generally considered to be the most exciting player in the game. Witnessing the proceedings from their respective dinner tables were two "old timers," Ford Frick and Branch Rickey. Frick looked on frostily as Governor Rockefeller praised the Mahatma for establishing yet "another landmark," the Continental League.[16] The dulcet strings of Sal Terini's orchestra could not smooth over the tension in the room between the Lords of Baseball and the irrepressible pitchman of the upstart new league.

Pittsburgh was the Steel City. In 1960 one could still see the shafts of light emanating from the open hearth furnaces along the Monongahela River. But Pittsburgh was no longer the grimy, soot-filled metropolis that an English visitor once called "hell with the lid lifted." The Gateway Project, begun just after the end of World War II under the leadership of the Equitable Life Insurance Company of America, had dramatically changed the skyline of the Golden Triangle. Where once had been seedy tenements, there were now three eighteen-story skyscrapers, housing the offices of U.S. Steel and the Mellon Financial empire. A twenty-acre park offered a beautiful vista of the forks of the Ohio—"the Point"—where, in November 1758, 2,500 Scottish Highlanders and colonial troops under the command of General John Forbes had stormed the French ramparts at Fort Duquesne. The $15 million Hilton Hotel, with its 22 stories and 807 rooms, was the latest jewel in the urban renewal project that had drawn nationwide attention. The town that General Forbes re-named Pittsburgh, two hundred years later was widely touted as the "City of Tomorrow."

The grand ballroom of the Hilton Hotel was the site of the 24th annual Dapper Dan banquet on Sunday, February 7, 1960. The *Pittsburgh Post Dispatch*, which hosted the charity event, had been trumpeting it in its pages throughout the month of January. About two thousand guests were in attendance, including Pennsylvania governor David Lawrence and Pittsburgh mayor Joseph Barr. The manager of the World Champion Los Angeles Dodgers, Walt Alston, was there, as was "Trader Frank" Lane of the Cleveland Indians. National League stars Hank Aaron, Ernie Banks, and Sam Jones were in among the crowd, although Aaron exited early, supposedly to continue his stalled contract negotiations with the Milwaukee Braves. Pirates TV and radio announcer Bob Prince was the master of ceremonies. The gala affair was broadcast live on local television.

Unlike the New York Baseball Writers Astor Hotel dinner, which had granted the laurels to out-of-towners, members of the local teams received the most important honors of the evening at the Hilton. Elroy Face won the Dapper Dan Award in recognition of his spectacular 18–1 season, seventeen victories in a row. Harvey Haddix, singled out for his twelve-inning perfect game, came in second in the balloting. Steeler quarterback Bobby Layne was third. White Sox first baseman Ted Kluszewski, an ex-Pirate first baseman, was honored for his record-tying three World Series home runs.

With the benefit of hindsight, one can see that the Dapper Dan banquet that evening was about more than just handing out awards. In the winter of 1960 it captured American professional sports at a crossroads in its history. Also present at the ballroom that night were Branch Rickey and Green Bay Packers coach Vince Lombardi. One of these men spoke to baseball's glorious past, and in moral terms, its finest moment. The other, although no one knew it at the time, was along with Johnny Unitas and Pete Rozelle one of the driving forces in the rise of professional football as America's premier team sport. Luckily for baseball, professional football still lacked a certain historical grandeur. In fact, one of Rozelle's tasks as NFL commissioner would be to choose a site for the yet non-existent Pro Football Hall of Fame. Baseball had no such problem. In the coming month, a conclave of baseball writers from all over America would assemble once again for yet another ceremony, this one to select new members for Cooperstown.

Chapter Three

"Don't crowd the Hall"

Cooperstown, New York, the home of the Baseball Hall of Fame, lies about 200 miles northwest of midtown Manhattan. In 1950, to get there by car, drivers were advised to take the Taconic State Parkway, hugging the east bank of the Hudson River up to the Rip Van Winkle Bridge, then cross over into Catskill. From Catskill two alternate routes were presented to the traveler. The first ran northwest to Lake Otsego into Cooperstown. The second proceeded on Routes 23 and 23A to Oneonta. By 1960, the New York State Thruway had been built, opening a third route to Cooperstown. The traveler could leave the Thruway at exit 19 at Kingston, and continue on Route 28 north over the Catskills, passing the tiny hamlets and villages of Fleischmanns, Margaretville, Andes, and Delhi, the heart of the upstate dairy country. After arriving at Oneonta, a college town soon to be inundated by baby boomers from Long Island, it was another 20 or so miles to Cooperstown. It was a ride full of twisting turns under a moving canopy of mountain greenery. Like the entry into the Hall of Fame, it was a journey beautiful to contemplate but not easy to negotiate.

On February 3, 1960, the Baseball Writers' Association of America concluded their deliberations, and adjourned without electing a single player to the Hall of Fame. Sam Rice, a Washington Senators outfielder who compiled a .322 lifetime batting average between 1915 and 1934, received the most votes at 146. Edd Roush, an outfielder for the Cincinnati Reds who finished with a lifetime batting average of .323 from 1913 to 1931, got 142 votes. Neither was anywhere near the 75 percent required for entry into the Hall. Two years earlier (the writers then voted every other year) the results had been the same. The scribes failed to elect anyone to the ranks of the immortals. In fact, no player had been elected since Joe Cronin, the Washington Senators star and current AL president, and Hank Greenberg, the Detroit Tigers great and now White Sox GM, entered together in 1956. In our age of manufactured sports events, such as the annual NFL draft and LeBron James' "decision," for a major sport to let the opportunity for free publicity slip by like this seems just short of incredible.

But this was not the case in 1960. "Is this bad?" asked *New York Times* writer Arthur Daley. Not necessarily, he thought (although he had lobbied for Rice, Rousch, and a third "R," pitcher Eppa Rixey). "The exclusiveness of the place," Daley wrote, "enhances its distinction." Shirley Povich, the long-time sportswriter for the *Washington Post* and father of TV personality Maury Povich, agreed. He doubted whether there were any genuine candidates among the current crop of players, beyond Ted Williams of the Boston Red Sox and Stan Musial of the St. Louis Cardinals. As for the rest, maybe Willie Mays might make it if he had several more good years. Jackie Robinson would command attention, of course. But Jackie might not get in on the first try — after all, Joe DiMaggio didn't. Beyond Yogi and Campy, Mickey Mantle and Hank Aaron, "others did not come easily to mind." The essence of Povich's argument was captured in the title of his article published in the *Baseball Digest* in April 1960: "Don't Crowd the Hall."[1]

Following the implementation of new rules later that year, future Hall of Fame electors would prove to be much more charitable with their votes. Four American League pitchers active on major league rosters in 1960 would eventually gain entry into the Hall of Fame:

Jim Bunning (Detroit Tigers)	Hoyt Wilhem (Baltimore Orioles)
Whitey Ford (New York Yankees)	Early Wynn (Chicago White Sox)

Of this group, only Wynn would become a 300-game winner, a criterion that ensures almost automatic entry into the Hall today. But Ford, with 236 lifetime wins, and Bunning with 224, would have fewer career victories than Eppa Rixey's 266. Wilhem (143 wins) was elected based on his accomplishments as a relief pitcher, although surprisingly he exceeded 20 saves on only three occasions in his 21-year career. In fact, it was not entirely certain in 1960 as to whether or not he would actually remain a bullpen ace. In 1959, pitching for the Baltimore Orioles, the knuckleballer started twice as many games as he relieved, including a no-hit game against the Yankees.

head by flying metal plate, hot rivets dropping inside his shirt. As a volunteer fireman, he had barely escaped entrapment in a burning building. But he came back from all of these troubles to launch a minor league managing career, and took over the Bucs' reins as skipper in 1957. He was Manager of the Year in 1958.[3] A calming presence in the dugout, the paunchy, tobacco-chewing Murtaugh was often referred to in the press as "the Irishman."

In an era in which there was a greater awareness of a player's or manager's ethnicity, Danny Murtaugh was often referred to in the newspapers as "the Irishman."

Today it is rare to hear a player referred to by his European heritage. Affirmative action categories have flattened out these ethnic differences into a single category of "white." But, in 1960, Americans were less removed in years from the immigrant experience. Many of them had parents who did not speak English well, if at all. In an age before political correctness, comedians like Chico Marx or Sid Caesar incorporated ethnic accents as part of their act. Hollywood character actors like J. Carroll Naish made a career out of playing ethnic types. Singer Rosemary Clooney's novelty records of the 1950s were sung in faux foreign accents. In short, given the *zeitgeist* of the times, Americans in general were more aware of ethnic distinctions. This was especially the case in 1960, the year during which an Irish Catholic from Massachusetts, John F. Kennedy, was running for the Democratic nomination for President of the United States.

Today, in the age of free agency, we are more likely to know more about the details of a player's contract than anything else. By contrast, the *Baseball Digest*, in its preview of the 1960 season, included not just a player's height and weight, color of hair and eyes, but often their ethnic heritage as well. For example, consider the scouting report for one "Jim McCarver [sic]" that reads "Irish ... Arm not real strong but gets rid of the ball quickly, runs real well, not much power ... as a catcher he batted leadoff in a big league game in 1959."[4] The *Baseball Digest* does not say whether the young Mr. McCarver had an alleged propensity for verbosity or for over-analyzing ball games. But his ethnic background is made perfectly clear. These ethnic categories are also reflected in many, if not most, of the official 1960 yearbooks published by the Major League teams. The *Baseball Digest* also provided a primer for pronouncing ethnic names: CUE-bek (for Kubek), cim-OH-li (for Cimoli), etc.

Another sign of this ethnic awareness was in the variety of nicknames by which ballplayers and managers were tagged. Bobby Thomson was popularly known as the "Staten Island Scot." Manager Al López of the White Sox was "El Señor," or the "Gay Caballero." "Dutch" Dotterer's nickname referred to his German ancestry ("Dutch," a corruption of "Deutsch," had also been Casey Stengel's nickname early on in his career). Carl Furillo was called "Skoonj" (scungili, an Italian dish). Not all nicknames were complementary, to be sure. Italian-American players were called "dagos" (a corruption of "Diego," and thus originally a derogatory term for Spanish people like Al López). And many a rhubarb began with "black bastard," or worse. The point here is not that Major League Baseball was a paragon of racial and ethnic understanding, but rather that there was a greater awareness of ethnic differences than there is today — and not just with regard to minority groups. Major League Baseball teams, always looking to make a buck, were keen to take advantage of these ethnic identifications in luring customers to the ballpark. The Braves were not unaware of the fact that second baseman Red Schoendienst, born in Germantown, Illinois, in 1923, was a big draw in Milwaukee, a city with one of the largest German populations in the United States. Stan Musial, who spent his entire career in St. Louis, was extremely popular with the Polish contingent in his native Pittsburgh area. In an age before free agency, it was not the size and length of a player's contract, but the extent of his lineage that mattered in selling tickets.

African Americans — Negroes was the polite word used in 1960 — represented about 11 percent of the American population (although they were grossly undercounted). Their numbers, however, were well documented and growing in Major League Baseball. In our list of future Hall of Famers, six are African American, all in the National League. The absence of future Hall of Famers on the American League side of the ledger reflects the junior league's later, and less aggressive, advance toward integration. By 1960, the color line had been effectively broken, but it had not occurred without a fight.

Take the case of Yankee catcher Elston Howard. Despite his self-effacing demeanor, Elston Gene Howard, born in St. Louis, Missouri, on February 23, 1929, at one time had been one of the most controversial of Yankees. Nearly a decade earlier, George Weiss, spurred by lobbying from civil rights groups, announced the signing of their first two "Negro" players. One was Vic Power, the other was Howard. Acquired from the Kansas City Monarchs of the Negro American League, Elston was assigned to Muskegon in the Michigan Central League. After two years of military service, the Yankees sent him to Kansas City, then a Triple-A team. By 1953 there was mounting pressure on the Yankees to promote a black player to the big club. Yankee co-owner Dan Topping announced that the Yankees would "bring up the first Negro who could make the team."[5] Power, a Puerto Rican by birth, was proud and outspoken and thus not considered to be "the Yankee type." He was soon traded to the Philadelphia Athletics. Meanwhile, in 1954, Howard hit .330 at Toronto and was voted the International League's Most Valuable Player. On April 15, 1955, he made his major league debut at Fenway Park in Boston, singling in a run in his first at-bat.

Like many a player of the Cold War era, Howard's progress to the Major Leagues had been retarded by military service. His path to the Majors was also slowed by his apprenticeship behind the plate. Howard was a sure-handed outfielder, with a rifle arm. But because he was slow afoot, Manager Casey Stengel decided to convert him into a catcher. In his first couple of training camps with the Yankees in Florida, Ellie would spend long hours learning the fine points of catching from Hall of Famer Bill Dickey, who had tutored Yogi Berra years before. Still, there's no doubt that Howard's ascent to the Yankees occurred with what can only be described as "all deliberate speed." If not out-and-out racists, the Yankee management was composed of men reluctant to defy the racial norms of the time. Two weeks before he made his big league debut, the Yankees played an exhibition game at Birmingham, Alabama. The team left Howard behind, adhering to local Jim Crow ordinances that outlawed athletic contests between "mixed athletes."

Howard's plight was par for the course. At one of the many baseball banquets that winter of 1960, a slim, young black man sheepishly introduced himself to Jackie Robinson. "Mr. Robinson," he said, "my name is Pumpsie Green." This moment brought together the first black in Major League Baseball with the last man to integrate a big league club. Elijah (Pumpsie) Green was a twenty-six-year-old native of Berkeley, California, who as Bill Brower of the *Los Angeles Sentinel* put it, had "figured in more controversy ... than any tan player [sic] since Jackie Robinson."[6] Green, a shortstop and second baseman, had performed admirably in spring training with the Red Sox in 1959 while enduring humiliating living conditions. He was not allowed to live in the same hotel as the other Red Sox players and had to jump in a taxi every morning to reach the Sox training camp at Scottsdale, Arizona. The crowning humiliation was Green's demotion to Boston's Minneapolis Triple-A team for "more seasoning." This action provoked a formal protest by the NAACP, which accused the Red Sox of blatant racial discrimination. The Massachusetts Civil Rights Commission, however, found no fault on the part of Sox owner Tom Yawkey. Green, a switch-hitter, finally made his Major League debut as a pinch-runner on July 7, 1959.

Pumpsie Green represented something relatively new in Major League Baseball: he was a black journeyman player in a sport that had hitherto limited itself to acquiring black stars. Run-of-the-mill black players for the most part remained in the minor leagues. Indeed, the advance of African Americans in Major League Baseball, as inspiring as it was, is tempered by a sobering fact. On the New York Yankee and Pittsburgh Pirate 1960 rosters, the number of foreign-born players is greater than that of native-born black players. For example, the New York Yankee breakdown is as follows:

Foreign-born players	*African American players*
Elmer Valo	Elston Howard
Héctor López	Jesse Gonder
Luis Arroyo	

The pattern is the same with regard to the Pirates:

Foreign-born players	*African American players*
Roberto Clemente	Gene Baker
Joe Christopher	Bennie Daniels
Diomedes Olivo	Earl Francis
Roman Mejías	

Neither the Yankees nor Pirates were particularly aggressive in signing foreign-born players, so the differences, admittedly, are not all that marked. However, two other ballclubs provide a more dramatic example of this trend.

The Washington Senators were the AL team with the most foreign-born players on their roster during the 1960 baseball season. As the list below shows, they far outnumbered American blacks:

Foreign-born players	*African American players*
Julio Bécquer	Earl Battey
Reno Bertoia	Lenny Green
Rudy Hernández	
Héctor Maestri	
Camilo Pascual	
Pedro Ramos	
José Valdivielso	
Elmer Valo	
Zoilo Versalles	

The two African American players, Battey and Green, were both starters on the 1960 Nats team, the former behind the plate, the latter in center field. This conforms to the usual pattern of black recruitment. There were not many black American utility players sitting on AL benches. On the international side of the ledger Pascual and Ramos were both starting pitchers, in fact, the anchors of the Washington staff. But of the position players, only Bertoia could be counted as a starter. In short, there were a lot of foreign-born players warming the bench.

The difference in number between American blacks and foreign-born players is even more startling on the Philadelphia Phillies' 1960 roster:

Foreign-born players	*African American players*
Rubén Amaro	Hank Mason
Tony Curry	
Rubén Gómez	
Tony González	
Frank Herrera	
Humberto Robinson	
Tony Taylor	

There were exceptions, to be sure. The Los Angeles Dodgers, the team of Jackie Robinson and Branch Rickey, was composed of many more African American players than foreign-born. (It was also, incidentally, the club with the largest number of Jewish players.) On the Chicago Cubs and St. Louis Cardinals (36–34), American blacks also outnumbered foreign-born players. But overall, the demographic advantage was slightly on the side of the outlanders in the National League. In the American League, the numbers were definitely skewed (24–12) in favor of foreign nationals. Today, the relative absence of African Americans in Major League Baseball is often commented upon, especially given the high percentage of American blacks in the NFL and NBA. But the ascendancy of foreign-born players in Major League Baseball was already an established fact fifty years ago. If not for the Cuban Embargo, which limited the number of players from that Caribbean island, the percentages would have been even higher in the 1960s.

The large number of foreign-born players in comparison to African Americans did not excite the same amount of comment as it would today. This is because, at that time, contemporaries did not view racial categories quite in the same way as we do. The 1960 census, the most comprehensive in American history, asked respondents questions regarding the number of television sets, washing machines, and air conditioners in American households. But it had no classification called "Hispanic" or "Latino." In fact, the ACLU's complaints over census categories centered on the categorization of Aleutian Islanders. Spanish-speakers were either "black" or "white," which is also how they were regarded in the baseball world. The Giants, for example, were considered to have the most blacks in their farm system, about 70 players. But many, if not most, of those players were not "black" if considered from the point of view of today's Affirmative Action categories. They were actually of Hispanic origin. When *Sport Magazine* listed a hypothetical lineup for an all-Negro all-star team, it included Cuban black Minnie Minoso and Puerto Rican blacks Orlando Cepeda and Vic Power. On the other hand, it did not include the White Sox's base-stealing phenom Luis Aparicio or Washington pitching ace Camilo Pascual.

This was not just the majority view of things. African American newspapers, such as the *Pittsburgh Courier*, *Chicago Defender*, and *Atlanta Daily World*, covered the exploits of black Spanish-speakers like Minoso, Power, and Cepeda in its pages, just as they celebrated Willie Mays, Ernie Banks, and Henry Aaron. There was nothing *phony* about Roberto Clemente being a black man, as well as Puerto Rican. By contrast, these black newspapers did not devote attention to Pascual, or to Aparicio. There is a very simple explanation for this: Hispanic at the time did not mean *automatically* non-white. In fact, in its scouting reports, *Baseball Digest* is very clear in distinguishing black and white Latins. Thus, Raúl Sánchez of the Reds was termed simply as "Cuban," while Tony Taylor of the Cubs was referred to as a "black Cuban."

This is not to say that there was a racial cleavage between black Spanish-speaking players and those of European or indigenous origin. When push came to shove, ethnicity trumped race. The *Pittsburgh Courier* sports columnist Wendell Smith related a story about Minoso and Cuban shortstop Willie Miranda, during the latter's brief stay with the New York Yankees. According to the story, Casey Stengel ordered Miranda to shout some nasty things in Spanish at Minoso in order to disrupt his concentration at the plate. What Willie actually said to Minnie was, "Why not meet me after the game at El Rancho for dinner and we'll eat some congrí [a Cuban dish] and talk it over." Minoso played along, pretending to be furious with Miranda while agreeing to meet for black beans and rice after the game.[7] The *Courier* story suggests the old black tradition of putting one over on Ol' Massa — or in this case, the Ol' Perfessor. However, this incident was not really about race. It was about culture. In Cuba, Minoso and Miranda were on separate ends of the racial divide — one black, one white. But, in America, they were bound together by a common cultural heritage — the Cuban Spanish vernacular, a Creole cuisine, and the sense of nostalgia that only expatriates can feel for their country of origin.

One person in particular looked forward to a continuing influx of international players into the United States. Branch Rickey claimed that players from the entire world would gravitate toward the Continental League. This sentiment was seconded by African Americans. The black press welcomed the upstart third league, for it would enhance the possibility of employment, not just for the Jackie Robinsons and Larry Dobys, but for the dozens of Pumpsie Greens presently frozen out of the Major Leagues. More than black players were involved. Jackie Robinson revealed at a *Sport Magazine* roundtable of prominent black athletes that he been contacted for a manager's job in the Continental League. If so, Rickey and Robinson would be making history once again. The new loop would also be shaping history in another sense. On February 18, 1960, Rickey announced a tentative 1961 schedule for the CL. The northern franchises of New York, Buffalo, Toronto, and Minneapolis would travel to Dallas-Ft. Worth, Houston, Denver, and Atlanta. It made practical sense to begin play in the warm weather cities in April, but there was something else to ponder as well. The Mahatma always said he preferred "turbulent progress over quiet stagnation," and by opening in Atlanta and Dallas, the CL would also be taking on Jim Crow on its home ground.

Unfortunately for Rickey and Bill Shea, at the moment the Continental League was facing more "quiet stagnation" than "turbulent progress." The new CL franchise in Houston was unable to come to an agreement on indemnity payments with the Triple-A Houston Buffs of the American Association. The Mahatma grimly admitted that the league might have to "bypass" that Texas venue and seek another site for its eighth franchise. Losing Houston would be a big blow to the CL's ambitions—but not a fatal one. Much more important to the league's survival was the establishment of a flagship franchise in New York. Hoping to create a distinct identity and generate excitement for their team, Bill Shea and Branch Rickey were pressing the City of New York to build a brand-new $15 million stadium at Flushing Meadows in Queens. These plans brought Shea and Rickey in direct conflict with the mighty New York Yankees.

Post–World War II America was becoming increasingly a "drive-in society." McDonald's and Holiday Inn, Disneyland and Jones Beach State Park all existed for and by the automobile. In California there were even drive-in churches.[8] For more and more fans from New Jersey and the Long Island suburbs of Nassau and Suffolk counties, the automobile, and not the "A" Train, was the preferred mode of transportation to the Yankee ballpark at 161st Street and River Avenue. As a result, the Yankee management was facing an ever more difficult parking situation. In 1960, the club parking lot could accommodate just 1,200 cars. Another 3,600 cars could be left in privately owned facilities within a six-block radius of the Stadium. But that was it. In an effort to solve the problem, Yankee owners Dan Topping and Del Webb petitioned Parks Commissioner Robert Moses to allow the seldom-used Macombs Dam Park, adjacent to the Stadium, to be converted into additional parking space.

Calling Robert Moses the Parks Commissioner is like referring to Nikita Khrushchev as the General Secretary of the Communist Party. In each case, an innocuous moniker belied an all-powerful individual. As

Parks Commissioner, Moses had the power of life and death over any large-scale building project in the City of New York. In fact, by building the Cross Bronx Express in the late 1950s — and destroying long established neighborhoods populated by Jews, Italians, Irish, and blacks — he had contributed mightily to the ever greater dependency on the automobile, thus adding to the Yankees' parking woes.[9] But Moses flatly turned down the Yankees' request. His nominal superior, Mayor Robert F. Wagner, was not about to force him to change his mind. In the light of this impasse, Topping and Webb suggested an alternative proposal: the City of New York should buy Yankee Stadium and build a larger parking facility on city-owned land. Having taken over the Stadium, the City could then provide monies for a triple-deck bleacher section. The renovated Yankee Stadium, its capacity now increased to 100,000, could then be used by *both* the Yankees and the new Continental League team. Bill Shea and Branch Rickey, however, would have nothing to do with the Yankee owners' proposal. The CL, the symbol of boldness and innovation, was not about to begin play in an "antiquated" park in the Bronx. They were holding out for a new, city-owned park in Queens.

On February 12, 1960, Weiss held a news conference at the Yankees' Fifth Avenue offices to announce the signing of Elston Howard. Ellie, driving in from Teaneck, New Jersey, agreed to a salary of $30,000. He was then photographed in the usual ritual of management-player harmony, juggling his contract along with three gloves — catcher's mitt, first baseman's mitt, and outfield glove. John McGraw, for whom Casey Stengel played on the old New York Giants teams of the 1920s, was a master at platooning. As Yankee manager, Casey would adopt his old mentor's methods, relishing players such as Elston, who could fill in at several positions. It was Parks Commissioner Robert Moses and the parking situation at Yankee Stadium, however, that was George Weiss' primary concern at the moment. The wily GM decided to use the city's supposed largesse to the Continentals as a wedge for forwarding the Yankees' parking agenda. Having dispensed with Howard, the wily Weiss brought up the subject of stadium parking. Unlike the Continentals, said Weiss, the Yankees were not asking for a single dollar from the New York taxpayer (the Flushing Meadows Stadium was to be funded by bonds issued by the City of New York). All the Yankees wanted, Weiss claimed, was the opportunity to buy, lease, or have the city operate a new expanded parking facility at the Stadium. After all, the city was prepared to shell millions in deference to Shea and

Rickey. With considerable chutzpah, the Yankee GM declared, "We're more or less the patsies in this thing."[10]

For the average baseball fan, the rivalry between the Continental League and Major League Baseball — even the looming shadow of pro football — was of secondary importance. The banquet circuit was ending. The Hot Stove League was over for another year. Players, managers, and coaches of the current sixteen Major League teams were beginning to pack their bags for the annual pilgrimage to southern Florida and Arizona.

CHAPTER FOUR

"I don't care for Florida"

In 1911, a forty-one-year-old man was told by his doctors that he would have to abandon his thriving laundry business in Pittsburgh, Pennsylvania, and move to a warmer climate for the sake of his health. Taking the doctor's advice, he went to California but found the weather too rainy. He then settled at St. Petersburg, Florida, a community located on the Gulf of Mexico just south of Tampa, where he lived for almost another half a century. Not long after arriving at St. Petersburg, the man ran for political office and served four years as town mayor. But his interests lay elsewhere. In 1914 he convinced Branch Rickey, then manager of the St. Louis Browns, to bring his ballplayers down to St. Pete to prepare for the upcoming season. The man's name was Al Lang, and what he pioneered, for better or worse, was spring training in Florida.

The New York Yankees began training at St. Petersburg in 1927. What had been a town of 3,000 people in the days of Babe Ruth, Lou Gehrig, and manager Miller Huggins (a local resident) was thirty-three years later a city of 180,000, swelled by thousands more during the colder months of the year. In the winter of 1959–60 visitors were descending on Florida in unprecedented numbers. Seven major airlines equipped with fast, direct-service jets, or turbo props, ran what amounted to a commuter service for sun seekers from the frigid North and Midwest. The St. Petersburg-Clearwater Airport terminal had been enlarged to accommodate six of these airlines. Visitors were treated to various diversions. One of the highlights of the winter season at St. Pete was the annual Sunshine Festival that began on February 4, and culminated with a parade on February 25. The Sun God and Goddess, two college kids crowned the previous night at the annual Sun Ball, rode a 150-foot float through cheering crowds.

For baseball fans, however, the real festivities began with the cavalcade of ballplayers congregating for the official start of spring training on March 1 (pitchers and catchers reported a week earlier). Some ballplayers arrived after a winter chasing the banquet circuit. Others came fresh from off-season jobs, which in this age were needed to supplement baseball incomes. Still others were flying back from Cuba, Puerto Rico, Venezuela, and the Dominican Republic, after months of playing winter ball. Sadly, there would be one less fan to greet them this spring; Al Lang had died on the last day of February. The Yankees, out of respect for his memory, limited their first workout to a light morning drill. In the afternoon, George Weiss, Roy Hamey, Casey Stengel, and several of the senior players attended the funeral. Ford Frick was also in attendance to pay his respects. Al Lang's familiar presence would be missed by all.

There were others missing on March 1. In this era of the Cold War, the peace time draft was in force, which meant that there were several players, such as pitchers Ralph Terry and Bill Stafford, who were still in military service. Then there were the holdouts. Roger Maris had finally "capitulated," signing for $20,000, a slight increase over his Kansas City salary. But ace reliever Ryne Duren was absent, as were second baseman Bobby Richardson, shortstop Tony Kubek, and third baseman Andy Carey. Mickey Mantle, still balking at the huge pay cut, was the most conspicuous absentee. So, on March 2, as the Yankee players exited the new clubhouse, with its pine floor and gray painted walls, and began their first workout at Miller Huggins Field, Casey was left with several key pieces and many questions up in the air.

The pitching staff alone was enough to keep the "Old Perfessor" up at night. Would Bob Turley, the Cy Young Award winner in 1958, return to form after a woeful 8–11 mark in 1959? Who would emerge in the starting rotation behind Turley and perennial ace Whitey Ford? The bullpen was just as perplexing. During a stretch in mid–July 1959 Ryne Duren had recorded 33 innings without allowing an earned run. But could the burly right-hander from San Antonio, Texas, with the dark shades and intimidating fastball, rebound quickly from the wrist injury suffered at the tail end of the season? The infield and outfield positions posed their own quandaries. Would the brittle Bill Skowron be able to withstand the rigors of a full campaign? (Behind him at first was Kent Hadley, possessor of a B.A.

in anthropology from Southern Cal and a .240 average with the A's.) Would Andy Carey, sick for most of last year's campaign, be able to assume fulltime duties at third base? Would Maris, who preferred right field, adjust to playing left? Would Héctor López, who had recently signed for $16,000 after driving in 93 runs in 1959, be able to handle right? Meanwhile, one of the most versatile of Casey's players, Tony Kubek, was nowhere to be seen.

Anthony Christopher Kubek was born into a Polish-American family at Milwaukee, Wisconsin, on October 12, 1936. His father, also named Anthony, had been an outfielder for the old Milwaukee Brewers of the American Association, and had struck up a friendship with Casey Stengel, then managing the Toledo Mud Hens. The "young man," as Casey called Kubek, was spotted by Yankees Midwest scout Lou Maguolo and signed for a $4,000 bonus. Tony garnered good reviews at the Old Perfessor's prospects' school at St. Petersburg in 1953, and moved quickly up to the majors. At age twenty he hit .297 and was voted AL Rookie of the Year for 1957. Kubek played five positions as a rookie: shortstop, third base, second base, left field and center field. When Casey was asked by the writers where he would play Tony in the World Series that year against the Milwaukee Braves, he responded by saying, "I'm waiting until he tells me in what part of the ballpark his family is sitting. Then I'll put him as close to them as I can."[1]

Kubek was not exactly the "milk drinker" of later repute. In February 1959, he was fined $20 by the Edison, New Jersey, Municipal Court for traveling 80 miles per hour on the Garden State Parkway, en route to his U.S. Army Reserve post at Ft. Monmouth. The tall, lantern-jawed, blue-eyed blond was no Midwestern hick. He liked Progressive Jazz (this being the "cool" era of Dave Brubeck and Stan Getz), went to see "the better movies," and read extensively. He was above all his own man. The Yankees were surprised when he sent back his contract unsigned in 1958; Tony believed he deserved more money for his rookie performance. In this 1960 political primary season, Democratic candidates John F. Kennedy and Hubert Humphrey would soon be descending on Wisconsin, debating questions of war and peace. But Kubek was not yet ready to leave the state, waging his own version of the Cold War from his snow-bound home in Milwaukee.

Then there was Mantle. As his teammates limbered their legs and practiced fundamentals at St. Pete, the Mick was shuttling between his bowling alley in Dallas and his motel business at Joplin, Missouri, issuing a stream of communiqués all saying basically the same thing. He would not report to camp at the $60,000 offered by the Yankees. On March 4, Ryne Duren finally signed (for $17,000, a $2,000 increase). Having dispensed with Duren, Weiss challenged Mantle to come to Florida and settle the business once and for all. There would be no negotiation over the telephone, he told the press. Former Yankee shortstop and team announcer Phil Rizzuto chimed in, criticizing Mickey for holding out.[2] On March 5, Andy Carey came to terms for $20,000 (a $2,000 cut). But Mantle and Kubek — the country and western music lover from Oklahoma and the jazz aficionado from Wisconsin — were united in opposition to management.

For Stengel, only the receiver corps seemed beyond reproach. Yogi Berra was no longer able to carry the fulltime catching load. But he was still a dangerous hitter in the clutch. In any case, Elston Howard was ready to take over after an 18-home-run season in 1959. The third string catcher, Johnny Blanchard, would have been a starter on practically any other major league club. It is fitting that these three men, the heart and soul of the Yankee team, were all reared near the Mississippi River, the geographical center of the nation. Berra, an Italian-American, and Howard, an African American, were both born in St. Louis, Missouri, which at one point was seriously considered as a replacement for Washington, D.C. as the capital of the United States. Blanchard (his name indicates French ancestry) was born at Minneapolis, Minnesota, which along with its sister city of St. Paul, was located at the northernmost reaches of the mighty "Father of Waters." In the 1830s, a slave named Dred Scott had been taken by his master, an army surgeon, from St. Louis to free territory at Ft. Snelling, Minnesota (today St. Paul). Upon returning to Missouri, Scott sued for his freedom in a now famous Supreme Court case.

Freedom — in the form of free agency — however was not something that ballplayers could very well exercise. With the Continental League vowing to work within the "canopy of baseball," there was not much leverage for a player to exercise. Time was on the side of management. On March 8, Tony Kubek finally came down to St. Petersburg and signed a contract for a reported $18,000, a $3,000 raise. His teammates marked his arrival by presenting him with a snow shovel (he had been pictured in an Associated Press photograph shoveling his driveway in Milwaukee). Mickey Mantle reported to camp on March 11 and inked a contract the following day for $65,000. It was not the original figure proffered by Weiss, but a $10,000 cut nonetheless.

With the full squad finally assembled, the Yankees opened their 1960 exhibition season, the so-called Grapefruit League, on March 12 against their St. Petersburg neighbors, the St. Louis Cardinals. The 5,027 paying customers at Al Lang Field were treated to one of Casey Stengel's most creative lineups. The great outfield experiment began with Maris in left and López in right. Since Mantle had just arrived, Kubek played center field. But, by far, the most curious spectacle of the afternoon was the man that the "Old Perfessor" slated to play third base. The keystone was manned by none other than Lawrence Peter Berra. Hitting-wise, the move made sense since it provided the Yankees with a spot for Yogi's potent bat. In fact, he ended up driving in the lone Yankees run of the day in a 5–1 loss to the Cardinals.

Unfortunately, things did not go so well in the field. Berra made a throwing error that resulted in one Cardinal tally, and he ran circles under a pop fly before deferring to shortstop Gil McDougald, who was so entranced by Yogi's circumnavigations that he managed to drop the ball. The last act in this comedy of errors began when pitcher Bob Turley attempted to pick the Cardinals' Bill White off first base. The return throw from first sacker Bill Skowron sailed over Turley's head in Berra's direction, but Yogi was taken completely by surprise. He was busy talking to the umpire. By the time he retrieved the ball, White was safely ensconced on second base. Berra was back behind the plate the next day as the Yankees came from behind to defeat the Cardinals, 3–2, for their first Grapefruit League victory. Hopefully, this signaled a return to form after the bitterly disappointing 1959 season.

The Yankees were not the only one trying to restore their grand reputation in the spring of 1960. Branch Rickey was attempting to do the same in launching the Continental League. It would not be an easy task. Rickey's biggest problem was the procurement of players. The sixteen big league clubs either owned outright, or had an exclusive relationship with, the minor league clubs. Commissioner Ford Frick had already served notice that the new loop would receive no help from the majors in landing players. But the Mahatma, his mind ever fertile, had found what he hoped would be a solution to this conundrum. On March 15, Rickey announced that the CL had negotiated an exclusive working arrangement with a new

Class D Western Carolina League. The Continentals would provide the eight North Carolina-based clubs with $60,000, the funds to be used for operating expenses. In a departure from the norm, the CL would deal with the Carolina League directly, not its individual clubs. The players would report together before being assigned to the respective teams. Rickey claimed this working arrangement had received the sanction of the National Association of Professional Baseball Leagues (the governing body of minor league baseball).

The Western Carolina League might alleviate one problem, but there were still other hurdles to contend with. The Buffalo club's largest stockholder, Sportsservice, Inc., a stadium and racetrack concession firm, was not satisfied with the new team's implementation plans. Questions still swirled over indemnity payments to the International League for the CL's takeover of its territory in Buffalo. Out west, the proposed merger of the new Houston franchise with the Triple-A Houston Buffs of the American Association was also a non-starter. Rickey and Bill Shea could only look with envy at the progress being made by the fledgling American Football League. AFL Commissioner Joe Foss announced that his league was ready to begin play in September 1960. Four hundred players were already under contract with AFL teams, and stadiums were available at all eight cities. Meanwhile, the National Football League, under its young commissioner Pete Rozelle, was doing its level best to spoil the party. Its new Dallas Rangers franchise, soon to be renamed the Cowboys, would compete head to head with the AFL's Texans. An outraged Foss said he would consult with the Department of Justice officials regarding possible NFL anti-trust violations. But Foss' problems were relatively minor compared with those faced by the Continentals. The "lack of enthusiasm" for Triple-A play on the part of "washed up veterans," claimed sportswriter Gordon Cobbledick, would effectively kill the CL. If it wasn't for Branch Rickey's "eloquence," scoffed George Weiss, "the idea of a third major league would never have gotten to the discussion stage."[3]

Ft. Myers, the training site of Branch Rickey's old team, the Pittsburgh Pirates, had its own share of spring spectacles. Thomas A. Edison had made it his winter home, and the locals took pride in memorializing the famous inventor. Between February 6 and February 13, 1960, the town residents celebrated the twentieth annual Edison Pageant of Light. The festivities included the annual parade, led by the King and Queen of Light, with a procession of fifty floats and twenty-five bands. All in all, it was not quite as impressive as the doings at St. Petersburg, but then again, the Pirates did not have the pedigree of the Yankees and Cardinals. They had last won a pennant in 1927, the same year that the Yankees first moved to the area. Terry Park, where the Pirates played their spring home games, was one of the smallest in the Grapefruit League. It was here that the Pirates assembled on March 1.

Pittsburgh Pirates manager Danny Murtaugh was not concerned—at least, publicly—about winning exhibition games. Who could tell what to make of spring training records, anyway? The previous year had seen the Pirates win big in the Grapefruit League and then plummet to fourth place during the regular season. Spring training was for getting players in shape and assessing new talent. There was even time for a little horse play; a United Press International photograph showed the Irishman being carted around in a wheelbarrow by pitchers Vern Law and Tom Cheney. Still, after the second-place finish in 1958, the 1959 collapse seemed to irk the Pirate brass. They were now in the tenth year of Branch Rickey's original five-year plan for pennant success. Some of the front office chagrin was reflected in one of the new rules for the upcoming season. Pirate wives would not be allowed to travel with their husbands on the road. Murtaugh alleged that there had been "too much sightseeing" in the afternoons before night games.[4] He did not specify what the sights were that had so depressed performance on the field.

There was one player that Murtaugh did not have to worry about, either on or off the field: right-handed pitcher Vern Law. Vernon Sanders Law, who turned thirty on March 12, was a native of Meridian, Idaho. Major league clubs had flocked to his door as soon as he graduated after a brilliant high school career. Babe Herman, one of Branch Rickey's enterprising Pirate scouts, got the jump on the others. Herman learned that *Going My Way* was one of Mrs. Law's favorite films. He got the star of the movie, Bing Crosby, who just happened to be one of the Pirates' minority owners, to place a call to the Law family.[5] That did the trick. Law came up to the big show in 1950 at the age of twenty. After spending 1952-53 in military service, he rejoined the Pirates, as they slowly made their way from mediocrity to respectability. In 1959 he tied Elroy Face for most victories (18) and led the club in innings pitched (266). Law resided at Boise, Idaho, with his wife VaNita and their sons Veldon, Veryl, Vance, and Vaughn. An elder in the Church of Latter Day Saints, the Deacon (as he was called by his teammates) did not smoke, drink alcohol, or drink coffee. He and his wife prayed together in the mornings and in the evenings. In the off-season, the couple was active in the Mormon ministry, although Law managed to find time to bag a bear or deer during his hunting expeditions. Law was as disciplined on the mound as he was in his private life. As a pitcher, he relied on pin-point control, keeping the batters off balance with a fastball, slider, and curve — all thrown at various speeds.

The Deacon didn't sit still for too many interviews with the press because he was always running — not to avoid reporters, but to stay in shape. The lack of physical conditioning among members of his pitching staff, in fact, had been one of the big headaches for Murtaugh the previous year. Bob Friend had gained a considerable amount of weight, and as a consequence slipped to 8–19 in 1959. Friend arrived in camp in February 1960 considerably trimmer than the year before, despite his six-week European vacation. But this did not solve all of the Irishman's problems. Beyond Law, Friend, Harvey Haddix, and the Baron of the Bullpen, Elroy Face, there was an unproven crop of youngsters: Benny Daniels, Earl Francis, Tom Cheney, Jim Umbricht, Joe Gibbon, and the Cuban Ed Bauta. On March 7, the Pirates signed a forty-year-old Dominican pitcher named Diomedes Olivo. Out of this bunch, a fourth starter would have to emerge to replace the departed Ron Kline, gone to the Cardinals in the Gino Cimoli trade.

By contrast, the receiver corps responsible for catching them would be vastly improved. The left-handed hitting Smoky Burgess had given the Pirates a scare by threatening to retire. The travel was too hard on his children's education, he said. Now, armed with a tutor for the kids, he was happily in camp. The right-handed hitting Hal Smith, acquired from the Athletics after the failed Maris trade, would platoon with Burgess. Smith, a former Yankee farmhand, could also play third base. Neither was spectacular defensively, but they could handle the bat. Burgess was also one of the National League's most accomplished pinch-hitters.

The right side of the Pirate infield was a study in contrasts: one of the best fielding second sackers in history played next to one of the worst defensive first basemen in the league. Bill Mazeroski had a rough 1959 season, but with his leg injury healed and his weight under control, was primed for a comeback. Dick Stuart was being tutored this spring by Coach Mickey Vernon, a high school teammate of Murtaugh's and a first-base standout in his heyday with the Washington Senators. The backup at first was Rocky Nelson. One of those minor league sensations that never quite made it in the major leagues, the well-traveled veteran had finally found a home in Pittsburgh. Nelson refused to wear a plastic batting helmet at the plate; he made do with a plastic liner stuck inside his regular cap. They called him "Rocky" for his supposedly hard head.

As for the rest of the lineup, the left side of the infield was set with Dick Groat, the team captain, at shortstop and Don Hoak at third. Groat was generally considered to be the best hit-and-run man in the league. Hoak had come from the Reds the previous year along with Haddix and Smoky Burgess — Joe L. Brown's best transaction ever. Tiger had proven himself to be a timely hitter, and an exceptional fielder; some thought he was the best third baseman in a Pirate uniform since Hall of Famer Pie Traynor had prowled the keystone at Forbes Field. Danny Murtaugh's outfield had Bill Virdon in center, flanked by Bob Skinner in left and Roberto Clemente in right. Virdon was a highly regarded defenseman, but had deteriorated at bat since his sophomore year at St. Louis. Skinner had also seen his batting average drop; he hit .280 in 1959 after hitting .321 and .305 the previous two seasons. Plagued by injuries, Clemente had been limited to 105 games in 1959. As usual, he had been absent on the first day of spring training, arriving on March 3 from Puerto Rico to sign his 1960 contract. Unsettling this outfield alignment was the presence of newcomer Gino Cimoli.

Gino Nicholas Cimoli was born December 18, 1929, in the North Beach section of San Francisco. North Beach would later be made famous by the presence of Beat writers Jack Kerouac and Allen Ginsberg, but when Gino was growing up it was a tough neighborhood populated by Italian and Chinese immigrants. "If you didn't have one fight a day you didn't belong," he later said. Branch Rickey visited the home of Abramo Cimoli, a shrimp and crab fisherman by trade, in an effort to recruit his son for the Brooklyn Dodgers. Abramo brought out his home-made wine ("the finest Dago red in San Francisco"). After several wine glasses, a tipsy Mahatma was soon demonstrating hook slides on the Cimoli living room rug with Brooklyn assistant Howie Haak. When the shenanigans were over, Gino had signed with the Dodgers for a $15,000 bonus.[6] Or so the story goes. It's hard to picture to picture Rickey tipsy. But sports editors, when given a choice between the truth and the legend, printed the legend.

Cimoli came up with the Dodgers in 1956 and hit .293 in their last year at Ebbets Field. He was the first player to bat in a big league game on the West Coast, leading off for the Bums against the Giants in his home town on April 15, 1958. In 1959 he hit .279 with St. Louis, driving in 72 runs. Cimoli was similar to Lou Piniella in his prime. Both possessed the square-jawed Mediterranean good looks (Cimoli Italian, Piniella Spanish). Like Sweet Lou, the "Latin Lover" Gino had a volatile temper. He made it known from the start of spring training that he did not intend to sit on the bench. Murtaugh, knowing Cimoli to be a fast starter, was leaning toward starting him in center instead of Bill Virdon. But the Italian's best position was right field, a position currently occupied by Roberto Clemente. Pittsburgh sportswriters and sports fans would gladly have kept Ron Kline as the Bucs' fourth starter instead of Cimoli.

In March, Ron's Kline's new teammates on the St. Louis Cardinals were making as much news off the field as on. The March 7 edition of *Sports Illustrated* contained an article written by former Cards pitcher Jim Brosnan (since traded to the Cincinnati Reds). Titled "You Can Consider It Came from Me," it consisted of excerpts from a diary that Brosnan had kept of the 1959 baseball season. Several Cardinals, including manager Solly Hemus and aging superstar Stan Musial, were prominently featured in the article. Another former Cardinal, the catcher-turned-sportscaster Joe Garagiola, would soon come out with his own insider's account called *Baseball Is a Funny Game*. But while Garagiola's book was mostly good-natured fun, Brosnan's article cast a more thoughtful, often cynical, gaze on his teammates and the sport.[7]

As Brosnan told it, spring training was an ordeal, not just for the ballplayers but for their families as well. For the Brosnans, it was a trek from the outskirts of Chicago to St. Petersburg, made in a station wagon loaded with dolls, a bat and ball, two blankets and four pillows, two large balloons, two baskets of small toys, writing pads and crayons, coloring books — all this in addition to suitcases and two small children squeezed in between. Once they arrived, his wife Ann was stranded for much of the time without transportation. At least the Brosnans could expect to find suitable, if tight, quarters in a beach house overlooking the Gulf of Mexico. Black ballplayers, restricted to the "colored section" of St. Petersburg, and unwelcome on the beaches, were reluctant to bring their families with them, not wanting them to bear the indignities of the Jim Crow South. One black ballplayer decided to hold out as long as he could in order to shorten his time in spring training. "I don't care for Florida," complained another black ballplayer.[8] And who could blame him?

That black ballplayers were literally a world apart from their white teammates was made abundantly clear in an article in the March 28 edition of *Sports Illustrated*, titled, "The Negro in Baseball." The writer, Robert Boyle, obviously gathered much of his material from the black players on the Cardinals team. This was a remarkable group. It included Bill White and Bob Gibson, both college educated men, as well as a future revolutionary, Curt Flood. However, the acknowledged black leader in the clubhouse, and mentor to White, Gibson, and Flood, was a part-time first baseman and pinch-hitter *de luxe* by the name of George Crowe. Although he was a burly six-foot-two, at two hundred and twelve pounds, Crowe's spectacles (like Brosnan's) gave him a professorial look. He had graduated from high school in Franklin County, Indiana, and studied at Indiana Central College (now the College of Indianapolis). Crowe and his counterparts — Bill Bruton (Milwaukee Braves) and Brooks Lawrence (Cincinnati Reds) — were the wise men who looked out for the younger black players.

As the *Sports Illustrated* article told it, Crowe and his cohorts lived a culture largely their own. Some major league cities were judged to be better than others. St. Louis was rated a "club members" town, meaning that it was a good place for blacks to hang out. Milwaukee, on the other hand, rated poorly. Upon arriving at a particular city, black ballplayers immediately headed for their favorite road hangouts. One of these was Ish Evans' Sportsman's Club in Los Angeles. Back at the ballpark, black players distanced themselves from their white teammates by employing their own arcane language. They roared with laughter at terms such as "mullen" and "hogcutter," which had a meaning and significance known only to themselves. Some of the terms blacks used at this time have since become part of the larger American vernacular: "pimp" (a flashy dresser) and a "foxy girl" (a real looker). Whites were called "squares." Blacks had their own nicknames for themselves: "Old Folks" (Crowe), "Snakes" (the Dodgers' Charlie Neal), and "Steelie" (Elston Howard of the Yankees).

Not everything, of course, was fun and games. Black major leaguers were acutely conscious of their exalted status in black society. Only a half of one percent of their fellow African Americans made the minimum big league salary of $7,500. Thus, they formed a vital component of the black bourgeoisie in America. Black major leaguers were, for the most part, "race men" — that is, dedicated to the advancement of civil rights for their people.

Many were card-carrying members of the NAACP. On the other hand, allegiance to the Democratic Party was not automatic; the Cubs' Ernie Banks supported Richard Nixon for president in 1960, while Jim "Mudcat" Grant of the Cleveland Indians stumped for Kennedy. Within the black community itself, these ballplayers were held to a different standard from black entertainers in the music, comedy, and acting business. Hollywood, Las Vegas — any club, set, or stage was the "house of Satan." The National Pastime was "an American sport, with an American respectability" to be upheld. Black entertainers could process their hair. Black ballplayers couldn't without incurring the strong disapproval of their peers. Black major leaguers reflected, said Howard University professor E. Franklin Frazier, the values of American middle class society.

As Boyle's article also pointed out, black ballplayers existed in an uneasy relationship with both their white and Latin American teammates. American blacks tended to get along better with southern whites than northern whites (a fact that may account for the higher rating they gave St. Louis, a southern city, over Milwaukee, a northern one). Blacks and southern whites knew the racial boundaries and adhered to them. Northern white teammates were not always so clued in. Jim Brosnan and a St. Louis teammate, pitcher Brooks Lawrence, shared a love of modern jazz. But Lawrence had refused to accept a party invitation to Brosnan's home. Social overtures extended by whites, however well intended, were met with suspicion. A major cause of resentment for African Americans toward their white teammates had to do with the lack of endorsements. Willie Mays and Hank Aaron were pitchmen for black magazines like *Ebony* (as was Martin Luther King), but not for mainstream publications. This rankled. After all, the consumer culture of post–World War II America was not monochrome. As one black sardonically put it, "Negro players shave too."[9]

One might assume that there was a natural affinity between African American and Latin blacks, born of a common Diaspora. But this is to read history backwards, taking the identity politics of the 1970s and later decades to be an established fact in 1960. American blacks recognized the *cultural* gulf that stood between them and their Caribbean counterparts. They spoke a different language and ate different food (Latins liked their food spicier, American blacks noticed). They, as did Anglos, tended to see them as "hotdogs." The biggest bone of contention between them, however, had to do with the Latin black's rejection of racial solidarity with African Americans. Latin blacks came to America, not just limited in language skills, but with an ignorance of the mores of the Jim Crow South. African American ballplayers took it upon themselves to explain the color line to Latin American blacks. Having explained the Negro's place in America, they naturally resented it when Latin American blacks chose to socialize with white teammates instead of themselves. The reason for their action was painfully clear to *Atlanta Daily World* columnist Marion E. Jackson: "to be a Negro in the United States is to be socially inferior." He added, "Latin players are not Negroes, as far they are concerned." They were Mexican, Cuban, Puerto Rican, etc. Still, the rejection hurt. "They think they're better than the colored guy," Boyle quoted one African American player as saying.[10]

Better than everyone else — that was something that the Yankees had always taken for granted. The third-place finish in 1959 had been a bitter pill for George Weiss, Casey Stengel, and company to swallow. The Bombers had staked much on the Roger Maris trade; although Roger came through with a great spring, Mickey Mantle was a gnawing concern. Trying to make up for the time lost holding out, the Mick had overdone his training regimen, and soon found himself sidelined by an inflammation of the knee. He did not make his Grapefruit League debut until March 24. He came to the plate five times, struck out twice, grounded out, flied out, and walked. On March 30, Mantle finally hit his first homer of the spring in a 6–2 loss to the Cardinals.

Pitching was Manager Stengel's other concern. There were some good signs. On March 19, pitchers Ralph Terry and Bill Stafford arrived in camp, having completed their military service obligations at Ft. Leavenworth, Kansas, and Ft. Sam Houston, Texas, respectively. While Terry and Stafford struggled to catch up, another pair of young Yankee pitchers was making a name for themselves. On March 23, Johnny James and Bill Bethel combined to pitch a no-hitter against the Philadelphia Phillies at Miller Huggins Field. But things were not going well with Casey's veteran pitchers. Whitey Ford, Bobby Shantz, and Duke Maas were all nursing sore arms.

New York's March 1960 record of six victories and thirteen defeats was one of their worst starts in years. In the past, such a dismal record might have been easily dismissed. But the Yankees' third-place finish in 1959 had erased much of the aura of invincibility that had always surrounded them.

Unencumbered by a glorious history, on March 12, the Pittsburgh Pirates traveled to Miami to face the Baltimore Orioles in their first Grapefruit League tilt of 1960. It was not an auspicious beginning. The Orioles beat them, 5–2. After losing two more games, the Bucs finally got into the win column in a manner that would characterize their season all the way through October. After falling behind the Kansas City Athletics, 11–0, the Corsairs stormed back to win 17–13. From here on, the wins started to pile up. On March 27 the Phillies finally broke the Bucs' string of victories at eleven straight. The Pirate streak was carried forward by some robust batting averages. Bill Virdon, wearing contact lenses in an attempt to maintain his job, turned in a .520 mark that March. The Virgin Islander Joe Christopher, tabbed for a utility role in the outfield, hit .436. Dick Groat hit .351 and Roberto Clemente .333. The major disappointments of the spring were Don Hoak (.233) and Dick Stuart (.227), but they were expected to come around.

As for pitching, Bob Friend showed every sign of returning to his 1958 form. Vern Law and Harvey Haddix were set in the starting rotation. And as always, there was Elroy Face in the bullpen. But the search was still on to replace the departed Ronnie Kline. Two young pitchers were showing some promise for Danny Murtaugh. On March 16 at Terry Field, Bennie Daniels and Jim Umbricht combined to pitch a no-hitter against the Detroit Tigers, winning 5–0.

The Tigers, managed by former Philadelphia Athletics star Jimmy Dykes, were hoping to break into the first division of the American League in 1960. They had an excellent nucleus of starting pitchers: Jim Bunning, Don Mossi, and "the Yankee killer," Frank Lary. At bat, the Bengals boasted the AL's defending batting champion, right fielder Harvey Kuenn, and a former batting champ and Gold Glove winner in center fielder Al Kaline. Left fielder Charlie Maxwell had made a practice of beating the Yankees with home runs. GM Bill DeWitt hoped to improve the club's middle defense with the addition of shortstop Chico Fernández, a black Cuban (there were no African Americans on the roster). Chico would play alongside dependable second sacker Frank Bolling. The pitching was thin beyond the three starters, however, with first base and catcher questionable. The team had little speed on the basepaths.

The only Tiger to reach base against the Pirates at Ft. Myers on March 16 was third baseman Eddie Yost. Born in Brooklyn on October 13, 1928,

Roger Maris during his first Yankee training camp in March 1960. The right fielder made his first run at Babe Ruth's home run record that season and was well ahead of the Babe's 1927 pace before he was felled by injuries.

Yost was one of a handful of college graduates in the Major Leagues. Signed out of New York University, Yost had spent most of his career with the Washington Senators. He was known as "the Walking Man," having led the American League in free passes six times, with a high of 151 in 1956. Detroit teammate Rocky Bridges joked that Yost came early to the ballpark every day to practice taking pitches.[11] Yost was also a member of the player's pension committee, and former AL player representative. We remember

Casey Stengel and Mickey Mantle's comic responses to the Kefauver Senate Committee in December 1958 as one of the most famous set pieces in baseball history. But it was Yost and NL rep Robin Roberts who carried the real weight of the hearings, walking the fine line between aiding the Lords of Baseball in their fight with Congress, while pressing them for better salaries and pension benefits. At the Winter Meetings in December 1958, Yost and Roberts introduced a proposal (rejected, of course) that would have set a salary budget for each club at 20 percent of its total receipts. At this point, major league players at the various training camps in Florida and in Arizona (where the Cubs, Giants, Red Sox and Indians trained) were more concerned with the coming season than with sparking a revolution.

On April 2, 1960, the New York Yankees and the Pittsburgh Pirates met for the first and only time that spring. The Yanks took the game, 5–0, at Miller Huggins Field behind the pitching of Bob Turley. The victory, however, brought the Bombers record to only 7–14, one of their worst springs in years. The Murtaugh men, their March hot streak over, fell to 11–9. The Pirates, however, rallied to win four of their last five spring exhibition games to finish at 15–10, the second best record among National League teams in Florida — the Cardinals were first. Despite their excellent Grapefruit League record, a pre-season *Scripps-Howard Sports* poll, representing 30 writers and 18 newspapers around the country, predicted a fourth-place finish for the Corsairs behind San Francisco, Milwaukee, and Los Angeles. *The Sporting News*' J.G. Taylor Spinks had them fifth. Danny Murtaugh waved off the pundits, insisting, "We will be all right." But Lester J. Biederman of the *Pittsburgh Press* thought the team had "peaked too soon" with their eleven-game winning streak in March. Al Abrams of the *Post-Gazette* thought they were as inconsistent as ever. The black press was no more charitable than the mainstream newspapers. The *Atlanta Daily World* found it "difficult, if not downright impossible" to share Murtaugh's optimism.[12]

The New York Yankees were the most successful team in the history of Major League Baseball with 24 pennants and 18 World Series championships to their credit. The *1960 Official Yearbook* predicted nothing less than a continuation of the Yankee dynasty. "Now as we turn the corner of a new decade," it read, "the Yankees are determined to bring baseball fans additional championships." But their Florida exhibition season had not been promising, characterized by poor pitching, poor hitting, and poor fielding. "The infield," complained Casey in his best Stengelese, "can't back up but has gotta turn tail and chase after the ball which Rizzuter was tree-menjous and Carey and Martin done good." The outfield presented its own set of problems for the Old Perfessor. Should he continue to use Roger Maris in left, where he was clearly uncomfortable, and Héctor López in right, where he was often overmatched?

Despite their mishaps, the Yankees fared much better than the Pirates in the pre-season poll of editors and writers held by the *Scripps-Howard Sports* syndicate. New York was picked to finish in first place, with Cleveland, Chicago, and Detroit rounding out the first division. *The Sporting News* also stayed with the Yankees.[13] At least one thing seemed clear: a collision between the Yankees and Pirates in the World Series was as problematic at this time as the launching of the Continental League.

CHAPTER FIVE

"The biggest decoy job in baseball history"

For Major League Baseball, April is a month of inaugurals. In 1960, for the first time since 1903, the National and American leagues did not begin their seasons at the same time. The expansion of the senior circuit to the West Coast in 1958 had put a crimp on the schedule, which could only be eased by the inclusion of additional open dates. Thus, the NL commenced play on April 12, with the AL starting six days later. April also saw the unveiling of the plans for a proposed Flushing Meadows stadium in New York City, the Continental League's ultimate card for big league respectability. Inaugurals, however, were just that — beginnings — for the Major League clubs as well as the Continentals.

As a relative of the first professional baseball club, the Cincinnati Reds were given the honor of hosting the season opener, the fifty-seventh time they had done so. Crosley Field had its share of quirks, such as the slight incline at the left field wall, and beyond it, the Siebler Clothing Store advertisement which exhorted batters to "hit this sign." Players who accomplished this feat (Wally Post did it the most times) received a free suit, courtesy of owner Jack B. Siebler. The 2:30 P.M. contest between the Reds and the visiting Philadelphia Phillies was preceded by two other long-established traditions: the pre-game concert by Smittie's Band and the parade to home plate led by the Findlay Market Association. Mayor Donald Clancy and City Manager C.W. Harrell served as the pre-game battery on this warm, sunshiny day.[1]

Manager Fred Hutchinson picked local boy Jim Brosnan, an Elder High School alumnus and now aspiring author, to start for the Reds. The

Prof did not have his best stuff on Opening Day. Philadelphia sent him to the showers after touching him for four runs in one and two-thirds innings. But, that was it for the Philly offensive. The crowd of 30,075 at Crosley Field was soon roused to its feet, as the Reds struck for five runs in the bottom of the second against Phillies ace Robin Roberts. The final score — Reds 9, Phillies, 4 — was achieved in a neat 2:34. Having completed their Opening Day chores, the Reds boarded a plane for Pittsburgh and the Pirates' home opener at Forbes Field.

The Pittsburgh Pirates began their season on the southwestern shore of Lake Michigan with a single game against the Milwaukee Braves. It would be the first of 30,000 miles they would spend in the air in the next six months. Several changes were in store for the Bucs when they landed at Milwaukee. The Braves' home, County Stadium, had undergone some major renovations. The wire fence in the outfield had been replaced with a concrete wall, well-padded with foam material. The Braves also had a new manager, Chuck Dressen. The peppery Dressen, a former pennant winner with the Brooklyn Dodgers in 1952–53, was predicting great things for his squad. The Braves boasted a murderous row of Hank Aaron, Eddie Mathews, and Joe Adcock. Aaron had led the NL in hitting in 1959 at .355, while Mathews was the pace setter in home runs with 46. The mound trio of Warren Spahn, Lew Burdette, and Bob Buhl was one of the strongest in the league, and might be even more formidable with the development of youngsters Joey Jay, Juan Pizarro, and Carl Willey. It didn't hurt either that Dressen had the best catcher in the National League in Del Crandall. But perhaps more than anything else, the Braves' spirits were buoyed by the return of second baseman Red Schoendienst.

That Albert Fred Schoendienst was of Teutonic descent could not have been more obvious. He was born at Germantown, Illinois, a village in the southwestern part of the state, on February 2, 1923. At six-foot and 170 pounds, the flame-topped, freckle-faced youngster must have looked like a grown-up version of Huckleberry Finn. In 1942 he crossed the Mississippi River into neighboring Missouri for a tryout at one of Branch Rickey's St. Louis Cardinals prospect camps. The Mahatma saw what he liked and signed him to a contract. After leading the International League in batting in 1943, the Redhead was drafted into the U.S. Army. He made his debut as a left fielder with the Cardinals in 1945, a position he soon vacated for his friend, roommate, and fellow parishioner, Stan Musial.

Schoendienst was the second baseman on the 1946 World Championship Cardinals team. In 1956 he was traded — by who else but Frank Lane, then the St. Louis GM — to the New York Giants. A year later he was swapped again, this time to Milwaukee. Schoendienst batted over .300 in helping the Braves to their World Series victory over the New York Yankees in 1957. He hit .300 in a losing cause in the 1958 classic against the Yankees. Shortly afterwards came the shocking news: Red had been diagnosed with tuberculosis.

After a year of inactivity, Schoendienst was back, and not a moment too soon. The Braves middle defense had suffered in his absence, a major reason for their second-place finish in 1959. At one point that spring, Charlie Dressen had even contemplated using Hank Aaron at second base (Hank's response: "I'll play second, if Dressen plays third").[2] But none of this would be necessary because if the switch-hitting Red could tighten the infield, and set the table for the powerful group of sluggers that followed him to the plate, the Braves might be able to resume their pennant-winning ways of 1957–58.

As the Pittsburgh Pirates got ready to face the rejuvenated Braves team, Danny Murtaugh tinkered with his Opening Day lineup. With the southpaw Warren Spahn pitching for the Braves, the Irishman decided to start Gino Cimoli in center field and Hal Smith behind the plate. Both were right-handed hitters. Another change was less orthodox. The left-handed hitting Bob Skinner would lead off against Spahn. Skinner was selective at the plate and a swift runner on the basepaths. In any case, what would it hurt? Pittsburgh had not done well on the road in 1959, finishing with a poor 38–46 record. Only two of those away games were won at County Stadium. Their fortunes weren't about to change any time soon. As 40,000 plus fans watched, Pittsburgh dropped its eighth game in a row to the Braves, 4–3. Spahn out-dueled Bob Friend. The deciding blow came on an opposite field home run off the bat of Joe Adcock. Spahn, one of the best hitting pitchers in the game, also hit a home run to aid his cause. Afterward the Pirates, covered by three million dollars of disaster insurance, boarded their four-engine United Airlines flight for Pittsburgh and their season opener against the Cincinnati Reds.

April 12, Opening Day for the National League, found the Yankees still down in Florida, hosting the Cleveland Indians who had come east after breaking camp in Arizona. While the Indians were beating the

Bombers, their general manager was holding court at Miller Huggins Field. Addressing the group of sportswriters crowding around him, Fearless Frank Lane breezily declared his predictions for 1960. The Tribe, of course, would win the pennant. But, now having seen the Bronx Bombers up close in action, Lane predicted that Casey Stengel's men would finish no better than third behind the White Sox.

As Lane was engaging in his favorite hobby, needling the Yankees, back in the Big Apple another irritant was vexing the Bombers. New York mayor Robert F. Wagner was holding court at City Hall before one hundred print, television, and radio reporters. The purpose of the press conference was to unveil a plastic model of the proposed $15,000,000 Flushing Meadows, Queens stadium. The new stadium would be located on the north end of Flushing Meadows Park, lying between the Grand Central Parkway and 126th Street, and extending from Roosevelt Avenue to Northern Boulevard. The reporters beheld an open end, three-tier, circular stadium designed to accommodate 55,000 people. The parking facility would accommodate 5,500 automobiles. The builders, Praeger-Kavanaugh-Waterbury, also envisioned a removable section, which would convert the stadium into a 65,000-person facility for football games. In fact, the New York Titans of the fledgling American Football League, coached by the legendary quarterback Sammy Baugh, were expected to join the Continental entry as tenants at Flushing Meadows.

According to Richard Praeger, the owner of the engineering-architect firm in charge of construction, the Flushing Meadows stadium would boast several engineering attractions. Unlike Yankee Stadium, there would be no seats obscured by columns in the new stadium. Escalators would move fans quickly from level to level. A fan sitting in the last row of the upper deck would only have to climb eighteen rows to get to his or her seat. A retractable roof, made of aluminum or light-weight steel, could be added later at an additional $3.5 million, to be financed by private capital. That would make the new park the first all-weather domed stadium in the United States. A beaming Mayor Wagner announced that there was "nothing in the way now" to prevent New York from having a second Major League team.[3]

The Yankees were not pleased by this turn of events. George Weiss said it was "damned unfair" that the Continental League was about to be the beneficiary of a multi-million dollar municipally-owned stadium. The financial plans for Flushing Meadows called for floating bonds outside the

Bill Mazeroski, the Pittsburgh second baseman, hit the first home run of the year for the Pirates on April 14, 1960, at Forbes Field. On October 13 he would also hit the last.

debt limit and then leasing the facility to the Continentals and, presumably, the Titans. The city would issue 30-year bonds to be paid off by collecting a minimum of $900,000 annually in rental fees from the new stadium tenants. But Weiss was not assuaged. "The city," he charged, "won't lift a finger to get us the parking space we need desperately at the Yankee Stadium, but it's ready to pour money down the drain to accommodate the Continental League."[4] But the Continentals had an ace in the hole in their battle with the Yankees. The engineering-architect firm doing the project was founded by Emil Praeger, who had built the Tappan Zee Bridge and Jones Beach State Park, initiatives associated with Robert Moses. Moses, in fact, was about to assume the presidency of the World's Fair Corporation, the Fair being located just north of the proposed Flushing Meadows Stadium.

In April 1960, Forbes Field was celebrating its fifty-first season. Babe Ruth had ended his career there as a Boston Brave with three successive home runs in 1935. Ralph Kiner, the great Pittsburgh slugger, hit 51 round-trippers in 1947 and 54 more in 1949. And Dale Long, now with the Giants, had set a Major League record as a Pirate by hitting eight homers in eight games in 1956. For all of that, Forbes Field was not a home run hitter's delight. Its dimensions — 300 feet to right field, 365 to left, and a whopping 457 to center — made it more of a gap hitter's park. With the exception of the hulking Dick Stuart, this is what the current Pirates basically were. A few changes had been made in Forbes Field since the previous year. A fresh coat of paint had been applied to the exterior. Inside the park, head groundskeeper Eddie Dunn had laid a new crop of grass in the outfield. The infield, however, remained as rock solid as ever. At 2:30 P.M. Central Standard Time on Thursday, April 14, 1960, following the singing of the National Anthem by Jeanne Baxter and the introduction of players, Governor David A. Lawrence, Mayor Joseph M. Barr, and the rest of the crowd of 34,034 spectators settled back to watch the home opener against Fred Hutchinson's Reds.

To inaugurate the season at their Oakland playground, Danny Murtaugh turned to Vern Law. The Deacon pitched a seven-hit shutout as the Pirates won their first game of the 1960 campaign with a 13–0 rout of Cincinnati in a swift 2:13. Law struck out just two batters, but he walked none. Cal McLish, dealt the previous winter to Cincinnati by Trader Frank Lane, lasted less than three innings against the Pirate barrage. Bill Mazeroski hit the first Pirate home run of the season — almost six months to the day, he would hit the last. Cincinnati came back to win, 11–3, in a Saturday afternoon game on April 16. But the Pirates avenged the loss by taking both ends of the Sunday doubleheader. In the first game, Clemente provided all the runs the Bucs would need with a two-run homer in the second inning. The victim was left-hander Joe Nuxhall, who in 1944 at the age of 15 became the youngest player to ever play in the Major

Leagues. Bob Friend evened his record at 1–1 with a four-hit shutout. After being shut out for eight innings in the second game, the Bucs rallied for six runs in the ninth to win, 6–5. With that, the Pirates had done something that would characterize their entire 1960 season: the ability to win games in their last time at bat.

On Monday, April 18, the American League finally inaugurated its 1960 baseball season. A full complement of Capital dignitaries was on hand at Griffith Stadium in Washington, D.C., for the game between the home team Senators and Ted Williams' Boston Red Sox. A crowd of 28,327 fans saw President Dwight D. Eisenhower throw out the first ball. Havana, Cuba, native Camilo Pascual, a right-hander with the big overhand curve, struck out fifteen batters in leading the Senators to a 5–1 victory over Boston. His strikeout total was a new Senators record, breaking the previous mark shared by Walter Johnson and Jim Shaw. Another milestone was reached that afternoon at the nation's capital. Any dedicated follower of baseball knows that Ted Williams hit a home run in his last at-bat in the Major Leagues. What is less well known is that Williams hit a homerun in his *first* at bat of his final season, a solo shot against Pascual in the top of the second inning. It was the Thumper's 493rd homer, tying him for fourth place on the all-time list with Lou Gehrig. Afterward, the Red Sox flew from the nation's capital to Boston for their season opener against their old rivals, the New York Yankees.

The Pirate home stand continued with the arrival of the Philadelphia Phillies on April 19. One member of the Phillies, however, failed to make the trip. Manager Eddie Sawyer had called it quits following the Quakers' Opening Day loss at Cincinnati. Before leading the Whiz Kids to their surprising pennant win in 1950, Sawyer had taught biology at Ithaca College. Professor Sawyer reputedly could recall each and every name of his 1,500 students. However, in the spring of 1960 there had been a noticeable lack of communication between Manager Sawyer and the veteran players. To replace him, Phillies general manager John Quinn chose Gene Mauch, who had been managing the Minneapolis Millers of the American Association. Like Cal McLish, the thirty-four-year-old Mauch had been one of Branch Rickey's wartime finds at Brooklyn. He also played briefly as an infielder for the Pirates in 1947–48. Mauch announced that his goal was to become "one of the greatest managers ever."[5] But that would remain to be seen as the Pirates took two of three from their Pennsylvania cousins.

On April 20, Vern Law, showing a knack for quickly-pitched games, dispatched the Phillies for his second victory in just 2:04.

The Pirates had opened the season at 5–3. They were in fourth place, trailing Los Angeles, San Francisco, and Milwaukee, who were in a three-way tie for first. Danny Murtaugh's team now faced their first big test of the young season, as they welcomed the Milwaukee Braves to Forbes Field. The Bucs had had their worst season's split in 1959 against the Braves, a dismal 7–15 mark. A good showing against Aaron, Mathews, and company could vault them into first place; a poor performance could send them hurtling into the second division.

Chuck Dressen and his Milwaukee Braves checked into the Carlton House in downtown Pittsburgh on April 21, full of vim and vigor. They would check out several days later with a sheepish and hangdog look. The Pirates avenged their Opening Day loss at Milwaukee by taking three consecutive games from the Braves. In the first game of the series on Friday, April 22, Bob Skinner provided the heroics, his homer lifting the Bucs to a 6–2 victory in a "spine tingling tilt."[6] Bob Friend upped his record to 2–1. The Pirates won their fourth in a row the next day with a close 5–4 victory. They stymied the Braves with excellent fielding on the part of Skinner, Clemente, Bill Virdon, and a surprising Dick Stuart, who speared Ed Mathews' high hopper and stepped on first to snuff out one potential rally. On Sunday, April 24, Harvey Haddix and Elroy Face combined to silence the mighty Milwaukee bats in a 7–3 victory.

Months later, third baseman Don Hoak would recall this series with the Braves as his first inkling that the Pirates had a chance to go all the way. But that was in hindsight. To be sure, the Pirates had now won five games in a row, their fastest start since 1938. And they were in first place for the first time, a game ahead of the pre-season favorite San Francisco Giants. But the Murtaugh men would now have to leave the friendly confines of their Oakland neighborhood for a grueling 19-game road trip.

As the National League schedule was getting underway, the Yankees were breaking camp and heading north. Casey Stengel took 31 players with him from Florida, three over the Opening Day limit of 28. He announced that Whitey Ford, Bob Turley, Art Ditmar, and Jim Coates would be his first four starters. The fifth had yet to be determined. Roger Maris would be the left fielder, with Héctor López playing in right. On April 14, as the Pirates were opening against Cincinnati at Forbes Field, the Yankees were taking on their Triple-A team at Richmond. It was their shortest barnstorming tour since the World War II travel restrictions were in force.

Arriving in New York, the Yankees split two exhibition games with the Red Sox at the Stadium on April 16–17. The real drama, however, was occurring off the field. During the second game with Boston, it was announced that Frank Lane and Detroit GM Bill DeWitt had just conducted a historic trade. Lane sent the previous year's AL home run king, Rocky Colavito, to the Tigers for the reigning AL batting champion, Harvey Kuenn. The Frantic One had a lot at stake in this last trade, for in dealing Colavito he had deprived the Indians not only of the reigning home run king, but their most popular player and gate attraction as well. But that was Lane's problem. Having finally completed their exhibition schedule, the Yankees and Red Sox both left for Boston and the season inaugural at Fenway Park.

On Tuesday, April 19, 1960, an Opening Day crowd of 35,162 — the second largest ever at Fenway — was on hand for the game between the Bosox and the visiting Bombers. High skies and a strong northwest wind prevailed as Mayor John F. Collins, confined to a wheelchair, threw out the first ball. The festivities began promptly at 1:30 P.M. Eastern Standard Time, a little too promptly, in fact. The two clubs barely had time to gather along the sidelines before the Harvard Marching Band launched into the National Anthem. Among the Red Sox scrambling to line up along the diamond was Pumpsie Green, the first African American on a Boston Opening Day squad.[7]

Despite the size of the crowd, this Yankee-Red Sox series did not spark the same kind of electricity that we see today. Very little was at stake, except perhaps for manager Billy Jurges' job. Boston was a second division club fighting to stay out of the cellar. There were a few bright spots. Third baseman Frank Malzone was considered the best at his position in the American League, for both his slugging and fielding. Second baseman Pete Runnels was a contender for a batting crown. But Williams, who had suffered through his worst season hitting .254 in 1959, had almost retired that spring and was now strictly a part-time performer. The team was known more for off-the-field high jinks than it was for its exploits on the baseball diamond. One wag quipped that you could drop a bomb on the Bosox hotel and still be able to field a team the next day. Owner Tom Yawkey, said some observers, was paying the price for his team's failure to sign black players.[8]

But it was the retirement of Boston's slugging right fielder, Jackie Jensen, which had the greatest immediate impact on the club's fortunes in 1960. The blond-haired Jensen was, in every respect, a Golden Boy. In the late 1940s he was an All-American football player at the University of California where he shined in the Rose Bowl. He married Zoe Ann Olsen, a stunning blonde who was a runner-up in the Olympic springboard competition at London in 1948. The Yankees signed Jensen as a $75,000 bonus player in 1950, but finding no place for him in their crowded outfield, sent him to Washington in 1952. Traded to Boston the following season, he became one of the AL's most productive hitters, leading the junior circuit in RBIs three times, and once in stolen bases. In 1958 he was voted the league's Most Valuable Player. But following a 112-RBI season in 1959, Jensen announced his retirement from Major League Baseball.

Tom Yawkey, known as one of the most generous employers in the game, paid Jensen $40,000 a year. But as Jackie put in an article he wrote for the *Saturday Evening Post* the previous year, "My ambition is to quit." His growing business interests had a lot to do with his retirement. But that was not the only reason. Jensen hated being away from his wife and children in California—"the endless goodbyes, see ya laters, and long distance telephone calls."[9] Zoe often kept bad news from him, fearing it would interfere with his play. Jensen also detested flying. Ironically, the Jet Age, which had made expansion and the new Continental League a possibility, only increased his woes. Train-travel had once been a bonding experience for Major League players. But Jackie traveled alone to games by rail, isolated from family as well teammates. Still, for fans and scribes alike, Jensen's decision to leave at the height of his career was incomprehensible. How many young men would not give their eye-teeth to be in his place?

Casey Stengel had his own problems staffing the outfield. After much thought, he decided to start Roger Maris in right and Héctor López in left. It was a temporary move only, he said, designed to give the weaker defenseman (López) a chance to play the easier field at Fenway Park. Stengel batted Maris in the leadoff position, and the young blond responded with a single, a double, two home runs, and 4 RBI, as the Yanks won their season opener, 8–4. Jim Coates, the beanpole right-hander with the mean stare, was the beneficiary of the Bombers barrage, going all the way for the victory. Coates yielded Ted Williams' second home run of the year, a solo shot in the eighth. With number 494 Williams now owned sole possession of fourth place on the all-time home run list. Yogi Berra would remain on the bench for all three games with the Red Sox. Casey loaded up his lineup with right-handed hitters in an all-out assault on the left field wall, the Green Monster. It was a new experience for Yogi watching from the dugout. "I never played sometime before," he said.[10]

After splitting the next two games with the Red Sox, the Yankees headed back to New York. Opening Day at Yankee Stadium took place on Friday April 22, 1960, under sunny afternoon skies. The fans passed through the turnstiles into the "House That Ruth Built" with tickets for their various stations: $3.50 for box seats, $2.50 for reserved seats, $1.30 for unreserved seats, and $0.75 for the bleachers. Some box seats now featured swivel chairs for their lucky occupants. Hours before, Head Matron Ann Bianchini had supervised the cleaning and scrubbing of every public facility for the Opening Day crowd of 60,000 gathered to see the Bombers play the Baltimore Orioles. The playing surface that lay before them still held to its original dimensions: 301 feet down the left field foul pole, 461 feet to straightaway center, and 296 feet down the right field line. It was a left-handed hitter's ballpark. Given the differences between the left field and right field power alleys (415 feet versus 367), one wonders why Mickey Mantle did not dispense with switch-hitting at the Stadium and bat strictly from the left side.

The pre-game festivities were a rather bland affair. They commenced with a performance by the 69th Veterans Band and the U.S. Drum and Bugle Corps, and a parade to the outfield flag pole. Lucy Monroe, who had sung the National Anthem at Yankee Stadium Opening Day festivities since 1945, performed it for the very last time. Ford Frick took a bow and AL chief Joe Cronin threw out the first pitch to fellow Hall of Famer and former Yankee catcher, Bill Dickey. For a presidential election year, there was a conspicuous lack of political brass at the Stadium. Mayor Robert Wagner and Parks Commissioner Robert Moses were both no-shows. The Yankee owners Dan Topping and Del Webb had been at loggerheads with Moses for his failure to approve additional parking at the stadium. Noticing Moses' absence, one wag cracked that the parks commissioner had missed the game because he had been unable to find parking.

Moses missed a good game, as Whitey Ford and Ralph Terry combined to shut out Baltimore, 5–0. Héctor López and Mickey Mantle hit their first home runs of the season off starter and loser Hoyt Wilhelm. Before the game, Casey Stengel officially dispensed with his spring experiment and announced that Roger Maris would be his regular right fielder, with López permanently in left. How well this scheme would work out remained to be seen, but meanwhile both men made their presence known with their bats. On Saturday the Yankees won again, 3–2. Roger got his first hit at Yankee Stadium, a single to right in the fifth inning which scored Héctor with what proved to be the winning margin. The Yankees swept the series on Sunday, 15–9. They scored eight runs in the bottom of the first inning before a single batter had been retired, tying an American League record. Yogi Berra started in right field in place of Maris who had a sprained ankle, and lashed out his first two RBIs of the season. The Yankees were now 5–1 for the young season.

Prior to the start of their long road trip, a reporter reminded Danny Murtaugh that the Corsairs, like the Confederate General Robert E. Lee, did not win away from their home turf. The Irishman may not have been a history buff, but he knew his team's recent history well enough and he wasn't about to panic. Except for Gino Cimoli, who had injured his right wrist, the Bucs were hale and hearty. Bob Friend and Bill Mazeroski had conquered the weight problems that had plagued them the year before. Their only power hitter of note, Dick Stuart, had yet to hit a home run. But as Murtaugh reminded the gentlemen of the press, a different hitter was stepping up in every game. Roberto Clemente, batting in the third position consistently for the time and free of the elbow and back woes that had ailed him in past campaigns, was driving in runs and playing with his usual flourish in right field. Mazeroski and Hal Smith (not for the last time) were demonstrating surprising power.

The hitting star of the month, however, was Bob Skinner. Called "Doggie" (a reference to his former service in the U.S. Marines) Skinner was born on October 3, 1931, at La Jolla, a seaside community near San Diego, California, where he made his off-season home. After a short stint in college (to please his father, a foreign language teacher), Skinner signed with Branch Rickey's Pirates. Following a two-year hitch in the service, he rose quickly through the minor league ranks, playing for Murtaugh at the Pirates' Triple-A affiliate at New Orleans in 1955. The string bean (6'4", 185 pounds) left fielder was noted for his pretty swing; he hit .305 in 1957 with the big club, and followed it with a .321 performance in 1958. In 1959 he had dipped to .280.

"The Duke of La Jolla" and his wife Joan, a former student at San Diego

State, had three boys, Mark (4), Craig (3), and Andrew (21 months). A fourth child was on the way. The road trips were just as tough for Joan Skinner as they were for her husband. While he was hitting the cover off the ball, she was finding it hard to get the kids to bed. They didn't behave as well when he was gone. When first married, Joan had jumped on the East Liberty trolley to see Bob play at Forbes Field. Now it was different. The kids were restless at the park and ate everything in sight. She didn't get to see as much of the game as before.[11] It was too bad. It was Skinner more than any other Pirate hitter who carried the club during its eye-raising April streak. Basically a line-drive hitter who took advantage of Forbes Field's cavernous dimensions, he proved he could hit on the road as well. His April ledger would show a .333 average with a team-leading four home runs and 16 RBIs.

The Pirates were hitting and fielding well, standing second in both categories in the National League. Clemente was batting .396 and Dick Groat .340. But there were still some question marks. The bench was thin and lacked punch. As for the pitching, Law and Friend had three victories each. But Harvey Haddix had yet to begin winning consistently and rookies Jim Umbricht and Bennie Daniels, who had combined for a no-hitter in Florida in March against the Tigers, had not been impressive in their initial starts. The Baron of the Bullpen, Elroy Face, was also struggling. Thankfully, newcomer Fred Green was having a fine season. There were rumors that Joe L. Brown was trying to trade Bill Virdon in exchange for a fourth starter. He was said to be close to a deal with the Phillies.

The Bucs' winning streak continued at Philadelphia. They took two more from the Phillies, as Law and Friend locked up their third victories of the season. Then it was on to Cincinnati where the Bucs beat Cal McLish again on April 30 for their eighth win in a row. As the first month of the season came to a close, the surprising Pirates sat atop the NL standings with an 11–3 mark. They were 1½ games ahead of San Francisco, the pre-season favorite, and three ahead of Milwaukee.

While the Pirates took to the road, the Yankee home stand continued. Casey decided to start Yogi Berra in right field in place of the injured Roger Maris. "I must get that gorgeous creature into the lineup," he said. Unfortunately, Héctor López was unable to contend with the treacherous shadows in left field. His two costly errors led to a 7–5 defeat at the hands of the Red Sox. This ended the Bombers' winning streak at four. The Yankees then suffered their second consecutive defeat, this time to the Washington Senators, 5–4. Rookie Jim Kaat, destined to become one of the few players to compete in four different decades, won his first Major League game.

The Yankee home stand concluded with a three-game series against Baltimore. The first game on April 29 was won by the Orioles, 2–1, the third Yankee loss in a row. The final day of the month, however, saw the Yankees take sweet revenge, walloping the Birds, 16–0. Jim Coates pitched a shutout for his second victory. Maris had two doubles, a home run, and four RBIs. The game, which saw 24 hits, 8 walks, 2 errors, 2 passed balls, and one wild pitch, took just 2:43 to complete. With that victory, the Yankees ended April in first place. Their record of 6–4, if not overly impressive, placed them one-half game ahead of the Chicago White Sox and the surprising Detroit Tigers. Newcomer Roger Maris was making good on George Weiss' December trade, pacing the team with a whopping .391 batting average. Whitey Ford joked that the club's dismal Grapefruit League showing was the "biggest decoy job in baseball history."[12]

Some might have said that Whitey Ford, at 5'10" and 180 pounds, was quite the decoy himself. Born in Manhattan on October 21, 1928, Edward Charles Ford grew up in a rough and tumble neighborhood in Astoria, Long Island. A restive soul, as kids he and another local phenom Billy Loes (currently pitching for the Giants) once took the BMT Subway from Queens to Coney Island and back — a journey 1½ hours each way. The undersized pitcher-first baseman would soon burst out of the confines of his native New York. After graduating from Manhattan Aviation High School, Whitey signed a minor league contract with Yankee scout Paul Krichell in 1947. He made his first start for the Yankees on July 1, 1950, and proceeded to go 9–1, winning the final game of the World Series against the Philadelphia Phillies. After completing two years of military service in 1951–52, Whitey returned to become the leader of the Yankee pitching staff. Ford was not an overpowering figure on the mound. But he kept hitters off balance with an assortment of pitches — curve, slider, changeup, and sneaky fastball. By 1960 Ford was living at Lake Success, Long Island, with his wife Joan and his three children. He had an off-season job on Wall Street. But he remained a free spirit. Whitey, it was said, "never runs away from a party," but then again, he never ran away from pressure situations either. Casey Stengel called him "his professional."[13] Troubled with an arm ailment, Whitey had gotten off to a slow start in 1960, but no one doubted that he would be ready when the chips were on the line.

Also on the line was the fate of the Flushing Meadows stadium. There was no Continental League without New York, and no New York franchise without the new ballpark. As Bill Shea readily acknowledged, if the Board of Estimate did not approve the preliminary plans, the CL was dead. But as it turned out, Shea and Branch Rickey had had no need to worry. On April 27 the Board of Estimate gave its thumbs up. The vote was a signal for the other Continental League owners to get going with the construction or renovation of their own parks. Ford Frick gave his usual guarded response. He pronounced the vote "a good thing," but insisted that there were many questions left to be answered. Would the CL be able to find big-league-worthy stadiums? Where was the money going to come from? Would they except the rules set up by the commissioner? Bill Shea was having none of Frick's doubletalk. "The Continental League," he stated, "feels it is in a powerful position because of Congress's displeasure over organized baseball's reserve clause contracts."[14]

These brave words belied the profound difficulties facing the new baseball loop. While the AFL was busy negotiating a television contract with ABC for all its teams — a first in professional sports — the Continentals were being tied in knots by the question of territorial rights. The International League franchises at Toronto and Buffalo demanded indemnities of $850,000 each. Minneapolis and St. Paul, entrants in the American Association, wanted half a million per city. In another development, there was a rumor that a National League team (perhaps the Pirates) was about to move to New York and play at Yankee Stadium. Bucs GM Joe L. Brown denied any such overture on the part of the Bucs. The only way the Pirates would play in Yankee Stadium, he said, was in the World Series.[15]

Chapter Six

"We're shooting for 1960"

On May 1, 1960, the Russians shot down an American U-2 spy plane over Soviet airspace and captured the pilot, Francis Gary Powers. While President Eisenhower and Premier Khrushchev sparred on the international stage, the baseball world was wondering if the high-flying Pittsburgh Pirates would be brought down to earth after their fast April start, or if the Yankees would stay aloft after plotting "the biggest decoy job in baseball history." Would the Continental League get off the ground? That also remained to be seen as the first full month of Major League play began in 1960.

The Pirate road show, which began with successful stops at Philadelphia and Cincinnati, arrived at St. Louis on May 2. Former teammate Ronnie Kline, whose absence was greatly lamented by Pittsburgh sportswriters, beat the Bucs, 4–3, ending their winning streak at nine games. Elroy Face continued to struggle, walking in the winning run in the ninth. His record fell to 0–2. Now it was on to the Windy City and a two-game series with the Chicago Cubs.

Wrigley Field, located on Chicago's North Side, was known for its ivy-covered outfield and for its day-only games — it was the only ballpark in the league without lights. Wrigley had received a $500,000 renovation since the Bucs last played there in 1959. Twenty-eight percent of the lower grandstand between first and third bases had been replaced. Stainless steel ticket booths had been installed, and new entrances opened on Addison and Sheffield Streets. Most important to the players was the new two-story clubhouse underneath the left field stands. It had seven rooms, including a lounge, a projection room for baseball films, and a spacious office for their new manager, Charlie Grimm.

The Cubs were hoping that Grimm would bring some of the magic back to the North Side. "The Kaptink" (an allusion to his German heritage) had been the manager on the Bruins' last three pennant winners in 1932, 1935, and 1945. His current club had one genuine superstar in shortstop Ernie Banks, the league's reigning MVP, who had hit 45 home runs and drove in 145 in 1959. Except for Cuban second baseman Tony Taylor, the supporting cast was composed of fading veterans (such as former Phillies star Richie Ashburn) and a bevy of untried youngsters. Outfielders George Altman (26) and Billy Williams (21), and third baseman Ron Santo (20), had yet to come into their own. (Danny Murphy, a bonus baby from Beverly, Massachusetts, would make his debut with the Cubs later that summer at the tender age of 17.) In the pitching department, Grimm had Glen Hobbie (a native of tiny Witt, Illinois), who was a 16-game winner in 1959, and Don Elston, one of the leading relievers in the league. But the rest of the cast, such as Moe Drabowsky, Jim Brewer, and Dick Ellsworth, were still unproven. To no one's surprise, the Bruins were last in the National League, seven games behind the first-place Pirates.

On May 4 the Pirates emerged from the visiting team's clubhouse, also recently renovated as part of the agreement reached between the owners and the Players Association at Miami Beach the previous December. They walked into the Wrigley Field sunshine and proceeded to lose to the lowly Cubs, 5–1, stymied by the pitching of rookie Ellsworth. It was the first time this season that Pittsburgh had lost two games in a row. But that was not the big story of the day. Before the game, Danny Murtaugh was interviewed on Chicago's WGN radio station by announcer Lou Boudreau, a former Cleveland shortstop and manager of the Tribe's 1948 World Championship team. What Boudreau knew, but neglected to tell Murtaugh, was that Cubs owner Phil Wrigley had engineered a move worthy of Frank Lane or Bill Veeck. Boudreau and Charlie Grimm were about to exchange jobs, the announcer going to the dugout, and the manager to the broadcast booth. It was only after the interview with Murtaugh that Boudreau called his wife with the news, "Honey, you're about to become a baseball widow again."[1] Boudreau's presence in the Chicago dugout was, at least for the moment, dubious as Pittsburgh returned to its winning ways, edging the Cubs, 9–7. Bill Virdon's triple with two out in the ninth inning brought in the deciding runs. The Pirates left Wrigley two games in front of San Francisco and three games ahead of third-place Milwaukee.

A short time later, the players were strapped tightly in their seats, as the nose of their DC jet sought the skies above Midway Airport and began its climb to the West Coast. The Murtaugh men would begin their Pacific swing with a weekend series at the San Francisco Giants' new digs at Candlestick Park.

The Bucs soon got a dose of the San Francisco Bay blues. The Giants took the first contest on Friday May 6, winning 5–1, behind ace Sad Sam Jones. The three Willies — Mays, McCovey, and Kirkland — all hit home runs. A frustrated Roberto Clemente was ejected in the ninth by plate umpire Shag Crawford for throwing his helmet after striking out. The next day, the Giants won again, 6–5, tying them with the Bucs for the NL lead. Giant shortstop Eddie Bressoud delivered an inside-the-park home run. Danny Murtaugh was given the heave-ho for arguing that Bressoud had failed to touch third as he rounded the bases. Later in the game, Dick Stuart was ejected for questioning a strike call. The hometown boy took his sweet time making his exit as exasperated umpire Frank Descoli chased him across the infield. The most humiliating blow, however, was delivered in the final game of the series on Sunday, as the Giants walloped Pittsburgh for the third time in a row. The 6'4" McCovey had four RBIs in a 13–1 romp. The usually sure-handed Dick Groat made three errors. Bob Skinner managed to have himself thrown out of the game, the fourth Corsair to walk the plank in three days. Pittsburgh said good-bye to the Bay Area with a 13–8 record, a game behind the 14–7 Giants.

The Pacific trip continued at Los Angeles on May 9–11. By all rights, Murtaugh's men would have been playing at a new 52,000-seat stadium spread over 300 acres at Chavez Ravine. Dodger owner Walter O'Malley, however, had encountered vigorous opposition by civil groups in Los Angeles. The challenges had finally been resolved in the California courts, but construction had been delayed, forcing the Dodgers to extend their lease on the Los Angeles Coliseum.

The Coliseum, built for the 1932 Los Angeles Olympics, was ideally suited for football or track and field events, but was a monstrosity for baseball. Converted for baseball play by the Del Webb Construction Company, it was a lopsided concoction. The dimensions in center (440 feet) and right field (300 feet) were of Major League proportions. The left field, line however, was closer to Little League, just 250 feet from home plate. Webb's builders had created a barrier of sorts: a steel mesh screen, 42-feet high, which extended 140 feet from the foul pole. One wag dubbed the screen "the Great Wall of China," for all the "Chinese [i.e. cheap] home runs" that would be tagged over the screen. (The wooden structure with a green canopy behind home plate, used by owner Walter O'Malley for entertaining dignitaries, of course became the "pagoda." The Coliseum wasn't baseball, critics said. It was "Screeno." In an Associated Press poll, 116 of 193 baseball writers declared that any home run records set as a result of playing in this monstrosity should carry an asterisk.[2] So far, the Babe's record had remained safe.

In fact, the previous year's World Series champions weren't even expected to repeat. The Dodgers were in a period of transition. Duke Snider, Carl Furillo, and Gil Hodges, the last remnants of the great Brooklyn teams of the late 1940s and early 1950s, couldn't be depended upon to play regularly; Furillo would soon be released. The team had up-and-coming stars, such as shortstop Maury Wills, outfielder Tommy Davis, and a 6'7", 250-pound monster in first baseman-outfielder Frank Howard, who was wowing scouts at Spokane. Between these two groups there were younger established veterans, such as third baseman Jim Gilliam, catcher John Roseboro, and second baseman Charlie Neal. Neal had swatted 22 home runs in 1959 and had taken the Gold Glove Award away from Bill Mazeroski. The Dodgers also boasted what was potentially the best mound staff in the National League, if not the Majors. Johnny Podres and Don Drysdale led the pitching, with Stan Williams, Ed Roebuck, and Roger Craig in the wings. Then there was Sandy Koufax, who recently had fanned 15 Phillies (and walked seven) in a ten-inning loss to Philadelphia. But the most celebrated hurler on the Dodger staff at this time — in fact, the most celebrated *Jewish* hurler on the staff— was not Sandy but a twenty-four-year-old named Larry Sherry.

Larry Sherry was raised in the Fairfax section of Los Angeles, a lower middle class Jewish neighborhood clustered with family-owned groceries, kosher butcher shops, delicatessens, bakeries, and fruit and vegetable stands — the kind of ethnic neighborhood that Robert Moses' Cross Bronx Expressway had been destroying in New York City in the 1950s. Sherry's father, formerly of the Inwood section of Manhattan, operated a dry-cleaning services, while his mother was a seamstress. As his parents struggled to make good in the Golden State, Larry and his three brothers honed their playing skills near their Orange Grove Avenue home. The idea of a sports career was not something that anyone could have envisioned for the young Sherry. He was born with a club foot, and underwent a succession of operations as an infant. Although he wore orthopedic appliances until age twelve, Larry soon made up for lost time. At Fairfax High School he was the number two starter behind Barry Latman (currently with the Cleveland Indians). The Dodgers signed Sherry after graduation, and although he did not have a sparkling minor league career, impressed them with his tenacity in spring training and brought him up in the middle of 1959. Sherry's two wins and two saves in the World Series had earned him a shot as a starter in 1960. After a spotty performance in the starting rotation, he was now back in the Dodger bullpen.[3]

Larry Sherry, of course, was not the only prominent fireman on the field at the Los Angeles Coliseum that week. Elroy Face was the other. Face hailed from Stephentown, a rural community outside Albany, New York, near the Massachusetts border. Born on February 20, 1928, he was of English, French, and German extraction. Both Elroy's father and older brother were carpenters by trade, and he figured to be one too before baseball intervened. Signed by the Dodgers without a bonus, Face began his minor league apprenticeship in 1948 at Bradford, New York, in the PONY League (Pennsylvania-Ontario-New York). Branch Rickey plucked him out of the Dodger chain in 1953. At 5' 8" and 155 pounds, Face was not overpowering like Sherry, but rather relied on guts, craftiness, and an exotic "out pitch," the fork ball. In 1957 he emerged as the Bucs bullpen ace, at one stretch pitching in nine consecutive games. In 1959 he was the toast of baseball.

During the winter of 1959-60, Elroy Face was busy collecting trophies and plaques on the banquet circuit. Fifteen of them, including the prestigious Dapper Dan Award, now adorned his house at Carbondale, Pennsylvania. Putting his carpenter skills to good use, Face built shelves with sliding glass doors to accommodate them all. The Pirates had made him their highest paid player at $35,000 a year. But Face was not resting on his laurels that winter. He remodeled homes, putting in walks and steps for clients. He also constructed game rooms and built cupboards and shelves. His future enterprises included a plan to rent part of his double lot, and buy more houses for resale. In these times before free agency and agents like Scott Boras, a ballplayer as feted as Elroy Face was not financially secure for life.[4]

It is not too much of an exaggeration to state that the modern-day concept of a relief specialist as a glamorous (if not lucrative) position began with Larry Sherry and Elroy Face. There had been great relief pitchers before: the Yankees' Joe Page, Ellis Kinder of the Red Sox, and Jim Konstanty of the Philadelphia Whiz Kids, the National League MVP in 1950. But Face's 18–1 season and Sherry's World Series heroics ensured the ubiquity of the position forever more. Although it was Hoyt Wilhelm who would make it to Cooperstown, Sherry and Face were truly the first relief stars of the Television Age.

Both men figured prominently in the opening game of the Pirates-Dodgers series on Monday, May 9, the first under the lights at the Coliseum that season. A crowd of 23,417 fans was on hand as the Dodgers beat Pittsburgh, 7–4. Right-handed ace Don Drysdale, an intimidating figure at 6'6", struck out thirteen Pirates and allowed only two balls to leave the infield in the first seven innings. The Bucs did themselves no favors, committing four errors, thus extending their string of miscues to 15 in five games. Bob Skinner put a ball over the left field screen with Dick Groat aboard to tie it in the ninth. Sherry, however, relieved Drysdale and put out the fire, winning his third game in relief in five games. A three-run homer by Charlie Neal (a "Screeno Job") ended the game in the bottom of the ninth. Face, the victim of the blast, was now 0–3.

Pittsburgh managed to eke out a victory the next night, ending a four-game losing streak that had begun at Candlestick Park on May 6. Mazeroski homered again, as did Hal Smith, as the Bucs beat the Dodgers and Johnny Podres, 3–2. Vern Law gained his fifth victory against a solitary defeat. The Pirates won the last game of the series, 6–3, before 27,926 fans. They struck for five runs in the eighth and ninth innings, with Face getting his first win of the season with three innings of shutout relief. The game featured sometime rare in Major League Baseball before or since — an all-Jewish battery. Catching Sandy Koufax and later Larry Sherry that day was Sherry's older brother Norm, also in his second season with the club.

Heading east, the Pirates made a stop at Milwaukee on May 13–15 and took three out of four games from the Braves. In the first game of the series, Dick Stuart finally hit his first home run of the season. But the real hitting star was Dick Groat, who went 6-for-6. Pittsburgh followed that win with a dramatic extra-inning victory over the Braves, which saw Roberto Clemente drive in the winning runs in the 11th with a two-out, two-run triple. The Pirates split a doubleheader with Milwaukee on May 15, giving them a season mark of 6–2 mark against the Braves. But they remained two games behind the league-leading Giants. Not that Danny Murtaugh was complaining. He had hoped to merely stay even on the road. The Pirates had exceeded his expectations, returning to the Golden Triangle after a seventeen-game road trip with a respectable 10–7 record.

Despite this success, the Pittsburgh press and anxious fans were still beating the drums for an additional starting pitcher. Spring training hopefuls Bennie Daniels and Jim Umbricht had failed to provide adequate pitching behind Law and Friend. Haddix beat no one except the Braves. One possibility got away on May 13, when the Phillies sent right-hander Don Cardwell to the Cubs in a trade for second baseman Tony Taylor. Two days later, Cardwell pitched a no-hitter against the St. Louis Cardinals. The Pittsburgh drumbeats for a fourth starter grew louder.

As Pirate GM Joe L. Brown was pondering roster changes, Estes Kefauver's Senate Anti-Trust Committee was calling into question Major League Baseball's entire operation for acquiring players. On May 4, 1960, Kefauver announced that he would introduce legislation designed to end what he called the "dog-in the-manger" hoarding of baseball talent by the Major Leagues. If enacted, his bill would limit each club to 100 players it could directly control. Sixty of those would be eligible to be drafted by other teams each year. Not surprisingly, Bill Shea expressed enthusiasm for the Kefauver bill, calling it a "step forward."[5] The legislation would provide the new Continental League with the opportunity to acquire players to stock its new franchises.

Branch Rickey, holed up in his Sutton Place apartment in New York City with a bronchial infection, was uncharacteristically silent. But Ford Frick had plenty to say on the matter. He let it be known that he considered the Kefauver bill "a vicious piece of legislation." And he denied that the Major Leagues were hoarding players. An inventory of big league clubs, conducted by the commissioner's office, showed an average of 193 per team.[6] League presidents Warren Giles and Joe Cronin, as well George Weiss and Frank Lane, also raised loud voices in protest. The bill, they insisted, would destroy any incentive to invest in players. The whole minor league system would cave in if the bill was enacted. And for what? The CL entrant, said Weiss, would be "laughed off the field" at Yankee Stadium.[7]

For the Continentals, desperate straits called for desperate measures. Shea noted that in the July 1959 hearings he and Rickey had defended the reserve clause as part of their pledge to work under "the canopy of baseball." But Frick had acted in bad faith. Thus, the Continentals were not so inclined to defend baseball's monopoly over players this time around. In any case, the bill was their "only hope" for procuring players and going into business. In this bare-knuckle fight even the hallowed reserve clause was not immune. "The reserve clause in a player's contract isn't worth the paper it's written on," declared Shea.[8] Major League Baseball, he added, wouldn't dare sue the Continentals if they went after Major League players.

As Al Abrams of the *Pittsburgh Post-Gazette* observed, it was the "lack of foresight and arrogance of officials of established leagues" that had "paved the way for newcomers." The decline of the minor leagues from 52 at the end of World War II to just 21 by 1959, the *New York Times*' Arthur Daley noted, was the result of the Majors' saturation of their territories by TV telecasts of big league games. To keep things going, they had been forced to subsidize 90 percent of minor league baseball operations. But the members of the Fourth Estate were not particularly charitable toward the Kefauver bill. Abram's *Post Gazette* colleague Harry Heck accused the Mahatma of "brainwashing" the Kefauver committee. Kefauver was being maneuvered into stripping the Majors of their investments in the name of an even playing field. "There hasn't been anything as confiscatory," said Daley, "since Fidel Castro expropriated foreign property."[9]

Two years earlier, Casey Stengel and Mickey Mantle had testified before the Kefauver committee. But the present doings of the Kefauver committee and the Continental League were of only passing notice to the New York Yankees, as they struggled to cling to first place in the AL standings during the month of May. After crushing Baltimore, 16–0, on the last day of April, New York began the new month with a 9–5 loss to the Orioles at Memorial Stadium, thus losing two out of three games to the young Birds. Rookie right-hander Chuck Estrada, a handsome Californian of Spanish-Italian descent, went all the way for the Orioles on an 11-hitter. With that loss the Yankees dropped a half game behind the White Sox, who vaulted into first place on May 1.

The Bombers returned to New York and prepared to face the first invasion of the western teams: Detroit, Kansas City, Chicago, and Cleveland, in that order. The homestand started well, with the Yankees taking two games from Jimmy Dykes' Detroit Tigers. On Tuesday, May 3, they chased Bengal left-hander — and Yankee Killer — Don Mossi. The jug-eared Mossi had beaten them six times in eight tries in 1959, going the distance in all but one game. Behind the plate, calling signals for the first time this season was "Mr. Berra," who was spelling Elston Howard who had a blister on his catching hand. The next day, Stengel sent rookie left-hander Bill Short, billed as the next Whitey Ford, against another Yankee Killer, right-hander Frank Lary. Short defeated the Tigers, 4–2. Again, revenge was sweet. Lary had won five of six decisions from the Yanks in 1959 and was 21–6 lifetime against them. Yogi's return to catching duties did not last long. He was ejected from the game for arguing a call. Howard replaced him, and, injured hand and all, managed an opposite field home run that proved to be the margin of victory. The Yankees then extended their winning streak to four straight, their longest of the season, by twice defeating the visiting Kansas City Athletics. The Stengel men were again in first place, percentage points ahead of the defending champion Chicago White Sox.

Now, it was the very same White Sox who were coming into town for a single game on Sunday, May 8. Long the property of the Comiskey family, the Pale Hose had been bought the previous year by the irrepressible Bill Veeck. This was the famed baseball impresario who had put ivy on the Wrigley Field wall, signed Larry Doby to the Cleveland Indians as the first black player in the American League, and sent the 3'7" midget, Eddie Gaedel, to bat for the St. Louis Browns. Veeck had lost a leg while serving in the Pacific Theater during World War II and had endured several more amputations on the same leg. But he was never short on creativity. When the White Sox took the field against the Yankees on this Sunday afternoon, they were sporting yet another of Veeck's innovations: their surnames were emblazoned in four-inch capital letters on the backs of their traveling grey uniforms. The White Sox uniforms had undergone some re-tailoring before the players made their sartorial debut at Yankee Stadium. In the initial batch of shirts, first baseman Ted Kluszewski's name was spelled KLUSZEWSXI, and the Z was sewn on backwards.

The game itself was played in miserable weather, the Stadium lights winking through the thick haze, as a chilly drizzle stung players and fans alike. When it was mercifully over, Chicago had beaten the Yankees, 8–3, in ten innings. The big blow came on a three-run homer by center fielder Jim Landis off Jim Coates in the top of the tenth inning. The game was notable (if that's the word for it) for a rare mental mistake by the usually astute Elston Howard. In the top on the ninth, Yankee reliever Johnny James threw a pitch low and wide to walk Chisox right fielder Al Smith. Howard turned to umpire Jim Honocheck for a new ball. While this transaction was being negotiated, Smith sped around first and landed safely on second. Howard was charged with an error. It was that kind of day. Chicago left town having taken first place from the Yanks.

Tuesday, May 10, the first night game of the season at Yankee Stadium, was also the fiftieth anniversary of Manager Casey Stengel's professional baseball career. The Cleveland Indians spoiled things for the Old Perfessor by beating the Yankees, 5–1, on a four-run explosion in the tenth inning off Ryne Duren. On May 12, Joe Gordon's team beat them again, 3–2, as the Bombers suffered their third straight defeat. In a switch, Stengel batted Mickey Mantle in the second spot in the lineup; he wanted his best hitters to get as many at-bats as possible in a tight game. Mickey received a lot of intentional passes, Casey noted, which provided more RBI opportunities for the power hitters behind him. One might argue that Mickey was a pretty fair RBI man himself. In any case, on this night the strategy proved ineffective against the Tribe.

New York now took to the road and what they hoped would be greener pastures at the nation's capital against perennial cellar dwellers, the Washington Senators. True to form, the Yankees took two of three games from the Nats. The middle game of the series on May 14, however, saw the Yankees suffer their first shutout loss of the season, 4–0. Their conqueror was Camilo Pascual, a pitcher much coveted by George Weiss. The Cuban dandy (who, playing for the Senators and the Cienfuegos team in winter ball, had pitched over 400 innings in a twelve-month stretch) struck out eleven and gave up just four hits in a lighting quick 2:08. Throughout the series Casey Stengel complained bitterly about the Washington fans throwing beer cans into the Yankee bullpen. One missile just missed hitting Ryne Duren flush in the face. The separation of patrons and players at Griffith Stadium had been another of the demands made by the Players Association at Miami the previous December.

In the middle of May, the New York Yankees' record stood at 12–9, hardly a spectacular showing. Fortunately, no one else was running away from the pack. Chicago, Cleveland, and the surprising Baltimore Orioles (who took the league lead on May 16) were all jammed up with the Yankees, in what looked like a baseball version of a roller derby match. There were bright spots: Roger Maris was hitting .368, Yogi Berra .358, and Bill Skowron .353. Among the pitchers Jim Coates was 3–0 and Art Ditmar 2–0. Casey still had his share of worries, however. Mickey Mantle, at .274, had not started to hit and was plagued by his usual leg ailments; Whitey

Ford, suffering from arm miseries, was just 1–1. The Yankees had to be at their best as they began their first swing to the western clubs, including a clash with the two teams that finished ahead of them in the standings in 1959, the White Sox and Indians.

The Pittsburgh Pirates, who, like the Yankees, had relinquished first place after a hot April start, now settled in for a two-week homestand at Forbes Field that would carry them to the end of the month. The Bucs began by beating Lou Boudreau's Cubs, 11–6, on May 17, as Bob Friend notched his fifth victory with help from Elroy Face. The Bruins left town, and the St. Louis Cardinals came in for a pair on May 18. The first game saw Vern Law defeat Ronnie Kline, 4–1, for his sixth victory of the season. With their win on May 19, a 8–3 laugher that saw Clemente go 4-for-5, with two doubles, the Bucs moved a half game ahead of San Francisco.

Now it was the mighty Giants' turn to invade Oakland. On May 20, a crowd of 39,439, the second largest night crowd ever at Forbes Field, was treated to a 5–4 Pirate victory. Bill Mazeroski tied the game with a home run in the ninth inning. Roberto Clemente, the "*Arriba Kid*, as Bob Prince called him,[10] drove in Dick Groat with a single to right to win it in the twelfth. Bob Friend lost on Sunday, but the Bucs came back the next day to down the Giants, 8–7. Hal Smith sent the first pitch delivered to him in the eleventh inning to the scoreboard to win it for the Bucs. Murtaugh's men (23–11) were now 1½ games ahead of San Francisco (21–12), having exacted sweet revenge for their embarrassment two weeks earlier at Candlestick Park.

The Pirates played host to the Los Angeles Dodgers for a three-game series on May 23–25. The visitors won the opener, a 1–0 squeaker. Sandy Koufax yielded just one hit en route to a complete game victory, his first of the season. He struck out ten and walked six. The much-maligned Bennie Daniels pitched almost as well, and got the only hit off Koufax to boot. The Angelinos took the second game of the series on May 24, dropping the Bucs out of first place, just percentage points behind San Francisco. Gil Hodges, the old Brooklyn war horse, settled matters with a two-run homer in the second inning. They next day Los Angeles completed the series sweep behind Don Drysdale's neat five-hitter. The awesome rookie Frank Howard hit a monstrous shot over the left field wall. The ball landed in Schenley Park as Pirate broadcaster Joe Tucker was parking his car. Tucker got out, paced the distance to the wall, and added it to the inside dimensions. The results: a 550-foot home run.[11] Fortune had continued to shine on the Bucs. Despite three straight losses, they remained a game behind the first-place Giants.

As the Pittsburgh Pirates were beginning their homestand, their owner was mobilizing opposition to the Kefauver bill. John W. Galbreath called together a meeting of the sixteen team owners for Chicago on May 17, 1960. Speaking afterward to the press, the group expressed its unanimous backing for Ford Frick. Buoyed by the owners' response, the commissioner returned to Washington two days later to testify before the Kefauver committee. He denounced the bill to limit the number of players under contract to any Major League club as a "farce."[12] Branch Rickey, his voice restored to its sonorous tones, was also present at the hearings. The bill, he insisted, was necessary in order to remove the "power of money" that was preventing the Continental League from gaining traction. Hopelessly deadlocked, the sub-committee referred the bill without recommendation to the Senate Judiciary Committee on May 24. Kefauver and his senatorial colleagues worked out a compromise that would drop the 100 player limit, but keep the draft, limiting each team to 40 "untouchables." And, so things remained for the duration of May.

As the Pirates' owner was mobilizing his forces against the Kefauver bill, the Yankees were beginning their western swing under less than auspicious circumstances. The team's duffle bags were rifled at Cleveland's Municipal Stadium, with Mickey Mantle's new glove stolen (he offered a $100 reward for its safe return). On the field, New York was a little more fortunate, splitting two games with the Tribe. In the meantime, the front office was engineering moves. On May 18 the Yankees got down to the 25-player limit, releasing veteran outfielder Elmer Valo. The next day George Weiss completed his sixteenth deal with the Kansas City Athletics, sending Andy Carey to the A's for Bob Cerv. A native Nebraskan, Cerv would provide the Yankees with power at the plate, and outfield insurance. Cerv's presence would also allow Stengel to return Yogi Berra to catching duties and give the battered Elston Howard a much-needed rest.

On May 20 and 21, New York had a return engagement with the Chicago White Sox at Comiskey Park. With its large dimensions — 352 feet down the left and right foul lines, 415 feet to dead center, and 425 in the power alleys — and punishing prevailing winds, the Old Comiskey rewarded a style of play which emphasized pitching, speed, and fielding excellence. Luis Aparicio, "Jungle Jim" Rivera, and the recently reacquired Minnie Minoso had all led the league in stolen bases in the 1950s. Jim Landis was third in 1959. Under Al López's tutelage, the Go Go Sox had parlayed the sacrifice hit, stolen base, and squeeze play into a surprising pennant victory in 1959. The player that best exemplified this kind of play was shortstop Luis Aparicio.

Luis Ernesto Aparicio was born on April 29, 1934, at Maracaibo, Venezuela. His father, also named Luis, was also a shortstop of renown in his native country. The younger Aparicio was signed by the Chisox in 1954. The next two years saw him sparkle on the diamond while struggling to master the English language off the field. At Waterloo in the Three-I League, he survived by following his teammates to the dining table and pointing at whatever looked good to eat. By the time he came to the big club in 1956 to replace fellow Venezuelan Chico Carrasquel at shortstop, Luis spoke reasonable English. He also married Jim Rivera's cousin Sonia, who joined the club's "coffee drinking set" at the Picadilly Hotel.[13]

The 5' 9", 155-pound Aparicio, who had finished second to the equally diminutive Nellie Fox in the Most Valuable Player balloting in 1959, had no peer as a fielder. A few weeks earlier, Little Looie had made an unbelievable play, sailing through the air to his left to snag a grounder off the bat of Detroit's Al Kaline, then flipping the ball to Fox at second base to complete a double play. Aparicio had led the American League in stolen bases each year since 1956, and was acknowledged to be one of the most exciting players in the game. Casey Stengel compared his running style to that of Willie Mays. According to the Old Perfessor, Willie always took a big lead when he wanted to steal. Everyone knew he was going, and he stole the base anyway. Luis, by contrast, was "a con man."[14] He would take only a couple steps off the bag and drop his shoulder toward first. Meanwhile, his feet were poised to steal the base.

Although old-timers like Ty Cobb loved it, "small ball" was not in owner Bill Veeck's plans for 1960. For Veeck, genuine champions, such as his pennant-winning 1948 Indians, were built on power and pitching, not finesse. Power is exactly what he and GM Hank Greenberg had set out to achieve since their World Series loss to the Dodgers the previous October. The 1960 White Sox bulked up their attack with the December acquisition of Minoso and third baseman Gene Freese (who came over from the Phillies for young outfielder Johnny Callison). Roy Sievers, the Washington Senators slugger, was added just before the start of the regular season for insurance at first base and the outfield. With catcher Sherm Lollar and first baseman Ted Kluszewski, the Pale Hose now had the lumber to complement the speed of Aparicio and Jim Landis.

Comiskey Park, which formally opened on July 1, 1910, was in Bill Veeck's own words located "in the grimy industrial back-of the-yards section of the South Side" of Chicago. During his short time at the helm, Veeck turned the park and its seedy environs into an "Isle of Light." During night games there was as much illumination on 35th Street and Shields Avenue as there was inside the park. But it was Veeck's latest promotional gimmick — an exploding scoreboard — which promised to really light things up. When right fielder Al Smith hit the first home run of the season in the third inning of a game against the Tigers on May 1, the scoreboard produced an éclat of ten aerial bombs, leaving the park shrouded in a canopy of colors.[15] The Yankees would not have long to wait for a display of Veeck's $325,000 investment. When Kluszewski hit a home run off Whitey Ford in the third inning, the scoreboard accompanied his home run trot with 32 seconds of weird displays. The scoreboard remained silent, however, when Mantle hit a round tripper off Early Wynn in the ninth. The Sox won 5–3, as Wynn, the previous year's Cy Young Award winner, picked up his 273rd career. The Yankee miseries continued. Play the next day began at 1:30 P.M. in the afternoon, and after two hour-long rain delays, finally concluded at 7:07 P.M., with the Pale Hose again defeating New York, 9–8.

After the twin defeats at Chicago, the Yankees were more than glad to go to Kansas City, the baseball equivalent of kicking the dog. They proceeded to whip the A's two straight on May 22–23 at Municipal Stadium. The first game featured two homers by Yogi Berra. It was then on to Detroit for the conclusion of the western swing. In the first game, on May 24, New York was shut out for the second time in the season, by their old nemesis Don Mossi. Another long time irritant, left fielder Charley Maxwell, homered to win the game for the Tigers. The next day New York wasted two Maris home runs in a 9–3 loss to the Bengals. Casey was not happy; his Yankees were not fielding well, pitching well, or hitting well. While the Bombers struggled, Paul Richards' young Baltimore Orioles had perched themselves into first place in the AL standings.

Despite the Pirates' surprising showing, it was clear that Pittsburgh would have to bolster its pitching staff if it were to remain a serious pennant contender. On May 27, Joe L. Brown finally swung the deal that the Pittsburgh sportswriters and fans had been clamoring for. The Bucs acquired left-hander Wilmer (Vinegar Bend) Mizell from the St. Louis Cardinals, in exchange for minor league second baseman Manuel Javier. A 22-year-old native of the Dominican Republic, Julián (as he would soon be known) was one of the brightest prospects in the Pirate farm chain. But the deal had to be made if the Bucs were to stay in contention. As Brown put it, "We're shooting for 1960."[16]

Mizell made his Pirates debut on the last day of the month. The burly left-hander hailed from Vinegar Bend, Alabama, a town of just 35 people. Pitching before a vastly larger crowd, he went eight innings against the Cincinnati Reds. The Bucs won the contest in the eleventh, on a bases-loaded single off Cal McLish. Delivering the big blow against the multi-named pitcher was Roberto Clemente. The Pittsburgh Pirates' May record of 16–11 was good enough to keep them in first place atop of the National League, 1½ games ahead of San Francisco. But it was too soon to pop the champagne. The Bucs had played sub–.500 ball against first-division opposition, finishing 8–9 against Los Angeles, Milwaukee, and San Francisco. Eight of those losses (four apiece) had come at the hands of the West Coast teams. The next trip to California was looming in June and might decide the fate of the Pirates once and for all.

Like the Pirates, the Yankees ended their May schedule at home. On May 26 they began a three-game series with the Baltimore Orioles. The Yankees took back the American League lead in the first game, as Whitey Ford shut out the upstart O's, 2–0. The next day, Baltimore squeezed by the Yankees, 3–2, behind knuckleball specialist Hoyt Wilhelm. For this game, Birds receiver Clint Courtney used a special catcher's mitt. It was 1½ times as large as a regular one, and four ounces heavier. A brainchild of Orioles manager Paul Richards (himself a former Major League catcher), it was developed in an attempt to reduce the number of passed balls created by Wilhelm's wicked knuckler. The mitt did its job, but the Bombers rebounded the next day, May 28, to take two of three from the Orioles.

The Yankees ended the month with a Memorial Day weekend series at the Stadium against the Washington Senators. Casey Stengel, however, was not there to make up the lineup. He was taken ill with a flu virus, and had to be hospitalized at Lenox Hill Hospital in mid-town Manhattan. First-base coach Ralph Houk directed the team in his absence. The Major

Mickey Mantle as viewed from the stands. At the end of a Memorial Day doubleheader against the Washington Senators on May 30, 1960, Yankee fans poured out of the stands, mauling Mantle and leaving him battered and bruised.

(as Houk was known) instituted several lineup changes. Clete Boyer was inserted at third base and Johnny Blanchard, the third-string catcher, was sent behind the plate. The Yanks won, 6–4, on May 29, the first victory under Houk.

The Memorial Day doubleheader on Monday was witnessed by 42,927, one of the largest crowds thus far at Yankee Stadium. The Bombers dropped the first game to the Nats, and then came back to win the second. The real drama that afternoon, however, occurred as the Yankees were exiting the field after the second game. Fans vaulted over the center field stands and attacked Mickey Mantle. A battered and bewildered Mick fought his way through the mob to the dugout. To add insult to injury, the phones began ringing at the Stadium from fans alleging that Mickey had deliberately struck their children. He vehemently denied it. Yankee brass vowed to create a roped phalanx of security guards, like the one that had been used for Joe DiMaggio, in order to avoid any further injury to Mickey or to the fans.

Mickey Charles Mantle was born on October 20, 1931, at Spavinaw, Oklahoma, and raised in Commerce, hence the nickname, "the Commerce Comet." Still only twenty-eight, he had experienced too much of the world too soon: the loss of his father at the onset of his career, the responsibilities of marriage and parenthood, debilitating injuries that would have crippled a lesser man, and the overhyped expectations of fans, press, and team alike. Having meant so many things to so many people during his lifetime, it is little wonder that it would take three autobiographies to tell his life story. In the first, *The Quality of Courage*, he portrayed himself in the mode of a classical hero. In *Whitey and Mickey*, written jointly with best pal Ford, he cast himself in the role of the fun-loving, late-night party animal. In the third, called simply *The Mick*, he was the fallen hero recognizing his mistakes and making a belated plea for redemption. But that was later. On this scary afternoon in May at the Stadium, years before John Lennon's murder, he was happy just to escape with his life, as crazed fans vented all their love and frustration on his rugged shoulders.

The month of May ended with the Yankees in third place. They had gone 13–13, leaving them three games behind Baltimore and two back of second-place Cleveland. Most distressing of all was their miserable 2–9 record against the first-division clubs, the Indians, Orioles, and White Sox. Their manager was in the hospital. Their best player had a swollen jaw and bruised ribs courtesy of overzealous fans, and was mired in a slump. Their ace pitcher was inconsistent. On the other hand, the Pirates, hale and hearty, had shown surprising resiliency, bouncing back from a discouraging trip to the West Coast to reclaim the top spot in the NL standings. While the eyes of the New York Yankees and Pittsburgh Pirates were fixed on the scoreboard, Branch Rickey, Bill Shea, and the Continentals had their eyes fixed on the U.S. Congress. All three organizations looked to June with great anticipation.

CHAPTER SEVEN

"As many as I can"

On June 2, 1960, the lights went out on the Great White Way. Unable to reach an agreement on a pension plan with the Actors' Equity Association, the League of New York Theatres closed down the last of the twenty-two productions currently running on Broadway. The Pittsburgh Pirates and the New York Yankees managed to keep their shows running in June. In fact, both teams enjoyed one of their best months of the 1960 season. While the Bombers and Bucs prospered, that consummate actor-director, Branch Rickey, was still trying to debut what he hoped would be the most successful production of his career, a third major league.

For the New York Yankees, June at first seemed to be nothing more than a continuation of May's miseries. With Ralph Houk at the helm in place of the recuperating Casey Stengel, the Yanks lost twice to Baltimore at Memorial Stadium. Their record dropped to 19–19, putting them in fourth place, six games behind the league-leading Orioles. The Bombers' return to the Bronx came with a change of fortunes. Between June 3 and June 11, they played a ten-game homestand, winning all but two games. The Yankees took three out of four from the visiting Boston Red Sox, concluding with a Sunday doubleheader sweep on June 5. In the first game, Mickey Mantle (who had been mired in a 7-for-50 slump) and Roger Maris both blasted round-trippers. Ted Williams notched career home run number 495. The Bombers now braced themselves for a showdown with their western pennant rivals, the Chicago White Sox and Cleveland Indians.

After losing to Chicago, 3–2, on June 6 (Houk's last game as interim manager), the Yankees welcomed Casey Stengel back to the dugout the next day with a 5–2 victory. Jim Coates went the distance to record his sixth victory of the season without a defeat. George Weiss, however, continued to tinker with the pitching staff. Before the game, the Yankees demoted lefty Bill Short to Richmond and brought up righty Eli Grba from the same club. Short's emergence as the "next Whitey Ford" had been derailed by wildness. The third game of the series, on June 8, saw a revived Bob Turley hurl a 6–0 victory, his first complete game of the year. Yankee Stadium didn't have an exploding scoreboard—just plenty of explosions in support of Turley. Mantle hit two home runs, while Héctor López and Roger Maris added one each. For Maris, it was his sixteenth round-tripper, matching his entire previous year's production with Kansas City. The Yankees made it three out of four over the Pale Hose, winning 5–2 on Thursday night. Mantle, beginning to surge, hit his third home run in two days, giving him twelve for the season.

Frank Lane was at the Stadium scouting the Yankees on the last day of the Chicago series. The Frantic One was in an expansive mood—and with good reason. His Indians had won five games in a row and had taken over first place on June 8, justifying for the moment his flurry of trades. The Yankees, however, were not about to lie down and play dead. On Friday, June 10, they defeated the Indians, 4–3, snapping the Tribe's winning streak while extending their own to four straight. A crowd of 46,030—the largest of the year—rose to its feet as Mickey Mantle hit two home runs, making it four in three games and eight in the last 16 for the Mick.

On Saturday, June 11, at the Belmont Stakes, jockey Bill Hartack brought Celtic Ash up from dead last to a take a 5½ length victory over Kentucky Derby winner Venetian Way. That same day saw the Yankees come from behind to whip the Indians once again. Elston Howard hit a two-out, two-run homer off Johnny Klippstein in the seventh inning to snap a 4–4 tie. Maris and Yogi Berra also hit round-trippers, while López was robbed of another on a spectacular catch in front of the center field bleachers by Jimmy Piersall. The Yankees' winning streak was at six. They lost a chance to extend it, and draw even closer to the league-leading Indians, when the Sunday doubleheader at the Stadium was rained out. However, Mickey Mantle, bedeviled by a groin injury, a thigh pull, and a bum knee, got a day of much needed rest. And so, the Yankees remained in third place, 1½ games back, as they began their second western road swing of the 1960 baseball season.

Like the New York Yankees, the Pittsburgh Pirates began the month of June on the road. But while the Stengel men had been mired in a slump, Danny Murtaugh's charges were still in first place, 1½ games ahead of the second-place San Francisco Giants. One of the major reasons for the Corsairs' fast start in 1960 was due to the emergence of their right fielder, Roberto Clemente.

Has there ever been a more glorious sight in baseball than Clemente? Who can remember him but as this impossibly handsome figure, approaching home plate like a modern-day Hercules sent to clean out the Augean stables? Yet, so much myth-making has been spun since his untimely, and still painful, death in 1972 that we forget that he was not always the most celebrated Latin, or even Puerto Rican player, in the Major Leagues. The island of Puerto Rico is only one hundred miles by thirty-five in area. But even within this tiny space, there are two Puerto Ricos. The one that is best known to tourists is the northern part of the island on the Atlantic Ocean. Here, the land is lush and verdant, and the palm trees sway in the moonlight, like one of those 1940s MGM musicals come to life. Carolina, Puerto Rico, the place of Clemente's birth, was a poor neighborhood located just east of the dancing lights of the capital city of San Juan. Turning southwest from San Juan over the Cordillera Central (or central mountain chain) is the old city of Ponce. Here the sun is hotter and the land is drier. The Plaza de las Delicias reminds us not of orchids in the moonlight, but rather of Andalusian Spain. Ponce, "the Pearl of the South," was the birthplace of the island's most popular player, Orlando Cepeda.

Known as the Baby Bull, Cepeda was the darling of the San Francisco Giant fans, and Latin fanáticos everywhere. He had enormous power, hit for a high average, and ran surprisingly well for a man born with flat feet. His obvious ability and his sunny disposition won him the lion's share of publicity among Anglo fans. By contrast, the often moody Clemente was still mostly an unproven talent in 1960. Everyone recognized his fielding brilliance and rocket arm, but he had not shown much power at the plate, and had yet to demonstrate that prized possession of a superstar, the ability to carry a team. Neither the *Pittsburgh Press* nor the *Pittsburgh Post-Gazette* devoted much newsprint to him that spring. But in fairness, the black press tended to pass over him as well, showering their attention on Cepeda, Vic Power, and Minnie Minoso.

It was hard to categorize Clemente. He didn't fit neatly into the usual Latin American stereotypes perpetuated by Hollywood. He wasn't the unschooled trickster that Minnie Minoso was. He wasn't the Latin lover in the Mediterranean mold like Pedro Ramos; he wasn't the courtly *hidalgo*, such as Al López was; he wasn't the naïf peasant boy that Cepeda was. But in May 1960 it was his bat that defined him. The previous month Clemente had transformed himself into "Mr. Clutch." Fully recovered from the various maladies that plagued him in 1959, he hit .336 with six homers, driving in 25 runs in 27 games. On June 11, at a brief ceremony at Forbes Field, Roberto (or "Bob," as he was known in the press) was honored with the National League Player of the Month Award for the month of May.

Danny Murtaugh was counting on Clemente to continue his hot hitting as Pittsburgh embarked on their biggest test of the young season. Starting on June 3 they played 16 games away from the friendly confines of Forbes Field, a road trip that would take them from the shores of the Delaware to the Pacific Coast, courtesy of the Jet Age. The road trip began auspiciously on June 3 with a 3–0 victory over the Philadelphia Phillies at Connie Mack Stadium. Vernon Law won his eighth game against a solitary defeat, and Clemente drove in two of the three Pirate runs. "Is there a more exciting player than Roberto Clemente?" asked Harry Keck of the *Post Gazette*.[1] Then, suddenly, the Pirate six-game winning streak came to a halt. The young Phillies stunned the Bucs by snatching both ends of a doubleheader on June 5. In the first game, the 6'8" Gene Conley, a member of Red Auerbach's Boston Celtics 1959–60 championship team, threw a 10-hit shutout against the Corsairs.

The Pirates moved on to Chicago on June 7 where they suffered their third loss in a row, 13–2. Bruins shortstop Ernie Banks, the National League MVP in 1958 and 1959, liked to have a breakfast of fruit juice, two eggs, bacon, or ham before a game. He ate the Bucs up that afternoon, going 3-for-4 with four RBIs, sending Law to his second defeat. Danny Murtaugh shrugged off the slump, saying, "If we hit rock bottom just once a month I'm going to be very satisfied."[2] The next day the Bucs justified his confidence, winning 5–3. Elroy Face stopped a Cub rally to preserve Vinegar Bend Mizell's first victory as a Pirate. The Bucs won the final game of the series at Wrigley Field, 11–3, leaving town on June 9 still nursing a two-game lead over the Giants.

Pittsburgh traveled to St. Louis for four games against the Cardinals on June 10–12. The Redbirds had been mired in seventh place on May 1. With nothing to lose, Manager Solly Hemus had benched a slumping Stan Musial (there would be some talk of "the Man" coming to Pittsburgh before the June 15 trading deadline). A miscast Bill White moved in from center field to replace him at first base. Curt Flood took over for White in center. Right-hander Ernie Broglio was shifted from the bullpen into the starting rotation. The revamped Cardinals moved into the first division for the first time by whipping the first-place Bucs three out of four games, beginning with the Friday night contest. Saturday was a day for stunning come-backs — Celtic Ash's win at the Belmont, Elston Howard's homer against Cleveland — and unfortunately, by the Cardinals against Pittsburgh. The Redbirds' lumbering left fielder, Bob Nieman, who had hit home runs in his first *two* at-bats in the Major Leagues in 1952, doubled in the winning run in the ninth for 7–6 Cards victory. On Sunday, June 12, the Pirates salvaged a doubleheader split at Busch Stadium, romping to a 15–3 victory in the first game. Dick Stuart had five hits (including two home runs) and 5 RBIs in support of Vern Law's ninth victory of the season.

Heading westward, the Pirates stopped at Salt Lake City where they played an exhibition game against their Triple-A affiliate and got in some fishing. Then, it was on to San Francisco. As their plane touched down in the Bay Area, Pittsburgh (32–20) was just one game in front of the Giants (32–22). When the Bucs-Giants series was over, only one team would remain in pennant contention.

After the completion of the Cleveland series at the Stadium on June 12, the Yankees boarded the Sunday night flight for Kansas City. They were in second place, two games behind the surprising Baltimore Orioles. As they traveled westward, the rumor mills were spinning. George Weiss was said to be interested in A's lefty Bud Daley, who had gone 16–13 the previous year for a seventh-place team. Gil McDougald and young Clete Boyer were supposed to be part of the transaction. Once back on the ground, the New Yorkers proceeded to take the first two games of the series from the A's at Municipal Stadium. On June 15, a Midwestern rain storm, buffeted by 28 MPH winds, caused the cancellation of the third game at 11:57 P.M. Central Time, with the score knotted at 7–7. The deal for Bud Daley was also at standstill, as the June 15 trading deadline expired. With eight straight wins and a chance to vault past the Tribe for undisputed possession of first place, the Yankees and Whitey Ford were routed by the Athletics, 9–1, on June 16. Ford (2–5) lost to Kansas City for the first time in his career. Daley, still in an A's uniform, utilized his slow curve to perfection, holding New York to four hits in running his 1960 record to 9–2.

During the sojourn at Kansas City, a group of New York area reporters decided to rent a car to take a side trip to the Harry S. Truman Library at Independence, Missouri. Yogi Berra spotted them in the lobby and asked where they were going. They told him, and asked if he wanted to come along. Yogi declined saying, "Why would I want to go there? I got my own books at home."[3] The Yankees, having closed their books at Kansas City, now headed for Chicago, trailing first-place Baltimore by 1½ games.

The Bronx Bombers swept four straight from the fourth-place White Sox in the Windy City. Art Ditmar beat the Chisox, 4–2, in the opening game on June 17, scattering four hits. He did not strike out a batter in going the distance, but did single in a run. Clete Boyer and Mickey Mantle hit home runs. Bill Veeck's exploding scoreboard remained silent, but not the Yankees. They celebrated their round-trippers in the dugout by lighting Fourth of July sparklers, and doing their best imitation of an Indian war dance. Veeck, the consummate showman, thought it was a neat trick and promised to "reciprocate in kind." That would have to wait. On June 18, New York wreaked havoc on Early Wynn and his would-be rescuers with a 19-hit attack in a 12–5 victory. Maris (number 19), Mantle (number 14), and Moose Skowron (number 8), all hit round-trippers. Eli Grba, "the Consonant Man," notched his first win with six innings of relief. With this victory the Bombers moved into first place, .002 ahead of Baltimore. On June 19, the Yankees completed their sweep of the Pale Hose, taking both ends of a doubleheader. As Chicago slipped into the second division, Yogi—"Mr. It Ain't Over Till It's Over"—declared the White Sox "are dead."[4]

The Yankees were in first place, eleven games over .500 at 33–22, with a thin .003 lead over the Orioles, as their western caravan rumbled into Detroit on June 21. The Tigers had stumbled after a fast start. But a recent streak had vaulted them out of the second division and into fourth place ahead of Chicago. The Bombers, unimpressed, took two out of three games from the Bengals at Briggs Stadium. Mickey Mantle and Whitey Ford led the Yankees to a 6–0 victory over their nemesis Frank Lary. There was one sour note. Bill Skowron, who had made it unscathed through the first 53 games of the season, injured his left wrist sliding into second base. But fortune continued to smile on the Yankees. The Moose's understudy, Kent Hadley, hit two home runs to help the Bombers defeat the Tigers, 7–3, on June 22. The New York winning streak was finally snapped at seven games the next day as another old nemesis, Charley Maxwell, ended the final game of the series with a leadoff homer in the ninth. But the Bombers remained in first place, one-half game over Baltimore. Now came a reckoning with the third-place Cleveland Indians on June 24–26.

While the New York Yankees were touring the Midwest, the Pittsburgh Pirates were playing the pre-season favorites, the San Francisco Giants, at Candlestick Park. San Francisco had been the first meeting place of the United Nations in 1945; according to the *San Francisco Chronicle*, the players that inhabited this new stadium were "the most polyglot collection of ball players yet assembled on one major league roster." There were at least twelve nationalities and ethnic strains represented. The manager, Bill Rigney, was an Irishman. Players of Irish descent included pitchers Mike McCormick and Billy O'Dell. Catcher Bob Schmidt was German, while shortstop Ed Bressoud was of French descent. Billy Loes was Greek. Georges Maranda was French Canadian. Pitcher Johnny Antonelli and infielder Joe Amalfitano (native of the Amalfi Coast) were Italian. Latin America was represented by Puerto Rico (outfielder Orlando Cepeda and shortstop José Pagan), Venezuela (Ramón Monzant), and the Dominican Republic (outfielder Felipe Alou, later to be joined by brother Matty and pitcher Juan Marichal). The Giants even boasted a former cricket player from the Bahamas, infielder André Rodgers. In all, the club had the largest percentage of blacks on its roster (black at the time meaning both African American like Mays and McCovey and Latin players such as Cepeda and Alou) of any Major League team.

San Francisco had the best player in the game in Willie Mays. The Say Hey Kid, however, did not enjoy a charmed relationship with the Bay City. Frisco in 1960 was not the liberal haven it is today. Realtors were reluctant to sell houses to either blacks or "Orientals." Mays, with some difficulty, had bought a house in an all-white neighborhood. There had been some ugly incidents, incendiary notes were left at this door and pranksters rang his door at will, prompting Willie and his wife Margueritte to move back to New York after the 1959 season.[5] In any case, Bay Area fans associated Mays with New York, and looked elsewhere for heroes. The fan favorite in 1958 was Orlando Cepeda. The Baby Bull had had a great sophomore season, hitting 27 home runs and driving in 105, while hitting .317, the last two categories surpassing Mays. He was lively and sensitive and made great ink for the press, who loved to mimic his Spanish accent (a common practice in both white and black newspapers of the time). But Cepeda was also bypassed in the 1959 poll. In an informal tally, the fans' favorite was the pitcher Sam Jones, a twenty-one game winner in 1959 and NL ERA leader at 2.83.

Sad Sam Jones, or Tooth Pick Jones as he was also called, was born December 14, 1925, in Stewartville, Ohio. He grew up in Monongah, West Virginia, a small mining town on the Monongahela River, one of the three rivers that form the Point at Pittsburgh. His father had died in a mining explosion, and his future father-in-law had been crippled by another. Jones was a large, powerful, slow-moving man, but the most striking thing about him was his color. Although African American, his skin resembled that of a white man and his receding hair was reddish brown. Jones never hid the fact that he was black, and suffered the hurts that went along with it. In the U.S. Army he played on the company team, but not the post club, which was segregated. The sportswriter Dick Schapp interviewed Jones at his West Virginia home. At the conclusion of the interview, Jones drove Schapp back to his hotel in the neighboring town of Fairmont. They stopped in at a tavern in town where Jones, a quiet and courteous man, introduced him to some of the patrons, all of whom were white. After one beer, Jones said his goodbyes and left. Sad Sam, so Schapp learned, was not comfortable drinking in an all-white establishment. Although Jones' celebrity and light skin gave him access to places barred to most blacks in Fairmont, he was not comfortable receiving privileges denied to most others of his race.[6] The Giants may have been a "sociologist's delight." White southerners, like Don Blasingame and Jim Davenport, coexisting peacefully with their black teammates, staying in the same hotel in Phoenix, Arizona, during spring training and on the road during the regular season. But there were limits on fraternization imposed by the world outside of baseball, which as Sad Sam Jones well knew, could not be overcome by celebrity or money.

Back in San Francisco, the "polyglot" Giants had every reason to be optimistic as the Pittsburgh Pirates came into town on June 14. At the last meeting between these two teams on May 6–8, the Giants had swept a three-game series from Pittsburgh, snatching the NL lead. But the Giants had their problems, too. The WOW trio (May, Cepeda, McCovey) had not hit consistently. Mays was Mays. But McCovey, after a fast start leading the league in RBIs, was in the midst of a prolonged slump. The bullpen with Stu Miller and Whitey Ford's former subway mate, Billy Loes, was spotty. *San Francisco Chronicle* writer Art Rosenbaum complained about their "listlessness afield." There was talk that Manager Bill Rigney's job was in jeopardy. However, the big bats seemed to be stirring at last. On June 12, San Francisco walloped Milwaukee, 16–7, with an 18-hit attack. The game took 3 hours and 52 minutes to play, breaking the NL mark and tying the Major League record for the longest game ever.[7] As the Pittsburgh series began the Giants were still only one game behind and eager to repeat their earlier success against the Bucs.

Many years later, having known it as one of the oldest and most derided baseball stadiums in the Major Leagues, it is hard to conceive of the hype that accompanied the opening of Candlestick Park in 1960. Bob Stearns, writing in *Baseball Digest*, called it "the Taj Mahal of the leather and lumber set."[8] Located at Candlestick Point at the extreme southern end of San Francisco Bay, it was the second largest facility in the National League after the Los Angeles Coliseum, with a seating capacity of over 42,500. Candlestick was the first ballpark built entirely of reinforced concrete. It was also the first to have a radiant heating system. It contained 11,000 box seats and 24,000 grandstand seats. The "golden horse shoe boxes" in the mezzanine section, with room for eight persons apiece, went for $4,000. The parking lot would be the envy of Dan Topping and Del Webb, holding 8,000 cars. On its opening day, April 12, 1960, Ford Frick and league presidents Warren Giles and Joe Cronin were in attendance, as was Vice President Richard M. Nixon, who threw out the ceremonial first pitch.

Candlestick Park's dimensions, 335 feet down the foul lines and 420 feet to dead center field, did not admit to any bias toward either left-handed or right-handed hitters. But geometric symmetry did not reckon with Mother Nature, for Candlestick soon proved to be problematic for fans and players alike. San Francisco in summer boasts a balmy temperature during the day. There is no more delightful city for sightseeing. It was one of those rare towns where visiting ballplayers were not confined to air-conditioned rooms. They could be seen roaming Market Street or Maiden Lane.[9]

The Giants, however, played mostly at night, and in the evenings the temperature dropped precipitously, often into the 40s. (On opening day, the heating system did not work). Ballplayers had their own miseries besides the plunging mercury. At the Giants' previous home, Seals Stadium, the prevailing winds at Potrero Hill blew fly balls into the seats in left. This had favored right-handed sluggers like Willie Mays and Orlando Cepeda.

At Candlestick the situation was reversed. A prevailing wind whipped across center field to right. What had been home runs at Seals Stadium all too often turned into pop flies at Candlestick — some were caught, others were not.

On June 14 a "wind-whipped crowd" of 35,465 saw the Pirates defeat the Giants, 6–3, in their first win ever at Candlestick Park. Sad Sam Jones was undone by four unearned runs in the first two innings, suffering his first loss ever at Candlestick. Things might have been different for Jones if not for the capricious winds. With one out in the second inning, Bucs catcher Smoky Burgess golfed an opposite field fly toward left for what seemed to be out number two. The ball, however, was caught in the swirls and drifted all the way back to the infield, where it fell in front of flummoxed third baseman André Rodgers for a single. This wonderment of nature ignited a three-run inning, boosting Bob Friend to his eighth victory of the season.

Danny Murtaugh's leprechauns continued to live their charmed life. On June 15 the Bucs pounded San Francisco 14–6 on a 19-hit attack, moving three games ahead of the Giants. Winning pitcher Harvey Haddix went the distance, and helped his own cause with a double, three singles, and two RBIs. Orlando Cepeda and Willie Mays hit mammoth home runs; Cepeda's 430-foot shot to center was the longest yet recorded at Candlestick Park, while Mays' traveled a mere 420 feet. Pittsburgh, by contrast, did not hit a single round-tripper, instead peppering Giants pitching with doubles and triples. Pittsburgh swept the series the next day, as Elroy Face held off a late Giant rally to preserve a 10–7 victory. Winning pitcher Vinegar Bend Mizell threw 167 pitches in eight and one-third innings. The hitting star was Bob Skinner who had a grand slam homer and five RBIs. In all, the Corsairs had outhit the Giants 42–34, despite hitting one-third fewer home runs. They were now four games in front of the second-place Giants, five ahead of Milwaukee.

Pittsburgh ended its West Coast visit at the Los Angeles Coliseum on June 17–19, grabbing two of three from the Dodgers. The big news of the weekend, however, was back in San Francisco. After the Pirate series, Giants owner Horace Stoneham fired manager Bill Rigney, and replaced him with head scout Tom Sheehan. The 66-year-old Sheehan was an imposing physical presence, well over 6 feet, about 240 pounds, and possessed of a deep cavernous voice. In 1916 he had had the dubious distinction of pitching on a Philadelphia Athletics team that finished with 117 losses.

His own contribution that year was 1–16. The red-faced Sheehan (known as Clancy) adopted the sartorial style of his former mentor. Like Connie Mack, he managed in street clothes. With Sheehan masterminding in mufti, on June 18 the Giants defeated Philadelphia, 7–4. The losing pitcher was the future Phillies and Yankees manager Dallas Green. After winning their second straight game under Sheehan, the Giants lost a heartbreaker to the Phils, 2–1, Tony Taylor singling in the winning run in the top of the eleventh inning. Robin Roberts went all eleven innings, striking out eleven, walking none. The only run scored against him came on a home run by Mays. The pre-season favorite Giants would go on to lose four more games in a row ("I don't die over these ball games," said Clancy[10]), as the Pirates tightened their hold on first place.

Municipal Stadium, fronting Lake Erie, was built in 1931. With a capacity of nearly 80,000 it was the largest park in the American League. The Yankees had seen their share of misfortunes here. On July 17, 1941, Cleveland hurlers Al Smith and Jim Bagby, Jr., had combined to end Joe DiMaggio's 56-game hitting streak. Even more poignant was May 7, 1957, when a line drive off the bat of New York's Gil McDougald struck Indian pitcher Herb Score in the face, effectively ending what might have been a Hall of Fame career for the young left-hander. Now on June 24–26, the largest crowds of the year gathered to see if the Tribe could dispose of the hated Yankees.

Trader Frank Lane had revamped the Indians in an attempt to improve on their second-place finish in 1959. The trades of Minnie Minoso to the White Sox in December and Rocky Colavito to Detroit in April had sacrificed power in favor of high average hitters like AL batting champ Harvey Kuenn and former Redlegs standout Johnny Temple. They would join a dependable core of hitters that included first baseman Vic Power, shortstop Woodie Held, and center fielder Jim Piersall. Then there was the man who replaced Minoso in left field, Tito Francona.

John Patsy Francona was born on November 4, 1933, in Aliquippa, Pennsylvania, a steel mill town about 30 miles north of Pittsburgh. His father, who was Italian, and his mother, who was Polish, married when they were sixteen and fourteen years old, respectively, John was nicknamed Tito, "little one" in Italian. Tito was a high school star in western Pennsylvania and was chosen to play in the Hearst All-Star game at the Polo Grounds, an annual event pitting high school standouts from the East against the West. Tito toured Broadway and had the best week of his life — until his honeymoon. Francona signed a modest contract with the St. Louis Browns. After the usual minor league stops and two years in military service, he joined at the parent club (now the Baltimore Orioles) in 1954. Following short stints at Chicago and Detroit he was acquired by Lane during spring training 1959. Tutored at the plate by manager Joe Gordon, Francona stopped upper-cutting the ball and began to hit — and hit, and hit.[11]

Tito finished the 1959 season with a .363 batting average, losing the batting crown to Detroit's Harvey Kuenn, who hit .353, because he did not have the minimum 477 plate appearances to qualify for the batting championship. Casey Stengel, however, had high praise for Francona, claiming he was "one of the five hitters in the league who kept us from winning another pennant" in 1959. The AL managers, in a secret ballot published in *Sport Magazine* in the summer of 1960, rated him the best left fielder in the league.[12] The 1959 season had been a productive one in another sense. The *Cleveland Indians Official 1960 Sketchbook*, which printed everything, including the names of the hotels that the Indians stayed in on the road, noted that Tito and his wife, the former Roberta Jean Jackson, had a two-year-old son named Terry, born April 22, 1959.

The player with the largest family on the Indians was Jimmy Piersall, with seven children. He was also the most controversial. In 1952, while playing for the Boston Red Sox, Piersall had suffered a nervous breakdown, an ordeal told in his autobiography *Fear Strikes Out*, that later was made into a motion picture. Eight years later, Jimmy's zany antics on the field were still driving teammates and opponents up the wall. A few weeks earlier, he hit a home run against Detroit's Pete Burnside. Expecting a brush back pitch in his next time at bat, he showed up at the plate wearing a Little League batting helmet. It almost got him thrown out of the game. Now, on June 24, he was up to his old tricks once again. As New York's Jim Coates was taking his warm-up pitches, Piersall got up close to get a good look at his stuff. Annoyed, Coates fired the ball in his general direction (it was "a curve that got away from me," he later claimed).[13] Jimmy retaliated by grabbing a couple bats and throwing them at Coates.

Once underway, a crowd of 36,675 then watched as New York beat the Tribe, 10–6. Tony Kubek contributed two home runs. The Indians had a chance to break the game open in the sixth, loading the bases with two out. But Roger Maris made the play of the game, with a spectacular grab over the right center field fence that robbed Tito Francona of a bases-clearing home run. The following day, June 25, New York lost 4–1 to the Indians, but managed to retain a half-game league over Baltimore. The Indians and Yankees split a Sunday doubleheader in front of a paid crowd of 57,261, the largest of the year. Whitey Ford spun a four-hitter, as New York took the first game, 6–2, with all of Cleveland's tallies coming on a two-run homer by Francona. In the second game, the ex-Indian Maris played the role of both hero and goat. Roger twice tied the game with home runs, numbers 21 and 22. But his error in the eleventh inning cost New York the game. Right-hander Jim Perry, whose parents had come up from North Carolina to see him pitch, got the victory with six innings of relief after being knocked out of the box in the first game of the series.

As the Bombers were splitting the doubleheader with Cleveland, Baltimore was thrashing Kansas City, 9–2. Despite a 10–4 road trip, the Yankees were out of first place, a game behind the Orioles, heading into the final week of June.

While Willie Mays, Orlando Cepeda, and company were getting acquainted with their new manager, and the second division, the Pittsburgh Pirates were streaking across the continent to the Golden Triangle. When their DC jet taxied into Greater Pittsburgh Airport at 4 A.M. on Monday, June 20, about 150 kids were on hand to greet them. Drinking soda pop and carrying autograph books, the excited bunch sought out their weary heroes for signatures. The team was a little embarrassed by all the attention; as one Buc put it, they hadn't won anything yet. Nevertheless, the Corsairs had a lot to be proud of. After a 4–6 start against poor competition, they had rallied to take five of six games on the West Coast for a 9–7 road tally.

It was a good thing that they had, for the Pirates completed their June schedule with a mediocre 5–4 homestand. On the last day of June, they split a doubleheader with San Francisco. The Giants took the first game, 11–0, with Willie Mays and Ed Bressoud hitting home runs in support of righty Jack Sanford. The Bucs returned the favor in the nightcap, 11–6. Mays homered once again, but the Say Hey Kid was overshadowed by Dick Stuart, who hit three round-trippers and collected seven RBIs. It had not been a *great* month for Pittsburgh — they finished at 15–11— but they had vanquished their West Coast rivals. The Giants were six games behind, the Dodgers 9½ games out. For the moment, the only team in the

Corsairs' rear-view mirror was the Milwaukee Braves, three games from the lead.

The western swing over, the Yankees flew back to New York to play Kansas City for the final three games in June. In the opener on June 28, Mickey Mantle hit home run number 17, in a 5–2 victory. The Bombers were back in first place, a half game in front of the Orioles. The next day Roger Maris hit numbers 23 and 24 off A's right-hander Ray Herbert, as the Yanks romped, 10–0. The pair of homers gave Maris 24 in 65 games. On the last day of the month, a 10–3 Yankee victory, he hit number 25 putting him four games ahead of Babe Ruth's 1927 pace. For many people, Maris seemed to have emerged out of nowhere to challenge the Bambino's home run mark in 1961. But actually, it was in the summer of 1960 that the Yankee right fielder made his first assault at the fabled record. Pestered by reporters as to how many homers he could hit, Maris simply responded, "As many as I can."[14]

Roger Eugene Maras (he changed the spelling of his surname after entering organized ball) was born on September 10, 1934, at Hibbing, Minnesota, a town in the northeastern part of the state, about one hundred miles north of Duluth. Hibbing was located in the midst of the Mesabi Range, whose soft sand-like iron had made it one of the richest deposits of its kind in the world. In the late nineteenth century, lake steamers laden with Mesabi iron would cross the Great Lakes from Duluth to Erie, Pennsylvania. From there, the precious ore would be carried by rail to Pittsburgh. Transformed into steel, it would help make Andrew Carnegie the richest man in the world.[15] Peering out at the world from his small eyes under a crew-cut, Maris often struck strangers as being aloof. A small town boy at heart, he had an uneasy time with the press. Perhaps there was something about the austere environment of Hibbing that produced contrarian talents. Victor Bugliosi, the controversial Los Angeles D.A. who prosecuted the Manson Family, was born there a year before Maris. In the late 1940s a young boy named Robert Zimmerman would move to Hibbing—the world knows him today as Bob Dylan.

By the time Bobby Zimmerman arrived at Hibbing, the Maras family had resettled at Fargo, North Dakota. It was in the midst of the sugar beet fields of the northern plains that Roger and his brother Rudy learned the fundaments of the game. A high school star in baseball and football, Maris signed with the Cleveland Indians and came up to the big show in 1957.

In December 1959, Pittsburgh GM Joe L. Brown had almost traded Pirate shortstop Dick Groat to Kansas City for Roger Maris. Both Groat and Maris would win the MVP award in their respective leagues in 1960.

But he was unhappy sharing right field with Rocky Colavito, and in June 1958 Lane traded him to Kansas City for the Tribe's current first baseman and former Yankee farmhand, Vic Power. It looked like he had finally found a home with the A's. Maris, his wife Pat, and their two boys loved their Raytown, Missouri, home in the Kansas City suburbs. The couple were expected a third child that summer. And the young blond outfielder was gaining a reputation as one of the best young talents in the game.

Maris was leading the AL in hitting with .344 in mid-season 1959 when he was sidelined by an attack of appendicitis. Although his average plummeted when he returned, there was no doubt among the experts of his ability to run (3.5 seconds from home to first), throw, and hit with power. The controversial trade that brought him to New York in December 1959 made Maris the target of press speculation. Many believed him to be the key to the Yankees' prospects in 1960. So far, he had more than matched expectations.

Maris was not the only Yankee displaying home run heroics in June. Mickey Mantle hit six round-trippers during the month, giving him 18 for the season. But the biggest slugging milestone of all was reached by the 41-year-old who patrolled left field at Fenway Park. On June 17, Ted Williams timed one of Cleveland's Wynn Hawkins' pitches and sent it through the mist and rain over the 365-foot sign at Municipal Stadium. In doing so, Williams became the fourth player to reach 500 home runs in his career. On June 30, he hit number 505, putting him just six behind New York Giants great Mel Ott. Waiting to pump Williams' hand as he returned to the dugout was the Red Sox's new manager Mike (Pinky) Higgins. Billy Jurges, handicapped by the sudden retirement of Jackie Jensen, had given up in nervous exhaustion.

Meanwhile, the Ol' Perfessor, who had begun the month in hospital clothes at Lenox Hill, had seen his Yankees post a handsome June record of 21–8. On the 30 of June his team was once again ensconced in first place, 1½ games ahead of Baltimore, three in front of Cleveland.

While Casey Stengel was following the Yankees in hospital garments, and "Clancy" Sheehan was directing the Giants in street clothes, that famous resident of Pittsburgh, Branch Rickey, was also "managing in mufti," strategizing over how to bring to life a third major league. In a bid to get the Continental League off the ground at last, the Mahatma was offering a compromise to Edward Doherty, the commissioner of the American Association, with regard to the Houston franchise. He suggested that the whole matter be submitted to arbitration. In other matters, Rickey announced that he was quite satisfied by the response to the Western Carolina League tryouts, which resulted in the signing of 130 of the 200 hopefuls. In two days the eight teams had stocked their players and were ready to begin play.

Back in Washington, however, things were not going well for the

Continental League. On June 13 the Senate Judiciary Committee sent the Kefauver bill to the entire Senate body without recommendation. The members simply could not agree on a plan. Kefauver was anxious to break what he saw as Major League Baseball's monopolistic practices. But other senators, like Alexander Lewis (Republican-Wisconsin), believed it was unfair to place greater restrictions on the operations of Major League Baseball than existed for the NFL, NBA, and NHL, since baseball had always had complete freedom to do as it pleased. The Senate defeated the bill, 45–41, although Rickey and Bill Shea used their influence to have it recommitted, a legislative move designed to keep the bill — and the Continental League — alive. The Pirates and Yankees, happily ensconced in first place in their respective leagues, could hope for even better things in July. Rickey, Bill Shea, and company could only be so lucky.

Chapter Eight

"The more I see of them, the more I like them"

As the Democratic Party National Convention at Los Angeles approached, Massachusetts senator John F. Kennedy appeared to have enough delegates to claim his party's nomination for president in 1960. Barring a late rally by the liberal stalwart and former standard bearer Adlai Stevenson, the nomination would be his by the middle of July. Like JFK, the Yankees and Pirates, both in first place at the end of June, also hoped to continue their winning ways. On the other hand, Branch Rickey was much more like Kennedy's rival for the nomination, Stevenson — an eloquent, much admired figure but no longer a major player. In fact, by the end of July the Mahatma's fate, and that of the Continental League, would be all but decided.

On July 2, 1960, the Yankees, still clinging to a one game lead over Baltimore, hosted the Detroit Tigers at Yankee Stadium. The result was a 7–6 victory, the winning runs coming in the bottom of the ninth against ex-Dodger relief ace Clem Labine. The rally featured two of the most unlikely Yankee batters. Pitcher Art Ditmar, inserted as a pinch-hitter by Casey Stengel, doubled sending Bobby Richardson to third. Little-used shortstop Joe DeMaestri, a throw-in in the Maris trade, then singled to left driving in Richardson with the winning run. The next day, the Bombers swept a doubleheader from the Bengals before a huge crowd of 50,556 fans at the Stadium. Roger Maris' peg to the plate cut off a Detroit rally in the ninth inning of the first game. Mickey Mantle's fifth inning three-run homer won the nightcap for the Yanks. New York now had six wins in a row, 23 in 28 games, since Casey Stengel's release from the hospital in early June.

The series completed, the Yankees and Tigers both headed out of town. They didn't get very far, however. The two teams were delayed for hours at LaGuardia Airport due to a bomb scare. Detroit skipper Jimmy Dykes got in the best quip of the night. Referring to their recent thumping by the Yankees, Dykes asked in mock innocence: "Why would anyone want to bomb us? We haven't hurt anybody lately."[1] When the situation was finally resolved Al Kaline, Rocky Colavito, and company took off for Chicago. Stengel and his men headed for the Potomac.

In 1960, what is now the Howard University Hospital was the site of Griffith Stadium, the home of the Washington Senators. The Nats were a perennial second division team, as the saying went: "First in war, first in peace, and last in the American League." They had not won a pennant since the first year of Franklin D. Roosevelt's New Deal. Old-timers still the cherished memories of the Big Train, Walter Johnson, opening the throttle on opposing batters. However, the most memorable moment at Griffith Stadium in recent memory had been provided by the Yankees. On April 17, 1953, twenty-one-year-old Mickey Mantle hit a colossal home run off lefty Chuck Stobbs, which cleared the left field wall and landed in a yard 565 feet from home plate.

The latest incarnation of the Senators were showing some signs of life under manager Cookie Lavagetto. The shortened dimensions of Griffith Stadium, 350 feet to the left field foul pole and 320 to right, proved a welcoming sight for the Nats' trio of sluggers. Third baseman Harmon Killebrew (the Killer) had tied Cleveland's Rocky Colavito for the AL home run championship in 1959, at 42, while outfielders Jim Lemon and Bob Allison had also slugged over 30 round-trippers. On the pitching side, right-hander Camilo Pascual had won 17 games and led the league with 17 complete games (including seven shutouts). A late April trade with the Chicago White Sox, which brought catcher Earl Battey to Washington for outfielder Roy Seivers, had provided the club with a tremendous shot in the arm. Given a chance to play regularly, Battey was soon recognized as the best defensive backstop in the league, while showing surprising heft as a hitter. Second baseman Billy Gardner and center fielder Lenny Green, acquired from Baltimore, shored up a weak middle defense. Shortstop was a problem, but there were high hopes for the Cuban rookie Zoilo (Zorro) Versalles.

The Senators boasted the league's most international cast. Two players, Reno Bertoia and Elmer Valo (picked up by the Nats after being waived by the Yankees), were born in Europe. Rudy Hernández was of Dominican descent. Then there were the Cubans. In July 1960, President Eisenhower and the U.S. Congress were moving toward an irreparable divorce with Fidel Castro by cutting Cuba's sugar quota to the United States. The baseball Senators, however, would have been hard pressed without their large Cuban crop. Besides Pascual and Versalles, they included first baseman Julio Bécquer, shortstop José Valdivielso, and the most colorful Senator of all, right-handed pitcher Pedro Ramos.

The Cuban Revolution had begun in the Sierra Maestra Mountains of eastern Cuba, in Oriente province, and worked its way westward toward Havana. Pedro Ramos was born in the most westerly of Cuban provinces, Pinar del Río, on April 28, 1935. A westerner, in the Cuban sense, Ramos fancied himself a westerner in the American mold as well. Off the field, he had preference for "shoot-em up" movies, through which he claimed he had perfected his English. His dress style ran to cowboy clothes, a black ten-gallon hat, and boots. His inevitable nickname was "Pistol Pete." Ramos, described as coming from "an old Spanish family,"[2] was like one of those Latin lover characters played by César Romero in MGM musicals in the 1940s, a man of obvious European looks whose brain had been addled by life in the tropics. He was in turns silly, maddening, and adorable — to the fans, the press, and opposing players.

On the field, Pedro Ramos was a talented all-round athlete. He claimed to be one of the fastest runners in the majors and set out to prove it. In spring training 1959 he challenged then Philadelphia Phillies center fielder Richie Ashburn to a 70-yard foot race. Ashburn had long been acknowledged as one of the most fleet-footed men in the big leagues, but Pedro left him in the dust, winning by eight yards. Ramos was also constantly badgering Mickey Mantle to race him. Mickey, plagued by his usual array of leg miseries, wisely put him off. The handsome, six-foot Cuban, who had recently married the daughter of a large tobacco factory owner in his native Pinar del Rio, was often used as a pinch-runner by manager Cookie Lavagetto. But Ramos' on-field business was pitching, and he was a good one. His 1959 record of 13–19 was more a reflection of a shaky defense than it was of lack of pitching prowess. Ramos had a live fast ball and a curve that broke more quickly than Whitey Ford's. His most exotic pitch, however, was the so-called "palmball." Held on the smooth part of the fingers like a slider, this Cuban concoction created howls of protest from opposing managers (especially the Orioles' Paul Richards) who accused him of throwing a spitball.[3]

The howls heard at Griffith Stadium on July 4, 1960, were those of joy. The Senators stopped New York's six-game winning streak despite four Yankee home runs, including the 300th of Mantle's career. Reno Bertoia, the native of St. Vito Udine, Italy, drew a bases-loaded walk in the ninth from Ryne Duren for a 9–8 victory. Afterward, an enraged Yogi Berra heaved his catcher's mitt into the visiting dugout, followed closely by Duren's glove. Pedro Ramos, used as a pinch-runner on the Fourth of July, came back the next day and held New York to three hits in eight innings. The Nats tied the game, 3–3, in the ninth and then won it in the tenth on Bob Allison's two-run homer off Art Ditmar. Chuck Stobbs, who served up Mantle's 565-foot home run in 1953, was the winning pitcher in relief of Ramos. The game was marred by two altercations. The first occurred in the third inning when Senator shortstop José Valdivielso rushed the mound after the Yanks' Ralph Terry just missed hitting him with a pitch. The second rhubarb occurred an inning later after Ramos hit Mantle in the side with an errant throw. The Yanks, who had hoped to pad their lead at the expense of the usually reliable Senators, instead left the nation's capital just two games ahead of Cleveland in the AL race.

New York recovered some of its equilibrium by defeating the third-place Baltimore Orioles twice on July 6–7 at Memorial Stadium. The first game featured Maris' twenty-seventh homer of the season, putting him six games ahead of Ruth's pace. Whitey Ford cruised to a shutout victory, evening his record at 5–5. But the Bombers were unable to pad their lead against the weaker clubs. The Boston Red Sox, trawling in the deep waters of the second division under new manager Pinky Higgins, beat New York three in a row at Fenway Park on July 8–10. The final contest saw Boston humiliate the New Yorkers, 9–5, the big blow coming on Vic Wertz's 400-foot grand slam homer over the high wall in the center field bleachers in the second inning. The victim was Ford, who had come on in relief of loser Ralph Terry.

At the All-Star break the New York Yankees were 2½ games ahead of the Cleveland Indians, three in front of the Chicago White Sox, and four ahead of the Baltimore Orioles. Their overall record was 45–30 with one tie. After a splendid June run they had thus far played .500 ball (5–5) in July. It would not get much better than this for a while.

Like the New York Yankees, the Pittsburgh Pirates opened their July schedule at the top of the standings, three games ahead of second-place Milwaukee. Also like the Yankees, they began July at home. On July 1 the Bucs beat their most troublesome 1960 opponent, the Los Angeles Dodgers. Then things began to unravel. They lost three games in a row, two of those at the hands of the Dodgers on July 2–3. The third loss came in the first game of a July 4 doubleheader at County Stadium against the Milwaukee Braves. Rookie outfielder Al Spangler singled in the ninth to win it, 7–6, against Elroy Face. Warren Spahn got the victory in relief, as the Braves inched within 2½ games of the Bucs. Hank Aaron predicted that the Braves would "pass the Pirates like they were on a jet."[4] Hank spoke too soon. Harvey Haddix continued to exact revenge for his 13-inning loss to the Braves the previous May, tossing a six-hitter en route to a 7–2 victory before 38,578 holiday spectators. On July 5, Rocky Nelson's tenth-inning home run (his second of the day) gave the Bucs their second consecutive victory over Milwaukee. Aaron's jet had had lost some fuel. The Corsairs' lead over the Braves was back to 4½ games.

The Pirates' pre–All-Star Game road show moved east to the Delaware River on July 8–10. Connie Mack Stadium, known until 1953 by its original name, Shibe Park, had opened in 1909. Located at 21st Street and Lehigh, it was the first baseball stadium built of steel and concrete. For most of its history, it was Connie Mack's Philadelphia Athletics that won pennants and World Series championships there. Mack's statue, in a park across the front entrance, stood in mute silence to those former glory days. But it was the Phillies, who moved in as tenants in 1938, who provided the last great moment, with the Whiz Kids stirring triumph over the Brooklyn Dodgers in 1950. The Phillies became the park's sole tenants when A's owner Arnold Johnson packed his team off to Kansas City after the 1954 season. Recent years had seen the Quakers at the lower rungs of the National League standings.

Danny Murtaugh and company expected to add to their lead at the expense of the young Philadelphia Phillies. Thus far, the Quakers' youth movement had produced a record of 32–45, the second worst record in the National League. Gene Mauch's men, in fact, were in a position not too different from that of the Branch Rickey-led Pirates in the mid–1950s. Dick Groat, Bob Skinner, Vern Law, Elroy Face, and Bob Friend had all undergone a long period of apprenticeship that was finally bearing fruit in 1960. On the Phillies, youngsters such as pitchers Chris Short and Art

Mahaffey, second baseman Tony Taylor and outfielders Tony González and Johnny Callison were about four or five years away from title contention. It was also an international group. González, Taylor, and first baseman Frank (Pancho) Herrera were all Cubans. Outfielder Tony Curry, who hailed from the Virgin Islands and spoke with a slight British accent, played cricket until age sixteen. Then there was shortstop Rubén Amaro.

Today, with all the focus on illegal immigration from South of the Border, it is hard to conceive of Mexico as a haven for immigrants. But in the 1930s and 40s Mexico was full of expatriates. As one of the major centers of Hispanic culture in the New World, it attracted talent from all over Latin America. Cuban Latin jazz pioneer Chico O'Farrill and Argentine singer-actress Libertad Lamarque found renewed fame in Mexico City. Another Cuban, Fidel Castro — and another Argentine, Ernesto (Che) Guevara — would plot a revolution from the former Aztec capital. Mexico was also a magnet for Cuban baseball players. Rubén's father, Santos, barred from the majors by his color, starred in the Mexican League. The elder Amaro (known as El Canguro, the Kangaroo) settled in Vera Cruz and married a Mexican woman.

In the sixteenth and seventeenth centuries, Vera Cruz, the "City of the True Cross," had been the destination of Spanish silver and gold from the mines of Guanajuato above Mexico City. Ships laden with plunder journeyed from Vera Cruz to Havana, and from there, to Spain. Rubén Mora Amaro's birthplace seemed to signal his own future journey. He was born in Nuevo Laredo, just across the Brazos River from Texas, on January 6, 1936. Signed as an amateur free agent in 1954 by the St. Louis Cardinals, he was traded to the Philies in December 1958. Amaro reported late to camp in spring 1960 (he was serving in the Mexican military), but by midsummer had won the starting shortstop job from Joe Koppe. A slick fielder, Amaro would figure on the offensive side of the ledger in the upcoming four-game series with Pittsburgh.

A crowd of 36,056, the largest at Connie Mack Stadium in three years, was on hand for the twi-night doubleheader with Pittsburgh on Friday, July 8. Missing was Phillies manager Gene Mauch, serving a two-game suspension for bumping plate umpire Ed Vargo two days earlier at Milwaukee. In his absence, the Phils defeated Pittsburgh, 6–5, in extra innings in the twilight game. Rubén Amaro, who had walked in his three previous trips to the plate, lined a double to left to open the bottom of the tenth. Reliever Dick (Turk) Farrell went up to bat and took two balls from losing pitcher Fred Green. On the next Green delivery, he singled to right field. Amaro, who was born on the Epiphany, perhaps felt he had some divine dispensation for he did something no sane person would do: challenge the arm of Roberto Clemente. The throw just missed nipping Amaro at the plate — at least according to umpire Vargo, who first hesitated, then spread his arms in the safe position. In the night game, Pittsburgh came back to rout the Pennsylvania cousins, 8–3, chasing Dallas Green. The Pirates and Phillies then split the last two games of the series. On Saturday, Vern Law lost a pitching duel to the towering Gene Conley, 2–1. The Bucs came back on Sunday to beat the Phillies ace Robin Roberts, to end the first half of the season.

The Pirates' mid-season record of 49–30 was four games better than that of the pace-setting Yankees in the American League. Murtaugh's crew was only 6–6 in so far in July as the All-Star Game approached. But they still led Milwaukee by 5 games, Los Angeles by 8, and San Francisco and St. Louis by 8½. It was a much bigger lead than that enjoyed by the Bronx Bombers, who were just 2½ games in front of Cleveland. From his lair in the Phillies clubhouse, the suspended Gene Mauch expressed his admiration for the Pirates. "The more I see of them, the more I like them," he said.[5] Not many people in the baseball world would have volunteered to say this when the Bucs lost to the Yankees back on April 2 in Florida.

As they had in the previous two seasons, the American and National Leagues played two All-Star games in 1960. The first contest took place at Kansas City on July 11; the second at New York on July 13. The players received 60 percent of the proceeds for the benefit of their pension plan. The owners took the rest. In 1960 the players, not the fans, chose the starting team. As announced by Ford Frick on July 2, they were:

Position	*National League*	*American League*
Catcher	Del Crandall, Mil.	Yogi Berra, N.Y.
First Base	Joe Adcock, Mil.	Bill Skowron, N.Y.
Second Base	Bill Mazeroski, Pitt.	Pete Runnels, Bos.
Shortstop	Ernie Banks, Chi.	Ron Hansen, Balt.
Third Base	Ed Mathews, Mil.	Frank Malzone, Bos.
Left Field	Bob Skinner, Pitt.	Minnie Minoso, Chi.
Center Field	Willie Mays, S.F.	Mickey Mantle, N.Y.
Right Field	Hank Aaron, Mil.	Roger Maris, N.Y.

The biggest vote-getter in the National League was Willie Mays; in the American it was Roger Maris.

There were some surprises, and perhaps, injustices in the player voting. In the American League, the heart of the Go Go Sox was shut out of the starting lineup. Baltimore rookie Ron Hansen was chosen over Luis Aparicio at shortstop and Boston's Pete Runnels over Nellie Fox at second. Yogi Berra, a part-time performer behind the plate, was selected catcher over the Nats' Earl Battey. There were no American blacks on the AL's starting squad. The NL had three African Americans, but no Latins of any color. Hank Aaron, a .277 performer, was selected over Roberto Clemente, who was hitting .325. Ernie Banks received the nod over the Bucs' Dick Groat, who was also in batting crown contention. The pitchers and reserves were picked by NL manager Walt Alston and AL skipper Al López. Alston tabbed Bucs Vern Law, Bob Friend, and Elroy Face to pitch. El Señor gave the nod to the Yankees' Whitey Ford and Jim Coates. Clemente, Groat, and Smoky Burgess were among the NL reserves. The AL had Elston Howard on the bench. Each manager selected a sentimental favorite: thirty-nine-year-old Stan (the Man) Musial of St. Louis for the Nationals and Boston's forty-one-year-old Ted Williams for the junior loop.

Kansas City, Missouri, was the 27th largest city in the U.S. and the smallest market in the Major Leagues. It was also cursed with a team currently 17½ games out of first place. When team owner Arnold Johnson had passed away the previous spring, there was talk that the new owners (whoever they might be) would try to move the club to Los Angeles. Not surprisingly, the All-Star Game created more baseball excitement in Kansas City than anything since the arrival of the Philadelphia Athletics in 1955. On the evening of July 10, Commissioner Ford Frick, league presidents Joe Cronin and Warren Giles, various ex-players, and at least 200 sportswriters gathered for a welcoming dinner in the grand ballroom of the Hotel Muehlebach. Absent from the festivities were the all stars themselves. A picture the next day in the *Kansas City Star* showed a weary group of Yankees and Pirates (including Mickey Mantle, Whitey Ford, Vern Law, Bob Friend, Smoky Burgess, Bob Skinner, and Roberto Clemente) alighting from their plane at 11:30 P.M. Central Time. By the looks of it, the future World Series rivals had only one thing in mind, a good night's rest.[6]

The twenty-eighth All-Star Game at Kansas City's Municipal Stadium was more memorable for the heat than anything else. The temperature at mid-day was 100 degrees, which overtaxed the stadium facilities. The air

Like Pittsburgh, mediocre play continued to plague the New York Yankees after the All-Star break. They began another western swing on July 15 by dropping three of four to the Detroit Tigers at Briggs Stadium, making it nine losses in the last twelve games. Meanwhile, the Cleveland Indians kept pace with the Bombers, 1½ games back. In New York's lone victory against the Tigers on July 16, Yogi Berra drove in five runs and Roger Maris blasted home run number twenty-eight.

The Yankees limped out of Detroit and headed for Cleveland for a return engagement with Frank Lane's Indians, still holding a 1½ game lead. As in so many previous must-win situations, Casey Stengel turned to Whitey Ford. On July 18, Ford scattered eight hits over nine innings in leading the Yanks over the Indians. Mickey Mantle's 22nd home run and Roger Maris' 29th sparked the Yankee attack. The Tribe suffered a severe blow when power-hitting shortstop Woodie Held went down with a broken finger. In another development, Jimmy Piersall, who had been sent home for a rest by Frank Lane in late June after a series of bizarre incidents, was fined by manager Joe Gordon for lackadaisical play. New York won again on July 19, a wild 13–11 slugfest. Bill Skowron's three-run double in the ninth was the clincher. Cleveland finally broke the spell in the last game of the series, winning 8–6. Maris (number 31) and Mantle (number 23) scaled the fences in a losing cause.

The Yankees' record for the month stood at an unimpressive 9–10 as they got ready to face the Pale Hose at Yankee Stadium on July 22–24. The New Yorkers had not faced the defending champions since the Yankee bench had mocked Bill Veeck's exploding scoreboard, by lighting Fourth of July sparklers in the visitors' dugout after hitting their home runs at Comiskey Park. At the time Veeck had vowed "to reciprocate in kind." The Yankees had not forgotten his threat. Prior to the first game on July 22, the New York Fire Department search the bowels of the Stadium and discovered a package that had been mailed to the visiting White Sox. In it was a cache of firecrackers, which the visitors planned to ignite following one of their home runs. An un-chastened Veeck claimed that he had arranged to have Yankee Stadium and its patrons insured by Lloyd's of London, in case of accident. Chicago managed just fine without the fireworks, beating Bob Turley and the Yankees, 11–5. On July 23, Family Day at the Stadium, Chicago won again, 5–3. The usually reliable Whitey Ford lasted just five and one-third innings. The Stengel men were now out of first place for the first time since June 26, one game behind Al López's White Sox.

Roberto Clemente (right) and Luis Arroyo, two Puerto Ricans, were part of a growing contingent of international players that outnumbered the African American players on most Major League teams.

In retrospect, the second game of the Sunday doubleheader against Chicago on July 24 was one of the crucial turning points of the 1960 AL campaign. The Yankees had lost the last game of the Cleveland series, and three straight to the Chisox at home. The former Cy Young winner (Turley) and their clutch pitcher (Ford) had both failed to stop the White Sox. With Chicago ready to administer a *coup de grace* against the reeling Yankees, Casey Stengel put the team's fortunes in the hands of Eli Grba, who a month earlier had been toiling in Triple-A at Richmond. A throng of 60,002, the largest of the year, watched as the Consonant Man pitched his first complete game of the season, an 8–2 Yankee win that salvaged the second game of the doubleheader. Roger Maris did not hit a home run, but his brilliant catch of a Gene Freese drive at the right field wall helped save the game for Grba. The defending-champion White Sox left town clinging to a one-game lead. But it could have been worse for the Yankees.

The weekend series against the White Sox is notable for another turning point of sorts. George Weiss, worried about the Yankee relief pitching, got bullpen help, indirectly, from an unlikely source — Fidel Castro. On July 7, International League president Frank Shaughnessy announced that the loop's Cuban franchise, the Havana Sugar Kings, was being moved from the island back to the U.S. "to protect our players." The team's remaining 35 home games would be played at Jersey City, New Jersey. On July 15, 1960, the newly-christened Jersey City Jerseys (a Cincinnati Reds affiliate) left their downtown quarters at the Journal Square Hotel and rode in an eight-car motorcade to Roosevelt Stadium. Miss Jersey City, 22-year-old Delphine Lisk, sat in the first car alongside manager Napoleón Reyes. Fearing interference from Castro supporters, fifty policemen were on hand at Roosevelt Stadium that night to patrol the stands in the event of pro-Castro demonstrations. In addition, two detectives were posted in the dugout to guard Reyes, the manager having been denounced by Fidel as a traitor. It turned out to be much ado about nothing, as a tiny crowd of 7,155 saw the Jerseys fall to a Pirates AAA affiliate, the Columbus Jets.

With the former Havana Sugar Kings just across the Hudson, George Weiss decided to scout out the team. There were eleven Cuban players on the Jersey City team, but the Yankee GM was interested in a player from the other wing of the Antillean bird. At 4:30 in the afternoon of July 22, the Jerseys' lefty pitcher Luis Arroyo answered the phone at the Journal Square Hotel. Three hours later, he was wearing number 47 at Yankee Stadium. Arroyo hailed from Peñuelas, in the southern part of Puerto Rico, where he was born on February 18, 1927. Peñuelas is known as the City of the Güiro, a Latin percussion instrument thought by many to be of Taíno Indian origin. Arroyo himself was a short, portly, easy-going pitcher of European looks. He, not Vic Power, would become the team's first Puerto Rican player. Looie had kicked around the National League in the 1950s, playing for the Cardinals, Pirates, and Reds, in addition to numerous other stops in the low and high minors. At 5' 8", 190 pounds, he was not overpowering, compensating for the lack of velocity by keeping the ball low and changing speeds. His out pitch was a screwball, which broke sharply away from right-handed batters. Arroyo's olive complexion didn't spare him from ethnic slurs emanating from the direction of the opposing dugouts. But he claimed not to be affected by the insults, saying, "If you survive Durocher, nobody else will upset you."[10] In the unflappable Arroyo, the Old Perfessor finally had the short relief man he had hungered for all season.

Luis Arroyo was in the bullpen as Frank Lane's Cleveland Indians followed the White Sox into Bronx for a three-game series on July 26–28. Casey Stengel came up with one of his more imaginative lineups, putting Roger Maris in the leadoff spot against All-Star left-hander Dick Stigman. In the sixth inning, Maris drew a walk from Stigman. Following a spectacular catch by Tito Francona, who fell into the left field seats clutching a Héctor López drive, Roger came home on Mickey Mantle's twenty-fifth home run. Arroyo made his debut in this game, blanking the Indians in the eighth and ninth innings to record his first save as a Yankee. On July 29 the Yanks took two more from Joe Gordon's men, 4–0 and 9–2. Whitey Ford and Bobby Shantz combined for the shutout in the first game. Bob Turley and Ryne Duren polished off the Tribe in the nightcap. With the doubleheader sweep, the Bombers were once again in first place, just three percentage points ahead of Chicago.

On the last day of July, Casey Stengel received a belated 70th birthday celebration at Yankee Stadium, conducted between games of a doubleheader with the Kansas City Athletics. The Old Perfessor, rocking back and forth on his heels, his hands clasped behind his back, looked on as Yankee broadcaster Mel Allen uttered encomiums in his honeyed southern tones. Casey received a shower of gifts, including a neckerchief and knife from the Boy Scouts. He was heard to mutter that he "might use it on himself" if the Yankees kept playing like they had so far, two straight losses to the A's.[11] Art Ditmar beat Bud Daley in the second game of the doubleheader, with home run help from Bill Skowron (number 19 for the Moose). But Casey's birthday celebration was spoiled, as the Yanks ceded first place to the White Sox.

Both Pittsburgh and New York slogged through a miserable July. The Pirates finished the month 15–14, .517, their National League lead just two games over Milwaukee. After an outstanding June drive, the Yankees finished July with a mediocre record of 13–14, a .481 percentage. Stengel's team was now 1½ games behind Chicago in the pennant chase. Both the Bucs and the Bombers would live to see better times. However, for Branch Rickey, Bill Shea, and the Continental League, things would only get worse.

Chapter Nine

"Kiss it goodbye"

In December 1959, Branch Rickey had arrived at the Fontainebleau Hotel in Miami Beach, Florida, trumpeting a third major league, set to compete with the American and National Leagues as early as spring 1961. Nine months later, on the morning of August 2, 1960, when the Mahatma and Bill Shea entered the $400-a day Imperial Suite at the Conrad Hilton Hotel in Chicago, it was to make one last desperate plea for an idea that he had once blithely announced was "as inevitable as tomorrow."

At their July 18 meeting in Chicago, National League officials declared that their expansion plans would go forward "only if it develops that a new major league is impracticable." In the two weeks since that conference, Rickey continued to argue that a third league was not only "practicable but highly desirable." In their "hearts of hearts," the Mahatma insisted, the Major Leagues did not favor expansion.[1] The reasonable alternative, of course, was the Continental League. The Continentals, said Rickey, had met all the requirements stipulated by commissioner Ford Frick but one — the territorial issues. If Major League Baseball gave its full support to the indemnification plan created by Rickey and Bill Shea, the CL could go forward, making the Major League expansion plans unnecessary.

At Chicago on August 2, the Mahatma and Shea, accompanied by the eight league owners, used all of their combined powers of persuasion in order to induce the American Association president, Edward S. Doherty, and the International League president, Frank Shaughnessy, to accept the Continentals' indemnification plan. Their pleas fell on deaf ears. The AL and NL expansion committees, led respectively by Del Webb of the Yankees and Walter O'Malley of the Dodgers, now assumed center stage. After consulting with Rickey, Shea, and the CL owners, the two expansion committees "voted to recommend" the admission of four Continental League cities into Major League Baseball. With that, the Continental League, for all intents and purposes, had ceased to exist.

Defeated but unbowed, Bill Shea put on a brave face for the waiting press. The CL's "principal mission," he insisted, had been achieved.[2] Without the pressure applied by the Continentals, Major League Baseball would not have taken any positive steps toward expansion. Not everyone was happy with the outcome in Chicago, however. U.S. Senator John Carroll of Colorado, whose Denver franchise had been left out in the cold, charged that Shea's objective all along was to get another team in New York. The rest be damned. The more charitable view would be that Shea and Rickey struck a compromise with the Lords of Baseball at the Conrad Hilton Hotel. Four of the CL clubs would be accepted as Major League franchises. In exchange, Frick and company could at long last put the threat of antitrust legislation behind them.

Reflecting on these events at his fishing island retreat near Sudbury, Ontario, the Mahatma might have been struck by a sense of irony regarding his late enterprise. As John Drebinger of the *New York Times* noted, many of the problems confronting the Continentals had been of the Mahatma's own making. Had minor league clubs been in a position to scout, develop, and sell ballplayers to the team of their choice, the new loop might have had a fighting chance. What made this impossible was the very farm system Rickey had invented in the 1920s.[3]

While the Continental League was passing from the scene, the new American Football League was eagerly anticipating the start of its inaugural season. To be sure, the pundits did not give the new football circuit much more hope for survival than they had given the Continental League. But AFL Commissioner Joe Foss had been able to do what Rickey could only dream of, secure a TV deal with ABC. In an innovative move, the AFL sold the league's games as a package. Pete Rozelle, astute public relations man that he was, quickly adopted this idea for the NFL. It is interesting to speculate what innovations might have sprung from the fertile mind of the Mahatma. At the very least, the CL's ground-breaking invasion of the Jim Crow South would have been worth headlines. But, at the moment, it was the AL and NL pennant races that were the focus of everyone's attention.

As the Continental League was saying adieu at Chicago, the Pirates were putting down the welcome mat for a seventeen-game homestand between August 3 and August 17. By this time, Pirate pennant fever had infected not just Pittsburgh, but western Pennsylvania, West Virginia, western Maryland, eastern Ohio, and lower New York State. Five busloads of fans arrived regularly from Bill Mazeroski's birthplace of Wheeling, West Virginia. Entire caravans of buses had begun lining up at Schenley Drive, stretching past the golf course and conservatory, up School Oval Road to the vicinity of the Panther Hollow Bridge. Inside Forbes Field, the crowds erupted with a thunderous ovation with every "blue darter" (as announcer Bob Prince liked to call line drives) and every run the Pirates scored. Things, in fact, were getting a little out of hand. A delegation of fans from Erie, Pennsylvania, waltzed in with ten cases of beer, prompting the Pirate brass to prohibit liquor at the ballpark for the rest of the season.

The Los Angeles Dodgers were the first to arrive at Oakland. The Bucs won the series opener on August 3, with Vern Law hurling a 3–0 shutout for his fourteenth win in a nifty 2:16. Los Angeles came back to win the next day, but the Corsairs seized the rubber game on a Rocky Nelson home run off loser Don Drysdale. Bob Prince's signature cry—"You can kiss it goodbye!"[4]—could be heard over the airwaves as Nelson's shot bent around the right field pole. The once mighty Giants were next. Vinegar Bend Mizell garnered his eighth victory in the first game on August 5, out-dueling Sad Sam Jones, 1–0. Prince's lopsided grin grew even more askew as the Pirates chased the Giants out of town by winning three more times. They then stretched their winning streak to eight games by twice dispatching the visiting Chicago Cubs. Danny Murtaugh's men had now won twelve of their last fifteen, as they prepared to host second-place St. Louis on August 11–14.

Like the Pittsburgh Pirates, the New York Yankees began the month at home. On August 1, they defeated the Detroit Tigers, 3–2. With Yogi Berra's stiff neck in a brace and Elston Howard plagued by a severely sprained left hand, third-string catcher John Blanchard got his first start of the season. The next day, as the fateful meeting between the Continentals and the Major Leagues was taking place in Chicago, the Yankees swept a doubleheader from the Bengals, again by identical 3–2 scores. Both games were decided in extra innings. Blanchard won the first game with a single in the 14th. In the nightcap, the Yankees chased Tiger starter Jim Bunning, as Roger Maris hit a homer with one on in the bottom of the ninth to send the game into extra innings. Bob Cerv won it in the tenth with a home run off Bob Bruce. If there was a hero of the day it had to be Blanchard. With Berra and Howard both out with injuries, the Minnesotan played all 24 innings, losing ten pounds in the process.

As the Continental League was disappearing from history in Chicago, Detroit's GM Bill DeWitt and the irrepressible Frank Lane were completing a transaction without precedent in the annals of Major League Baseball. In a "face to face meeting under the catacombs," DeWitt informed Tiger manager Jimmy Dykes that he had been traded to the Indians for the Tribe's field boss Joe Gordon.[5] Neither team was doing well. The Tigers, after a fast start, had stopped hitting (their best player, Al Kaline, was mired in the .220s). The Bengals' current eastern swing had seen them lose 10 of 14 games, 9 by one run. The Indians, despite Frantic Frank's flurry of trades, were in fourth place, seven games out. The two general managers decided the swapping of the easy-going Dykes and the more aggressive Gordon (who had been fired and re-hired by Lane the previous September) might be just the tonic each club needed. Meanwhile, on August 3, Dykes was just one of the 22,621 spectators at Yankee Stadium who watched from the stands as Coach Billy Hitchcock led his former team to a 12–2 victory over the Yankees. Less than a week later, Hitchcock would join Dykes at Cleveland, with Jo Jo White, who had served as interim manager on August 3, reuniting with Gordon at Detroit. Lane and DeWitt, you might say, had also concocted the only trade of bench coaches in baseball history.

The Yankees left the Tigers and Indians to acquaint themselves to their new managers, and headed to Kansas City to play the Athletics on August 5–7. This was one of Yogi's least favorite stops on the August calendar. The weather was so hot and humid in Kansas City that time of year that he and his teammates rarely ventured from their rooms, praying that the air conditioning wouldn't break down.[6] The Yankees won the opener behind Roger Maris' two-run homer. On August 6, the mercury rose to 97 degrees and the Bombers were equally torrid, torching the A's, 16–4. Maris had two more home runs and six RBIs against his former team. With 35 round-trippers, he was seven games ahead of Babe Ruth's 1927 pace.

The Yankees now headed for Chicago and a reunion with the White Sox at Comiskey Park on August 8–10. Al López's team was just 1½ games behind the Bombers. The Yanks received a rough welcome, losing 9–1 in the series opener. Veteran left-hander Billy Pierce faced just 31 Yankee batters, and Minnie Minoso had three RBIs against Whitey Ford. The Yankees' lead over Chicago shrank to half a game. The next day, the usually sure-handed Nellie Fox uncorked an errant throw with the bases loaded in the seventh, leading to a 7–4 Yankee victory, dropping the Chisox into a second-place tie with Baltimore. Luis Arroyo recorded his first Yankee win. On August 10 New York took the rubber game, 6–0. The largest weekday crowd in Comiskey Park that season, 48,109, watched Art Ditmar, Eli Grba, and Bobby Shantz (the AL MVP in 1952) combine for the shutout. The Yanks left the Windy City for New York in first place, 1½ games ahead of the Baltimore Orioles. The defending AL champions dropped to third in the standings.

Tim O'Toole, known familiarly as "Mooch," probably knew more about the human side of the opposition than any other person in the Pirate organization. It is said that no man is a hero to his valet, but you would be hard pressed to hear this from the man who ran the visiting locker room at Forbes Field. There were few players he didn't like, but there were three he especially admired. O'Toole's holy trinity consisted of Stan Musial of the St. Louis Cardinals, Robin Roberts of the Philadelphia Phillies, and Al Dark, the former Giants standout now with the Milwaukee Braves. All three men tipped well, and, despite their star status, didn't ask for special treatment. The best visiting team, in Mooch's estimation, was the Los Angeles Dodgers. The Giants' Willie Mays was "a good guy," who also didn't ask for much and was a great kidder. Frank Howard of the Dodgers and Ernie Broglio of the Cardinals were "good kids." Howard's teammate Don Drysdale took losing harder than anyone, except perhaps Reds manager Fred Hutchinson. They didn't call Hutchinson "the Bear" for nothing! The instituting of the interleague trading period had brought a larger number of players over from the American League. Former ALers like Billy Martin (Reds) and Bob Nieman (Cardinals) were initially puzzled by the "swindle sheet." This was the ledger with which O'Toole kept track of the players' expenditures — gum, chewing tobacco, soda pop and sandwiches. The newcomers went along amiably with the NL system.[7]

The Cardinals' Stan Musial, Ernie Broglio, and Bob Nieman may have been nice guys, but they came to Forbes Field determined to gain ground on the first-place Pirates. St. Louis ended the Pittsburgh eighth-game winning streak on August 11, winning 3–2 in twelve innings. Broglio bested Bob Friend in a pitching duel that saw both pitchers go the distance.

Musial teed off on Friend with an upper deck job in right field in the top of the twelfth to drive in the winning runs for St. Louis. A disconsolate Pirate batboy, Bob Recker, put it best: "Darn, we had them all the way and shoulda won."[8] The following day the Cards did it again, winning 9–2. Bob Gibson, who had entered the previous game as a pinch-runner, scattered 10 hits in a complete game victory. Ken Boyer hit a three-run homer, and Musial had an RBI single. The Cardinals received a scare when second baseman Julián Javier was stunned by a throw as he was sliding into second in the third inning. Manager Solly Hemus sat him down for the remainder of the game. In winning, the Cardinals ran their own winning streak to six games, and reduced the Pirates' lead to three.

Pittsburgh now faced one of the most important challenges of the 1960 season. If the Cardinals could win the next three games at Forbes Field, they would pull abreast of the Pirates for the NL lead. The Corsairs, however, began to right their shaky craft. The next day, Saturday, August 13, they turned back St. Louis, 4–1, behind Harvey Haddix's seven-hit pitching and Roberto Clemente's four RBIs. The game is also notable, if that's the word for it, for the fact that both starting catchers that day were named Hal Smith — Hal Raymond Smith for the Cardinals and Hal Wayne Smith for the Pirates. On Sunday, the Bucs stopped the St. Louis challenge in its tracks, taking both ends of a doubleheader, 9–4 and 3–2. Vern Law won his seventeenth game in the first contest. The Bucs lead was stretched once again to six games over St. Louis. Milwaukee was 6½ out. In this magical season, the Pirates always seemed to find someone to step up and take charge in a tough spot. During the St. Louis series that man was Don Hoak.

Don Hoak was born at Roulette, Pennsylvania, a tiny hamlet in the north-central part of the state, on February 2, 1928. Joining the Marines at age 16, Hoak saw action against the Japanese at Saipan and Okinawa. Mustered out in 1945, he hung out at Key West, Florida, eking out a living as a professional prize fighter. Abandoning boxing for baseball, he signed with Branch Rickey's Dodgers in 1947. Hoak came up to the big club in 1954, and, after stops in Chicago and Cincinnati, finally found a home with the Pirates in 1959. Hailed for his fielding, the Bucs third sacker didn't do badly with the bat either, hitting .294 in 1959. But the ex-Marine's value went far beyond his skills with the bat and glove. He was a take-charge kind of guy in the Billy Martin mode, who goaded pitchers like Bob Friend toward better performances. Once, when the whimsical

Dick Stuart failed to run out a ground ball, Hoak screamed at the top of his lungs: "If you can't give me 90 feet, why don't you go back to bed!" Dick Groat referred to him as the "straw boss."[9]

Hoak's leadership, savvy, and physical toughness were clearly in evidence in the second game of the twin bill against St. Louis on August 14. In the top of the seventh, with the score knotted at 2–2, the Cardinals put men on first and second with none out. At this point, with St. Louis in a sacrifice situation, Hoak called Dick Groat over to plot a pre-arranged play. The batter, Joe Cunningham, bunted Joe Gibbon's pitch down to third base. Hoak charged in, fielded the ball, and threw to Groat who had broken for third base. Groat beat the Cardinal baserunner Curt Simmons to the bag to stymie the Redbird rally, all according to Hoak's plan. In the bottom of the eleventh inning, with the game still tied at 2–2, Hoak swung at and missed two pitches, then lined a single to center to score Bob Skinner with the winning run.

Don Hoak, the Pirate third baseman, was the fiery vocal leader of the team. In August 1960 he starred in an important series against the St. Louis Cardinals, playing on a gashed foot that had required eight stitches to mend.

It was incredible that Don Hoak was even playing at all in that game. The night before, he and several other Pirate players had been invited to a pool party at a friend's house. While getting out of the water, Hoak gashed his foot badly on the pool ladder. Anxious teammates volunteered to escort him to a clinic, but the stubborn ex-Marine didn't want to give Danny Murtaugh any excuse to sit him down. He insisted that a doctor at the scene stitch his foot back together. The injury required eight stitches running from beneath the foot through webbing of the second and third toes. "Tiger" endured the procedure without the benefit of anesthesia, allegedly puffing on a cigar. Danny Murtaugh, trainer Danny Whalen, and the majority of Hoak's teammates remained unaware of these gruesome details until long after the St. Louis series was over.[10]

The Pirate homestand came to an end on August 16–17 with three straight wins over the Philadelphia Phillies. After 114 games Murtaugh's men were 7½ games ahead of Milwaukee, and 8½ in front of St. Louis. Dick Groat (.327) and Roberto Clemente (.314) were third and fourth in the batting race behind Norm Larker of Los Angeles and Willie Mays of San Francisco. Mooch would not have many visitors to attend to for a while. Groat, Clemente, and their teammates would be on the road for the remaining fourteen games of August.

Casey Stengel and his men returned to the Bronx from Chicago on August 12, winners of 10 out of the last 11 games, and 14 out of their last 18. The team was healthier than they had been in a long time with Yogi Berra and Elston Howard back in the fold. And they were playing the Washington Senators in a three-game series. The pesky Senators, however, did not cooperate with the Yankees' plans, winning the opener, 12–7. Berra dropped a fly ball in left to let in three runs in the fifth. Yankee pitchers contributed eleven free passes to the debacle. With the loss to Washington, the Yankees' lead over the Baltimore Orioles had suddenly shrunk to just five percentage points.

Saturday, August 13, was Old-Timer's Day at Yankee Stadium. The day's festivities featured a reenactment of the 1938 All-Star Game, which had been played at Yankee Stadium. The Bombers' Joe McCarthy and the Cubs' Gabby Hartnett were on hand to manage the clubs once again. The AL team included the likes of Joe DiMaggio, Bobo Newsom, Lefty Grove, Bob Feller, Red Rolfe, Luke Appling, and Doc Cramer. On the NL squad were Johnny Vander Meer, Stan Hack, Joe Medwick, and Billy Herman, among others. Mel Allen was the master of ceremonies and Tony Martin sang the National Anthem. Mrs. Babe Ruth, Mrs. Lou Gehrig, and Mrs. John McGraw were special guests. Former president Herbert Hoover threw out the ceremonial first pitch. Public address announcer Bob Sheppard informed the fans that attendance at Yankee Stadium had reached a million for the fifteenth consecutive year. In the regular game later that afternoon,

Whitey Ford pitched a three-hit shutout for his eighth victory, aided by Roger Maris' thirty-third home run of the season.

The Sunday doubleheader on August 14 was painful in more ways than one. The Yankees lost twice to Washington. Camilo Pascual hit a grand slam in the opener to help his own cause. Then, in the sixth inning of the second game, Roger Maris slid into second baseman Billy Gardner's knee trying to break up a double play. He ended up with severely bruised ribs, which put him out of the lineup for an undetermined period. Meanwhile, an irate Casey Stengel benched Mantle for failing to run out a ground ball. The Yankees, who had returned hale and hearty, and in first place, to the Bronx, had fallen into third place. Chicago and Baltimore shared the AL lead with an identical .580 percentage. The Bombers now faced another crucial series, as they welcomed the red-hot Orioles to the Stadium for a two-game series on August 15–16.

Baseball games, the pundits agreed, were taking longer and longer to complete. Several reasons were advanced to explain this phenomenon: more pitching changes, extended mound conferences, pitchers fussing around the mound, and batters stepping out of the plate.[11] But there were exceptions. At the Stadium on August 15, Art Ditmar won his twelfth game for the Bombers, 4–3, in just 1:56. He gave up five hits, walked one, and struck out one. A chastened Mantle responded to his recent rebuke by Stengel by hitting two home runs (numbers 28 and 29), good for four RBIs. With this victory, the Yankees climbed back into first place. The next day Whitey Ford threw his second three-hit shutout in a row, beating rookie phenomenon Chuck Estrada, 1–0. Pitching on just two days' rest, Whitey dispatched the Orioles on 106 pitches. With Maris out with bruised ribs, Stengel started Berra in right field and placed Johnny Blanchard behind the plate. Blanchard responded by driving in the winning run of the game. The Yankees now held a narrow half-game lead over Chicago and 1½ games over Baltimore, as they began a short road trip against the Boston Red Sox and Washington Senators.

On August 18, the Bucs boarded a plane for Cincinnati and the beginning of their 14-game road trip. Gino Cimoli immediately started a pillow fight. This was mild stuff compared to the fireworks the Redlegs had produced so far in August. Jim Brosnan's book, *The Long Season*, had recently come out in print. Although reviews were favorable, the baseball world was not so pleasant. Joe Garagiola, whose own book *Baseball Is a Funny*

Game was a best seller that summer, found little to laugh about in the "kookie Beatnik's" diary of the 1959 season. Frank Lane called Broz "an intellectual meathead," and forbade any of his Cleveland players from writing books. According to Brosnan, the source of their anger was his revelation of one baseball's darkest secrets: managers ordered pitchers to deliberately throw at hitters. Just as provocative was the professor's contention that hitters had every right to retaliate against "dusters." He asked, "Why shouldn't they be allowed to take a poke at us?"[12] One of Brosnan's teammates, in fact, had recently done just that.

The *Cincinnati Reds 1960 Yearbook* displayed pictures of various players gearing up for spring training. Billy Martin, the new second baseman acquired in December from the Cleveland Indians, was pictured working out on a punching bag. Whether this was an in-joke alluding to Martin's bellicose past, one can't tell. But it certainly proved to be prophetic. On August 4, in a game against the Chicago Cubs at Wrigley Field, Martin took umbrage at an inside pitch thrown by righty Jim Brewer. Following a short exchange of words near the mound, the former Yankee favorite let loose a punch to Brewer's right eye, fracturing his cheekbone and shelving him for the season. NL president Warren Giles suspended Martin for five games and fined him $500. Martin claimed self-defense—"I was only protecting myself"—but the appeal was denied. In any case, Martin's problems were far from over. Brewer's teammates regarded him "as a scoundrel who had escaped with a light punishment."[13] As the Reds were battling the Pirates at Crosley Field, Brewer and the Cubs were preparing an unprecedented $1,040,000 suit against Martin.

Martin was back with the Reds when the Pirates arrived at the Rhineland (as Cincy, with its large German population, was called) for a four-game series on August 18–21. The two teams split the difference. Vern Law got his eighteenth win in a starting role, and Elroy Face his eighth victory in relief in the two Pirate victories. Jim Brosnan saved both Cincinnati wins. The Bucs then proceeded to Chicago, where they won two of three from the cellar-dwelling Cubs. The Pirates were 3–4 thus far on their road trip. Now it was on to the Mississippi River for another reckoning with the Cardinals on August 26–28.

The Cards, an NL powerhouse in the 1920s, '30s, and '40s under the guidance of Branch Rickey, had fallen out of pennant contention after his departure for Brooklyn. In 1960 St. Louis had a genuine All-Star in the slick-fielding, power-hitting Ken Boyer (the brother of the Yankees' Clete

Boyer), and two solid pitchers in Larry Jackson and relief specialist Lindy McDaniel. That spring the baseball pundits had judged Solly Hemus' crew to be too slow afield and their pitching too poor to compete in the first division. However, the Redbirds had been one of the real surprises of the season, fighting the Braves for second place behind the Bucs. The Cards made a number of key adjustments. The most important move of all, it was agreed, was the one that sent Vinegar Bend Mizell to the Pirates in late May for second baseman Julián Javier.

Javier hailed from Ciudad Trujillo (formerly Santo Domingo) in the Dominican Republic. The city, the oldest continuous settlement in the New World, had been renamed in honor of Generalissimo Rafael Leonidas Trujillo Molina, the dictator who had ruled the Dominican Republic for thirty brutal years. The Dominican Republic was a mostly mountainous country occupying the eastern two-thirds of the island of Hispaniola. On its 19,333 square miles lived about three million people in 1960, 15 percent of whom were white, 20 percent black, and the rest of mixed parentage. It was a land of appalling contrasts: blocks of handsome one-story framed houses in the big cities of Ciudad Trujillo and Santiago co-existed with villages of squalid shacks built of palm leaves, where adults went about barefoot and children played naked in the dirt.

Well acquainted as Americans are with Fidel Castro and the Cuban Revolution, we forget that in the late 1950s and early 1960s Trujillo's dictatorship was one of the most destabilizing forces in Latin America. Venezuela accused the Dominican dictator of subsidizing an assassination attempt on its president, Rómulo Betancourt. On August 21, 1960, the Organization of American States passed drastic measures against the Dominican Republic, calling for the cessation of diplomatic ties and economic sanctions. On August 26, the day that the Pirates began their series with St. Louis at Busch Stadium, the United States officially broke diplomatic relations.

As the United States was distancing itself from the Trujillo regime, Dominicans were making a name for themselves in the National Pastime. Before the season was over, Matty Alou would join his older brother Felipe in the San Francisco Giants outfield. Juan Marichal had already made a stunning debut with the Giants. On July 8, 1960, Felipe Alou was in left field for San Francisco and Julián Javier at second base for St. Louis, the first time that Dominicans competed against each other in a Major League game. The Alous, Marichal, and Javier, like other Latin players, had to deal with language barriers, culture shock, and discrimination. As with the Cuban players, they were competing at the highest level while worrying about the safety of loved ones living under the cloud of revolution and counter revolution at home. Despite these difficult circumstances, Javier managed to help solidify the Cardinals middle defense. He did not hit for average, but he provided an added dimension of speed on the basepaths.

Julián Javier's home away from home was Busch Stadium. Originally called Sportsman's Park, it was the oldest standing structure in the Major Leagues, going all the way back to the 1860s. It had been the scene of many memorable moments in Cardinals and Browns history from the likes of Rogers Hornsby, Dizzy Dean, and Stan (the Man) Musial and Satchell Paige. But perhaps the most memorable event of all had occurred nine years earlier when Bill Veeck, then the owner of the St. Louis Browns, sent a midget, Eddie Gaedel, to bat in a game. Veeck's extravaganzas, unfortunately, did not make up for the Brownies' poor play on the field. In April 1953 he sold the stadium to beer magnate August A. Busch, Jr. The new owners undertook a $1.5 million reconstruction of the old ballpark, renaming it Busch Stadium. The new owners retained Sportsman's Park's most distinguishable feature, the screen in front of the right field pavilion, extending 156 feet from the foul line toward center field. Its days were numbered; a new park was planned for 1964.[14]

A crowd of 24,436 was present at Busch Stadium on August 26 as the Cardinals took the opening game of the series from the Pirates, 3–1. Stan Musial's two-run homer atop the pavilion in the seventh inning off Bob Friend, provided the margin of victory. Ernie Broglio went all the way, winning his sixteenth game, two less than Vernon Law. The next day, Stan the Man did it again, knocking a 2–0 pitch for a home run in the last of the ninth to beat the Corsairs, 5–4. Former Pirate Ron Kline got credit for the win before the largest crowd of the year. On August 28, the Cardinals came from behind to sweep the series, sending Pittsburgh to its fourth straight defeat (the longest streak of the year), 5–4. Julián Javier, who scored the tying run, was kept busy in the field. The Cards' outfielders did not make a single putout all day.

A bruised Pittsburgh team left for the West Coast, their lead over the Cards and Braves cut to 5½ games. On August 29, they snapped their four-game losing streak by beating the Dodgers at the Coliseum. Vern Law won his 19th game, five of which had come at the expense of the Angelinos. The next day the Bucs helped the Dodgers top the 2,000,000 attendance mark, winning once again as Roberto Clemente and Dick Groat clouted home runs. The last day of August found Pittsburgh at Candlestick Park. Former Dodger Clem Labine, signed as a free agent on August 16, recorded his first win as a Pirate, with two and two-thirds innings of relief against the woebegone Giants.

The Pirates produced a road record of 7–6 mark in the second half of August. A 12–4 start, including a seven-game winning streak, however, allowed them to finish the month with a gaudy 21–10 record. There were some lingering concerns. The Bucs did not do particularly well against their first-division rivals, with a combined 7–5 record versus Los Angeles and St. Louis (they did not play Milwaukee in August). However, they made up for it by beating up on the second-division teams, finishing 14–5 against them, including a 5–0 slate against San Francisco. With an overall record of 78–49 they had already exceeded their previous year's mark by two victories. Could they remain injury free and hold on for one more month?

Having faced down the Baltimore challenge on August 15–16, the Yankees took to the road against Boston and Washington. New York won two at Fenway to gain a 1½ game lead over Chicago, which had squeezed into second place ahead of the Orioles. However, the Senators once again proved to be a nemesis for the Bombers, beating them on August 19 behind Camilo Pascual. New York came back to win the next day, rallying for four runs in the eleventh. But the Nats captured the rubber game, with Pascual, who had pitched a complete game victory two days earlier, getting credit for the save. The Cuban, however, was soon shelved with a sore arm for the remainder of the season. Since he had pitched almost continuously the entire year in the majors and Cuban Winter League, it's a wonder he had lasted this long!

Stengel and company returned to New York for an eleven-game homestand against the western teams. First to arrive at the Stadium were the White Sox. One and a half games back, the defending champions could take back the league lead with a sweep of the Yankees. The Pale Hose got off to a good start, beating New York, 5–1, on August 23 in one of the strangest starts to any game ever. Left-handed ace Billy Pierce took his warm-up pitches in the top of the first, before suddenly being pulled out by Al López in favor of right-hander Early Wynn. The Major League rule book states that the announced starter must pitch to at least one batter, unless injured. That is what the White Sox claimed in making the switch.

The Yankees later filed an official protest with the league office, alleging that it was ploy by the "gay Señor" to induce Casey Stengel into fielding a mainly right-handed hitting lineup.[15] Pitching in what amounted to nine innings of relief, Wynn recorded his 281st lifetime decision. New York lost the protest, but won the next day, 3–2. Art Ditmar gained his thirteenth victory with help from Luis Arroyo in the ninth. The Yankees remained 1½ games ahead of Chicago and Baltimore.

Now came one of the most difficult stretches of the 1960 season for the New York Yankees. Stengel's men would have to play three double-headers in a row at home, six games in the space of fifty hours. The Cleveland Indians were the first to invade the Bronx. Luckily for the Bombers, the Tribe had failed to live up to Frank Lane's extravagant spring predictions. They were mired in fifth place under new manager Jimmy Dykes. The Indians were hitting well enough, with four players (Harvey Kuenn, Ken Aspromonte, Jimmy Piersall, and Vic Power) in the top ten in batting. However, none of their hitters ranked among the leaders in home runs or runs batted in. Clearly, the trading of Rocky Colavito and Minnie Minoso had resulted in a power outage. Meanwhile, injuries to second baseman Johnny Temple and shortstop Woodie Held had hurt the middle defense. Jim Perry was vying with Baltimore rookie Chuck Estrada for the AL lead in victories, but the rest of the young pitchers had failed to deliver. One of their most promising hurlers, Gary Bell, was on the disabled list with a tendon injury.

The Yankees spoiled Jimmy Dykes' return to the Stadium as the new Cleveland manager, whipping the deflated Indians twice on August 26. Yogi Berra's eleventh-inning home run won the first contest. With Roger Maris still on the sidelines, Mickey Mantle continued to carry the team on his broad back, swatting his thirtieth home run in the second inning to pace the New York victory. The Yankees also tied a record by producing four consecutive pinch-hits, with Maris, Gil McDougald, Clete Boyer, and Bob Cerv all delivering from the bench. Meanwhile, Bob Cerv's wife was delivering their eighth child, tying Jimmy Piersall and the Reds' Gus Bell (Gary's brother) for the Major League lead in that department. The next day, August 27, the proud father helped the Yankees sweep a double-header from the Tribe, hitting his fourteenth home run of the year in the second game in support of Bob Turley, who hurled a two-hit shutout.

The Yankees now hosted the other principal of the managers trade, Joe Gordon, and his new team, the Detroit Tigers. In gaining a split with the Tigers, the Bombers managed to win five of the six doubleheader games, and remained 1½ games ahead of the Baltimore Orioles, who shut out the White Sox on August 29 behind right-hander Jack Fisher.

Bob Elliot and his Kansas City Athletics came into town on the last two days of August. The A's were dismissed in many quarters as a Triple-A farm club of the New York Yankees, with every trade concocted by George Weiss seeming to improve the Bombers at the expense of the Midwesterners. The incestuous relationship between the two clubs took a new twist when the Athletics arrived at Yankee Stadium on August 30 — without their uniforms. The team's bags had not been removed from their Boston flight, and wound up at Washington instead. League rules provided that, in event of this happening, the visiting club would wear the grey uniforms of the home club with the shirt turned inside out. This odd sense of poetic justice was not lost on bystanders. One of them quipped, "I wonder what Bill Veeck and Frank Lane will have to say about this!"[16] Luckily, the A's uniforms arrived at the Stadium from Washington at 6:45 P.M., just in time for the game.

The Yankees took two of the three games played against the A's. Fans watching the first game of the twin bill on Wednesday, August 31, focused their attention on the fine four-hit shutout hurled by rookie right-hander Bill Stafford. A close inspection of the box score for this game, however, reveals something that is quite startling. Thirteen years after Jackie Robinson had broken baseball's color barrier, there was not a single black player on the field during the entire game. The Yankees had two black players on their roster at this time: Elston Howard and Héctor López. Neither one played in the game. The Kansas City Athletics did not have a single black player on their roster during the *entire* 1960 season.

This had not always been the case. In 1955, their first year in Kansas City, the team had three blacks on its roster: López at second base, first baseman Vic Power, and outfielder Harry (Suitcase) Simpson. The three still held most of Kansas City's batting records in 1960. The last black to play on the A's was López — like Power, a Latin American. He had been traded to the Yankees on May 26, 1959. One of the A's best minor league prospects was a Latin player named Leo Posada, but he would not join the club for another several weeks. However, Posada, uncle of current Yankees catcher Jorge Posada, was not a black Latin.[17]

To call Héctor López a Latin, while accurate, doesn't quite describe his ethnic background. Born in Colón, Panama, on July 9, 1929, López was a product of one of the most ambitious engineering feats of the twentieth century. Colón was the Caribbean terminus of the Panama Canal, built between 1903 and 1915. This great engineering feat was accomplished at a terrible price. Teeming jungle and preying mosquitoes resulted in the deaths of thousands of Panamanians from disease and exhaustion. Faced with a critical labor shortage, the project's directors began to import blacks from the British West Indies.[18] López's full name, Héctor Headley López Swainson, betrays that ethnic mixture created by the building of the Panama Canal.

López and his teammates had every reason to be satisfied with their performance after their mediocre play in July. As the book closed on August, the New York Yankees were in first place with a 75–50 record. Their record for the month was 22–11, a .667 percentage. Their lead was tenuous, however. They held a one-game margin over the Baltimore Orioles and four games over the Chicago White Sox. Over in the National League the Pittsburgh Pirates had also recovered from their July doldrums, posting a 21–10 record and a winning percentage of .677. The Bucs, 78–49, were seven games in front of the Milwaukee Braves and 7½ ahead of the St. Louis Cardinals.

August had been a month characterized by arrivals and departures. Joe Gordon and Jimmy Dykes exchanged managerial positions. The Yankee Old-Timers returned to the Bronx. Former Bronx hero Billy Martin was suspended for fighting. On August 2, the Continental League disbanded. And then on August 30, the American League announced it would expand to ten teams, no later than 1962. Branch Rickey and Bill Shea had exited the stage. But their influence on baseball's future direction could not be discounted. Without them, Major League Baseball would have remained asleep at the wheel as professional football continued its steady rise to American sports hegemony. As September beckoned, neither the Pirates nor Yankees could yet afford to sleep quietly. They still had several barrels of their own to jump before claiming their respective league pennants.

Chapter Ten

"The gateway to the rainbow"

If the Major League season is a marathon, and September the last six-mile leg of the race, then we can say that in 1960 the Pittsburgh Pirates and New York Yankees had very different experiences in reaching the finish line. The Pirates, leading for most of the race, shook off various injuries in September to keep their rivals at bay and win their first pennant in thirty-three years. By contrast, the Yankees, who had been jockeying for position with the lead pack since the start, suddenly broke free from their competitors at the twenty-mile mark, and never looked back until breaking the tape.

Before the season began, the New York Yankees had regarded the Chicago White Sox and the Cleveland Indians as their greatest obstacles to winning their tenth pennant under Casey Stengel. But, for months, the Old Perfessor and his men had had to contend with a challenge from an unexpected source, the Baltimore Orioles.

The City of Baltimore did not have a Major League Baseball club from 1903 to 1953. After the 1902 season the original Orioles franchise was moved to New York, where they were known as the Highlanders, and eventually the Yankees. After World War II, the city fathers began a concerted effort to lure a Major League club to the Chesapeake Bay area. With this goal in mind, Memorial Stadium was built in 1950. Three years later, it was remodeled as an all-purpose facility with an unroofed second deck. The St. Louis Browns moved to Baltimore for the 1954 season. The newly-christened Orioles won their debut at their new home, as future Yankee Bob Turley pitched a complete game victory against the Chicago White Sox.

The current O's were led by their cool and cerebral manager, Paul Richards. The fifty-one-year-old Richards came from Waxahachie, Texas, a suburb of Dallas. A catcher by trade, he made his Major League debut in 1932, a teammate of White Sox manager (and fellow backstop) Al López. After an undistinguished career with the Dodgers, Giants, Athletics, and Tigers that ended in 1946, Richards turned to managing. He led the White Sox (1951–53) before moving on to Baltimore to 1954, where he served as both GM and field manager until 1958. For some time now, Richards had been predicting the "end of the Yankee dynasty."[1] As manager in 1960, the slender Texan was doing his best to make that forecast come true.

Richards had done wonders with a collection of young kids and grizzled veterans. The Baby Birds' infield was populated by third baseman Brooks Robinson (23), shortstop Ron Hansen (22), second baseman Marv Breeding (26), and first baseman Jim Gentile (also 26). Hansen and Breeding were rookies. The pitching corps was led by 22-year-old rookie Chuck Estrada. Behind him were Milt Pappas, Jerry Walker, and Jack Fisher—all of whom were a mere 21 years of age. To complement the youth movement, Richards had a small group of veterans among the Flock: catcher Gus Triandos (30) and left fielder Gene Woodling (37)—both former Yankees—and two pitchers, knuckleball ace Hoyt Wilhelm (37) and Hal (Skinny) Brown (35). They were not to be confused with Johnny Unitas and the Baltimore Colts. But six years after the Browns had arrived from St. Louis, Maryland's baseball fans finally had a baseball team to be proud of.

Memorial Stadium's dimensions—309 feet down the foul lines, 380 in the power alleys, and 425 to dead center field—did not make it a particularly congenial park for sluggers. Consequently, apart from newcomer Jim Gentile, Richards had assembled a team of line-drive hitters. As with the Pirates in the National League, most were having career years at the same time. It was the hitters that carried the Flock during the first half of the season. With their wealth of young arms emerging in the second half, Baltimore posed as a dangerous threat to the Yankees' hopes for returning to the Fall Classic. As they got ready to host the Yankees for a three-game series at Memorial Stadium on September 2–4, the Orioles trailed the Bombers by just one game.

Casey Stengel had reason to be confident. Pitching the opening game would be his "professional," Whitey Ford, who already had scored three shutouts over the Orioles that year. On the mound for the Birds was

Miltiades Stergius Papastedgius, otherwise known as Milt Pappas. A Detroit native, he was half of the Orioles' all-Greek battery with catcher Gus Triandos. Baltimore, in fact, had the major league "monopoly" on Greek players, before trading Ford's old pal Billy Loes to the Giants the previous December.[2]

While the plump and cocky Pappas had gotten off to a slow start in 1960, he had found command of his pitches in the second half of the season. In the opening game of the series on September 2, Pappas held the Yankees to just three hits en route to a 5–0 victory. The capacity crowd of 44,518 (5,000 fans had been turned away) witnessed the Orioles' 77th win, their most ever in one season. New York's lead, meanwhile, had been reduced to a minuscule .003 in the percentage column. The next day, September 3, the Yanks were shut out again, 2–0, this time by Jack Fisher. Brooks Robinson led the way with a ninth-inning home run off Luis Arroyo (Luis made the mistake of throwing Robby a fast ball instead of his screwball). With the loss, New York fell a full game behind Baltimore. Unable to solve the Birds' pitching, the Bombers leveled their most damaging blows at home plate umpire Larry Napp. The arbiter was hit by two foul tips in a row, the first off the bat of Roger Maris, the second off Mickey Mantle's. The latter knocked the wind out of Napp, forcing him off the field on a stretcher.

The mighty Bombers had now suffered three shutouts in a row (the first was at the hands of the Athletics' Ned Garver in the second game of a doubleheader on August 31). That made for a total of 29 scoreless innings. New York finally put some runs on the Memorial Stadium scoreboard on September 4, but it was not enough to avoid a series sweep by the O's. They lost, 6–2, as Chuck Estrada, with help from Hoyt Wilhelm, won his sixteenth game of the season. Only Bill Skowron's seventh-inning single to right field averted another shutout. Whitey Ford and Luis Arroyo both failed in relief of rookie Bill Stafford. With the win, Baltimore extended its lead over New York to two games.

Reeling from the shutdown by the Oriole pitching, the Yankees came back to the friendly confines of Yankee Stadium and finally flexed their muscles against the lowly Red Sox. On September 5, they took both ends of a doubleheader from Boston. Mickey Mantle's double in the first game was, incredibly, the first Yankee extra-base hit in four games. Joe DeMaestri singled in the ninth inning of the second game off Cuban relief specialist Mike Fornieles to win the nightcap. DeMaestri had only two RBIs all season — both were game-winners. The Red Sox took the final game of the series. Pumpsie Green hit a ball that eluded Héctor López in left, bouncing off the auxiliary scoreboard. By the time the Yankees retrieved it, Green had crossed the plate with an inside-the-park home run. Ted Williams chipped in with his 26th homer of the year, number 518 of his career. Meanwhile, Roger Maris, his ribs still heavily bandaged, had fallen off Ruth's pace. Having scored just 10 runs in 8 games, New York found itself 1½ games behind the O's as they began their last western swing of the 1960 campaign.

As the Yankees struggled, the Pirates continued their seemingly inexorable (and amazing) march toward their first pennant since 1927. Teamwork personified the Pirate drive to the flag. In a confidential scouting report, conducted by *Sport Magazine*, no member of the Pirate club was judged as the best at his position in the National League.[3] In fact, the first of September found none of the Bucs leading in any offensive categories. Dick Groat (.323) and Roberto Clemente (.319) were third and fourth in the batting race, respectively, behind Norm Larker of Los Angeles (.339) and Willie Mays of the San Francisco Giants (.326). Clemente with 86 RBIs was as a distant fifth behind the league leader, Chicago's Ernie Banks, who had 105. No Corsair was anywhere near challenging Banks's 37 home runs. All Pittsburgh seemed to be able to do was win, as they did on September 1 against San Francisco. Harvey Haddix and Clem Labine allowed the Giants 14 hits, but only gave up a single run while stranding 15 men in a 6–1 victory at Candlestick Park. From San Francisco, the Pirates flew back to the Golden Triangle for two games with the Philadelphia Phillies on September 3–4.

Writing in *Ebony Magazine* the previous month, Bill Veeck had pooh poohed the idea of American blacks dominating the ranks of Major League Baseball. African American participation in the National Pastime, he argued, would "level off" in time. Like the increasingly affluent white youth, who drove to school and instead of walking, "the Negro" would become "less physical" as new employment opportunities opened up. Moreover, a new diet regimen would eventually bring "Oriental" players into the mix to compete for Major League jobs.[4] To note from Gene Mauch's Philadelphia lineup on September 3, the international invasion had already begun. To face Vinegar Bend Mizell, the Phillies manager placed four players with Cuban roots in the lineup: Pancho Herrera (first base), Tony Taylor (second base), Rubén Amaro (shortstop), and Tony González (center field.) Taylor and González drove in the winning runs, and Amaro scored one, in helping Phils rookie Art Mahaffey to his fifth straight victory, a 2–0 shutout. Vern Law failed once again to record his 20th win. But Mauch's Cuban contingent was no help against Mizell as the Corsairs returned to their winning ways the next day.

Danny Murtaugh's Pirates had thus far benefited from a number of good breaks: a second-half schedule played mostly in their home park, the disarray of the pre-season favorites like the San Francisco Giants, and the lack of major injuries. The luck of the Irishman, however, was about to change. The Milwaukee Braves came into town on September 5 and split a Labor Day doubleheader with the Bucs. The Corsairs took the rubber game the next day, September 6, but it was a pyrrhic victory. Lew Burdette hit Dick Groat in the arm with a pitch in the first inning. Burdette, known for his pin-point control (he walked 1.14 batters in 1960), later said he had thrown a slider too fast and it had gotten away from him. Groat stayed in the game until the third inning, when the swelling became too much for him to bear. After the game he went to the hospital, where doctors confirmed the bad news. He had suffered a broken left wrist and would be out for the rest of the regular season.

Dick Groat was in the U.S. Army in 1953 playing for the Fort Belvoir, Virginia, basketball team, when he overheard two boys talking excitedly in the stands before a game. The first boy asked, "Which one is Dick Groat?" The second one replied, "I dunno, let's ask the bald guy." The "bald guy" was the future Pirates shortstop. With his bare pate and spare frame, Groat certainly was not an impressive physical specimen. Lester J. Biederman of the *Pittsburgh Press* thought he resembled a bank clerk. Born November 4, 1930, in Wilkinsburg, Pennsylvania, Groat had been playing sports ever since his older brothers had put up a makeshift basket in the backyard of their home. Groat was two-sport star at Duke University, and, after graduation, signed with both Branch Rickey's Pirates and the Fort Wayne Pistons of the young National Basketball Association.[5]

Mustered out of the military in 1955, Groat decided to give up basketball and concentrate on becoming the Pirates' starting shortstop. Observers were not impressed with his skills. He was slow afoot, did not have a strong arm, and lacked power at the plate. But Groat made up for his shortcomings in other ways. He had quick hands and excellent peripheral vision, skills honed from years of playing basketball. Lacking fielding range, he learned to play the hitters to gain the maximum advantage. Don Hoak said he had never been impressed when playing against him, but as a teammate the Tiger had gained appreciation for what the Bucs team captain could do. Groat was super smart in the field, as evidenced by the rally-killing play against the St. Louis Cardinals the previous month. At bat, Groat was adept at hitting behind the hitter — he was generally acknowledged to be the best hit-and-run man in the National League. Laying down sacrifices and breaking up double plays, he was a "team man through and through." Even so, he would lead the club in on-base percentage in 1960.

Like so many other ballplayers of his era, Dick Groat scrambled to make a living in the off-season. He was a salesman for Imperial Oil and Grease, a Pittsburgh industrial lubricating company, a job which he approached with his usual intensity. He, his wife Barbara, and their three daughters resided in the Pittsburgh suburb of Swissvale. Back in August, Barbara had made one of her rare appearances at Forbes Field to watch Dick play in an evening game against the St. Louis Cardinals. Groat proceeded to strike out four times against Ernie Broglio. Identifying his wife as the cause of his humiliation, Groat — like many players, deeply superstitious, not necessarily male chauvinist — decreed that she could not return to Oakland that year unless the Pirates won the World Series. Now, both the season and the World Series had been cast into doubt by his injury.

As Dick Groat was bemoaning his fate, the New York Yankees were making their final western incursion, beginning with two games at Comiskey Park. They started on the right foot on September 7, downing the White Sox, 6–4. The winning run came on an error by second baseman Sam Esposito. Subbing for the ailing Nellie Fox, Esposito bobbled what would have been a sure double play. Instead his error created a bases-loaded opportunity for the Yankees. Yogi Berra singled in two runs, and Johnny Blanchard doubled in a couple more. At this point, an irate fan jumped on the field and attacked Esposito. Blows were exchanged between player and fan before the park police were able to restore order. With this win, the Yankees cut the Orioles' lead to half a game. However, Chicago exacted revenge the next day, the big blow coming on Ted Kluszewski's two-run double in the eighth. Luis Arroyo suffered his first loss as a Yankee. Roger Maris and Héctor López hit home runs in a losing cause, with the one by Maris an inside-the-park affair. The Yanks still trailed Baltimore by 1½ games.

Briggs Stadium, located on Michigan and Trumbull Avenues, was the home of the Detroit Tigers. It was here, on May 2, 1939, that Lou Gehrig's 2,130 consecutive-game streak came to an end, foretelling the end of Major League Baseball's Second Golden Era. The park's dimensions — 340 feet down the left field line, 440 feet to straight center, and 325 to right — made a congenial place for sluggers like Gehrig, Ted Williams, and the Tigers' own Hank Greenberg. Although Detroit's Rocky Colavito was among the league leaders in home runs, with 28, the current group of Bengal belters was mired in sixth place under new manager Joe Gordon. The most exciting news emanating from Briggs Stadium was the arrest, two weeks earlier, of a seventeen-year-old youth who had thrown an egg at Cleveland outfielder Jimmy Piersall.

For once, New York did not go into Briggs Stadium having to face the Yankee killers Frank Lary and Don Mossi. Bill Stafford twirled a six-hitter on September 9, the rookie's third win since being called up from Richmond. Stafford, a resident of tiny Catskill, New York, also drove in the initial Yankee tally in the first inning. López and Maris homered in successive times at-bats for the second consecutive day. September 10 was Maris' twenty-sixth birthday, but it was Gil McDougald who supplied the heroics, hitting two home runs. Mickey Mantle blasted a colossal shot of his own. With the count two balls and no strikes, the Mick took a Paul Foytack serving and put it over the right field roof, the ball rising 94 feet up from the ground. The ballpark-clearing feat had been accomplished only three times in Briggs Stadium history: twice by Mantle and once by Ted Williams, back in 1939. The victory allowed New York to claim first place, a half-game over the Orioles.

Cleveland was next on the schedule. The Indians, long out of the pennant race, went down quietly twice in a twinight doubleheader. Maris slugged home run number 38 in the first game, and a red hot López hit his fourth homer in four games against loser Jim Perry. Bobby Richardson's RBI single in the eleventh inning won the second game for the Yankees. Mantle had earlier hit his 34th home run. Ryne Duren came out of the Yankee pen and snuffed out an Indian rally in the bottom of the eleventh, striking out Woodie Held to end the game. New York, which had finished third behind the Indians in 1959, completed their season series against the Tribe by whipping them in sixteen of their twenty-two meetings in 1960. Frantic Frank Lane was already packing his bags to leave.

As the Yankees toured the Midwest, back in New York the new AFL franchise was making its debut at the Polo Grounds. The New York Titans overcame mud, wind, and rain to defeat the Buffalo Bills, 27–3. However, as far as the Lords of Baseball were concerned, the launching of the AFL was but a small blip on the horizon compared with the ultimate event of the Major League season. On Tuesday, September 13, Commissioner Ford Frick announced the 1960 World Series schedule. The first game would begin on October 5 in the NL pennant winner's home park. Two AL teams, the Yankees and Orioles, were permitted to print World Series tickets. It was too early for the Yankees to begin collecting World Series checks. But there was another revenue stream of sorts. Major League players collected royalty checks for autographed baseballs, a commercial venture in which all sixteen clubs participated. The Yankees, from Mickey Mantle on down, each received $145.12. The low men on the totem pole, the Kansas City A's, each got $6.08.

The poorly-paid Athletics were the last stop on the Yankees' final western swing. Any hope Stengel may have had of extending the team's two-game lead over Baltimore, however, was upset by the dismal A's. On September 13, Kansas City routed the Yankees, 12–3. Dick Williams, one of Branch Rickey's Brooklyn farmhands and future Hall of Fame manager, had a single, double, and home run, for six RBIs. Luckily, the Orioles lost to the Tigers, keeping New York's lead over Baltimore at one game. The Bombers were not so lucky the next day, September 14, when A's right-hander Ray Herbert out-dueled Art Ditmar, 2–1. Former Yankee Andy Carey's screaming liner over the left center field fence provided the margin of victory. It was Ditmar's 24th gopher ball of the season, breaking the old Yankee record held by Tommy Byrne. In the meantime, Baltimore defeated the Tigers in a slugfest, 11–10, shaving the Yankee lead over them to a microscopic one percentage point, .590 to .589. The Old Perfessor was infuriated by his team's performance. "The main problem," he growled, "is that our guys aren't mad at anyone." He added, "We'd better learn that we can't watch the scoreboard and still make a living." An anonymous Yankee admitted that the team lacked a team leader to stir them up. "What this club needs right now," he said, "is a Billy Martin."[6]

All season long, there had always been a Pirate to step up to the mark when the going got tough. Bob Skinner, Roberto Clemente, and Don Hoak had all taken turns carrying the team. No player had provided steadier play and leadership than Dick Groat. With Groat now on the sidelines, all eyes were on his understudy, Dick Schofield. Ducky, as Schofield was called, was at shortstop as the Pirates continued their homestand by hosting the St. Louis Cardinals for a single game on September 8. Vern Law failed once again to win his 20th game of the season. Ernie Broglio won his 18th, with help from Lindy McDaniel, who posted his 23rd save. The Corsairs returned to their winning ways by beating the visiting Chicago Cubs, 4–3, on September 9. Elroy Face came on in relief of Vinegar Bend Mizell, and ended a Cub ninth-inning rally with just one pitch. It was *his* 23rd save of the season. Bob Friend won the next day, 4–1, for his 15th victory. The game, which featured 17 hits, two errors, and one wild pitch, was completed in 1:59. Five Pittsburgh double plays speeded things along. Who supplied the winning runs? It was none other than Ducky Schofield.

Pittsburgh now said their good-bye to the West Coast teams. The Pirates-Giants series at Forbes Field on September 12–13 had a certain poetic justice to it. Before the season began, the pundits had been predicting a pennant flag flying over Candlestick Park. The Bucs were picked for fourth, at best. On September 12, the Pirates bested San Francisco, 6–1, and mathematically eliminated Willie Mays and company from the pennant race. That same day Ford Frick authorized the Pirates to print World Series tickets.

The current Pirate homestand ended with two games against the Los Angeles Dodgers on September 14–15. The Dodgers had played the Pirates even all year; predictably, the two teams ended their season series by splitting these last two games at Forbes Field. The first game was distinguished (if that's the word for it) by one of Dick Stuart's most flamboyant defensive boners. It happened like this: in the fourth inning, with the score tied, 0–0, the Dodgers' Maury Wills singled; Vern Law, going once again for his twentieth victory, tried to pick Wills off first. Stuart missed the tag, but had Wills caught in a rundown. The lumbering Stuart decided to chase Wills all the way to second, faking throws all the while to a perplexed Bill Mazeroski. Upon approaching second, Wills dived head first into the bag, with Stuart diving right in after him. He missed the tag, of course, and shortly afterward Wills scored what proved to be the winning run. The Pirates, however, came back the next day to beat the Angelinos behind Bob Friend. The magic number, the combination of Bucs victories and second-place team defeats needed to win the pennant, was now at ten.

Four days later at Crosley Field in Cincinnati, Vern Law finally gained his 20th victory in the first game of a doubleheader against the Reds. Vinegar Bend Mizell followed him with a masterful three-hit shutout in the nightcap. Further north on the Ohio River in the Golden Triangle, World Series tickets officially went on sale at 4:30 P.M. A crowd of 3,000 fans waited at the downtown post office to make ticket requests by mail. The 12,625 lucky winners would be chosen at random. The Pirates' race to the pennant had brought 1,521,251 fans through the turnstiles thus far at Forbes Field, a new attendance record. Visiting the city, *New York Times* columnist Arthur Daley noted, "In buses, cabs, hotel lobbies, and store windows, posters reading 'Beat 'Em Bucs' smack you in the eye. The question of the day is 'How do you like our Pirates?'" The campuses of Carnegie Tech and the University of Pittsburgh, which flanked Forbes Field, were aflame with pennant fever. One professor, puzzled by all the pennant talk among his students, was inspired to ask, "What is this magic number?"[7]

The New York Yankees' magic number — in fact, their entire season — rested on the four-game series with the Baltimore Orioles scheduled for the Bronx on the weekend of September 16–18. The two teams played single games Friday night and Saturday afternoon, concluding with a doubleheader on Sunday. With the Bombers holding a razor-thin .001 lead over the Birds, the upcoming clash overshadowed all other sporting events in the Big Apple. New York Titans owner Harry Wismer asked AFL Commissioner Joe Foss to allow his team to postpone their Friday night game at the Polo Grounds against the Boston Patriots until Saturday night. Wismer did not want his team to have to go head-to-head with the Yankees-Orioles contest. Paul Richards, who thus far had guided the O's to an 83-win season (the Bombers had 82), called the series "the most important I have ever managed." An Oriole sweep, the Texan added, would be "the gateway to the rainbow."[8]

To stem the Baltimore challenge, Casey Stengel turned once again to Whitey Ford. The Yankees' longtime ace had had an up and down year, brilliant performances followed by woeful starts. Troubled with arm ailments, his record was just 9–9. But this was a situation that called for clutch pitching, and Stengel had to go with his best. Unlike his start at Baltimore earlier in the month, Ford did not disappoint. Over 50,332 fans were on hand on Friday, September 16, as Whitey pitched the Yankees to a 4–2 win over the Orioles. He went eight and two-thirds innings. Bobby Shantz came on to get the last out in the ninth. Héctor López's opposite field, wind-blown home run, and a round-tripper by Roger Maris (only his fifth against lefty pitching) helped sink young left-hander Steve Barber.

Bobby Richardson greeted at home plate by Gil McDougald (12), Elston Howard (32), and Bill Skowron (14). The Yankee second baseman was the 1960 World Series MVP, but his pivotal role came in the crucial September 16–18 series with Baltimore at Yankee Stadium, where he helped break open what had been a tight pennant race.

Saturday's game was even better than Friday's. Gene Stephens, the Oriole lead-off batter, had set a Major League record in 1953 by getting three hits in one inning playing for the Red Sox. On Saturday afternoon at the Stadium, Stephens led off the game with a single. From here on the game was played with a continuous roar from the crowd. Even the vendors stopped hawking their wares in anticipation of a big rally. It was a seesaw battle. Mickey Mantle slugged a two-run homer in the first inning off Oriole ace Chuck Estrada. Gus Triandos' solo home run off Bob Turley, leading off the top of the sixth, tied the score at 2–2. The Yankees regained the lead in the bottom of the inning when Yogi Berra hit his fifteenth round-tripper off Estrada. In the top of the seventh, Maris made a circus catch on a Gene Woodling drive to right. But then Jim Gentile put a Bobby Shantz pitch where Maris couldn't reach it, an upper deck job that tied the score at 3–3.

All of a sudden, the Orioles' pennant hopes were undone by two freakish plays. Yogi Berra opened the eighth against Estrada with a bad bounce double that caromed off the elbow of first baseman Gentile. Estrada then gave Bill Skowron an intentional pass. John Blanchard also walked, loading the bases. Then Bobby Richardson (who went 5-for-11 in the series) singled off Estrada's glove, the ball bounding crazily toward right field for two runs. Paul Richards looked on in disgust. If the ball had traveled unmolested, it would have been a sure double play. Instead, it was a 5–3 victory for the Yankees.

The unlikely hitting star of the game, Robert Clinton Richardson, was born at Sumter, South Carolina, on August 19, 1935. As a youngster, Richardson had starred on his Salvation Army and American Legion teams. Signed to the Yankees after graduating high school in 1953, he was assigned to Norfolk, Virginia, in the Class D Piedmont League. By 1956 he was a standout on Ralph Houk's Triple-A Denver Bears, batting .328. Richardson was brought up to the big club the following year as the logical successor to Billy Martin, who was showing signs of slipping even before the infamous Copacabana incident in May 1957, which exiled him to Kansas City. Richardson certainly was a marked contrast to the volatile Martin. The South Carolinian did not smoke, curse (his strongest language was "dad gum"), or prowl the streets after curfew. He did share one thing with Billy, though, a love for hunting. Earlier in the 1960 season, he took his roommate, the equally diminutive Bobby Shantz, to a gunsmith store in Kansas City to look at a 28-gauge shotgun.

During the baseball season Richardson, his wife Betsey, and two boys Bobby (3) and Ron (2) lived in a rented home in the Bergen County community of Ridgewood, New Jersey. Back at Sumter during the offseason, he hosted a local radio sports show and served as a general secretary for the YMCA. His ambition was to coach a YMCA or college team. But a keen eye might have discerned larger ambitions. Richardson took an active part in the 1960 presidential politics, campaigning for Richard Nixon alongside the Reverend Billy Graham. That Bobby was guided by the highest principles was not to be doubted. His motto since his American Legion days was to "keep a stout heart in defeat ... a sound soul, a clean mind, and a healthy body."[9] Richardson's resolve had certainly been tested so far in 1960. The previous year he had been one of the few highlights in an otherwise dismal season, leading the club in batting at .301. But prior to the Baltimore series, he was batting .250 and had not driven in a run in 38 games.

Richardson would continue to figure in the scoring as the Yankees had their final reckoning with Baltimore on September 18, a doubleheader before 53,876 raucous fans. The first game, played in a cold drizzle, was a 7–3 laugher. Art Ditmar won with help from Jim Coates. Ditmar, who was scheduled to pitch the second game, was not supposed to be at the ball park until later. But when Casey saw that the second game might be rained out, he had trainer Gene Mauch place a call to Ditmar at his River Edge, New Jersey, home. Art took off, crossing the George Washington Bridge, wending his way through traffic on the Cross Bronx Expressway, and made it to the Stadium in plenty of time. Despite a back injury to Bill Skowron, the Yanks came back to the locker room after the game brimming with confidence.

The second game, indeed, put the nail in the Orioles' coffin, New York shutting out Baltimore, 2–0. The Yankees' Ralph Terry, a rangy right-hander from Big Cabin, Oklahoma, had a perfect game until the eighth inning. He faced just twenty-nine batters in a game completed in 1:56. Milt Pappas hurled a fine game in defeat, giving up two runs on only five hits, but he was undone by mishaps in the field. The most damaging came in the third. Bobby Richardson was again the agent of the Orioles' demise. The Yankee second baseman led off with a low fly ball to short center. Three Birds — Ron Hansen, Marv Breeding, and Jackie Brandt — converged, collided, and went sprawling, with the ball dropping for a double beyond Hansen's desperate reach. After Terry sacrificed Richardson to third, Bobby came home on Tony Kubek's sacrifice fly.

The AL pennant race was effectively over. The Baltimore Orioles had arrived at 161st Street and River Avenue one percentage point behind the Yankees, and one game ahead of them in the win column. The Flock left four days later four games behind the Bombers, with "the gateway to the rainbow" effectively closed. Paul Richards later insisted that the Orioles would have won the pennant in 1960 if they had been able to acquire a young outfielder from the Dodgers' farm chain in 1955. But the Pirates beat them to him. The player? Roberto Clemente.[10]

On September 18, Clemente and his Pirate teammates began a six-game winning streak with a doubleheader victory at Cincinnati. They then dispatched the Phillies twice at Philadelphia, and returned home to Oakland to win two more from the Chicago Cubs. The Bucs, 7½ games in front of the St. Louis Cardinals with the magic number at two, packed their champagne and headed for Milwaukee for their final three games of the season with the Braves.

Hank Aaron, reminded by the Pittsburgh sportswriters of his boast that the Braves would pass the Pirates "like a jet," smiled graciously and said, "Well, we did pass you for a few hours on July 23rd." Now, two months later, it was too little, too late. On September 23, Milwaukee defeated the Bucs, 2–1. The next day, they beat Pittsburgh again, 4–2, on an 11-hit complete game victory by Lew Burdette. After this second straight loss at County Stadium, the Bucs came back to the locker room anxious to know how second-place St. Louis had done that afternoon against Chicago. Someone yelled, "Turn on the radio." Roberto Clemente, his face full of shaving cream, twirled the dial.[11] Suddenly, the air was filled with a whoop and a holler as news of the Cubs' victory over the Cardinals came over the air waves. The magic number was one.

The Bucs, who had backed into a tie for first, next backed into the National League pennant on September 25. This last game of the series at Milwaukee was a pitchers' battle between lefties Warren Spahn and Harvey Haddix. Always tough against the Braves, Haddix had allowed just four hits until the bottom of the eighth. With the score tied, 2–2, Milwaukee manager Charlie Dressen sent rookie catcher Joe Torre up to the plate to bat for Spahn.

A Brooklyn native, Joseph Paul Torre was barely two months past his twentieth birthday when he went up to swing for Spahn on September 25. A few years earlier he had been a tubby, 240-pound first baseman, third baseman, and pitcher for the Brooklyn Cadets of the New York Federation. As Torre recalled, his older brother Frank, a first baseman with the Milwaukee Braves, "was always after me to become a catcher."[12] Upon graduating from St. Francis Prep in Queens (Vince Lombardi and Frank Serpico were also alumni) he signed for $15,000 with the Braves. Two years in the Florida Instructional League helped him hone his skills as a catcher. Assigned to Class C Eau Claire, Wisconsin, in 1960, now a relatively slim 215 pounds, he led the Northern League in hitting with .344. Facing the Kitten on this Sunday afternoon, Torre singled to center in his Major League debut. Lee Maye was sent in to run for him. Two more hits and a throwing error by catcher Hal Smith knotted the score at 2–2. In the tenth inning, a two-run shot by Eddie Mathews off Elroy Face won it for the Braves. But again, it didn't much matter. An hour earlier, the Cardinals had been eliminated by the Cubs. At 4:43 P.M. Central Time, the Pittsburgh Pirates were officially the National League champion for 1960.

The visitors' locker room at County Stadium was a soggy mess as the Bucs celebrated their first pennant in thirty-three years, with the players dousing each other with champagne, beer, water, and other assorted spirits. Vern Law slipped on the wet locker room floor and sprained an ankle, but no one paid much attention at the time. While the Bucs were celebrating, a more poignant scene was taking place in the Braves' clubhouse. Red Schoendienst, a nice guy to the last, shook hands with the Pittsburgh sportswriters and thanked them for all the nice things they said about him in the press. The Redhead, who had overcome tuberculosis to return to baseball, and on whom Chuck Dressen had placed much of his World Series hopes, would not be returning to Milwaukee in 1961.

As the Pirates were celebrating, the National Football League was kicking off its 1960 season. Buddy Parker's Pittsburgh Steelers spoiled the debut of Tom Landry's Dallas Cowboys with a 35–28 victory at the Cotton Bowl. But it was the Pirates and Yankees, not the future "America's Team," who grabbed the headlines this Sunday. When the Bucs' chartered plane landed at Greater Pittsburgh Airport at 10:25 P.M. the Pirates were greeted by a crowd of between 70,000 and 100,000 well wishers. Crowds of this size had not been seen in the Golden Triangle since the V-E Day and V-J Day celebrations at the end of World War II. A thousand lights were aglow in the Golden Triangle as the team bus cut a swath through the downtown crowds. Large signs hanging from buildings exhorted "Bring on the Yanks." The U.S. Steel-Mellon Building had its top row of lights spelling BUCS in huge letters. A beatnik (or, at least, what passed for one) rode alongside the bus and yelled to Dick Stuart, "Man, you is the greatest. Like, man, you'll hit 61 in '61."[13]

After taking three straight from the Baltimore Orioles at Yankee Stadium on September 16–18, the Bombers went undefeated for the rest of the season. With fifteen victories in a row, they made a shambles of the AL race, finishing eight games ahead of Baltimore, 10 games ahead of Chicago, and a whopping 21 games ahead of the Cleveland Indians. During the second half of September, the only real question remaining regarding the New York Yankees was which one of its sluggers, Roger Maris or Mickey Mantle, was going to win the league home run crown.

Maris had stalled at 39 homers after connecting off lefty Steve Barber in the first game of the Baltimore series on September 16. From here on, it was all Mantle. The Switcher hit his 36th round-tripper off lefty Jack Kralick in the Bombers' victory over the Washington Senators at Griffith Stadium on September 20. The next day, Mantle switched to the right side and put number 37 in the seats off Pedro Ramos. The Nevada legal bookmakers made the Yankees a 5-to-7 favorite to win the World Series. The Pirates were listed as 6-to-5 underdogs.

The Yankees flew from Washington to Boston and their last visit of the season to Fenway Park. In the second game of the series on September 24, Mickey Mantle hit home run number 38, a tenth-inning shot on a cold New England afternoon. On the September 25 New York prevailed for a third straight time over Boston, a 4–3 squeaker. Luis Arroyo saved the game for Ralph Terry with just one pitch in the ninth. He induced Pete Runnels to fly out to third base where Bobby Richardson was playing that afternoon. The Cuban right-hander Mike Fornieles set a new American League record by appearing in his sixty-ninth game in relief.

It was over. The Yankees had clinched their twenty-fifth pennant since 1921. It was the tenth flag for the Old Perfessor, breaking a tie with Connie Mack of the old Philadelphia Athletics. The team popped champagne in the visitors' clubhouse and continued to party at the Statler-Hilton Hotel, before taking the 10:20 P.M. train out of Boston (the Yankees under George Weiss did less flying than any other major league team). Calling the win "something special," Casey Stengel pointed to the acquisition of Luis Arroyo in mid–July and the improved play at shortstop by Tony Kubek as reasons for the Yankees' success.

The Yankees' last three road games were played against the Washington Senators at Griffith Stadium. Ryne Duren, given a rare start by Casey on September 27, struck out five men in a row to start the game, tying a record held jointly by Walter Johnson, Dazzy Vance, and Lefty Gomez. The victory, however, went to rookie Bill Stafford, who won his third game since being recalled from Richmond. "He don't even look like a rookie," exclaimed an admiring Yogi Berra. The next day, Mickey Mantle overtook Roger Maris in the AL home run derby, hitting two home runs, numbers 39 and 40. Both shots were off Chuck Stobbs, the lefty who had yielded the mammoth 565-foot homer to Mantle in this same park in 1953. With this victory, the Yankees took the season series from the pesky Nats, 12 games to 10.

The Yankees now entrained for New York and the final three games of the 1960 baseball season against the visiting Boston Red Sox. Tony Kubek's fourteenth round-tripper on September 30 allowed the Yankees to set a new team record in home runs, 191, breaking the old record set in 1956. Dale Long's home run on October 1 made it 193. With this final win against Boston, the Yankees finished the 1960 season with a 97–57 record.

On September 25, the same day that the Yankees and Pirates clinched their respective pennants, Ted Williams made his last appearance in a Major League game. Playing at Fenway Park against the Baltimore Orioles, he finished the season as he began it — with a home run. The victim was O's right-hander Jack Fisher. September had been a month of retirements in the world of sports. The hockey great Maurice (the Rocket) Richard had hung up his skates two weeks earlier. Lou (the Toe) Groza, the greatest placekicker in NFL history, also called it quits. One player, however, was about to return. Minutes after Williams' announcement, Red Sox owner Tom Yawkey revealed that Jackie Jensen had ended his one-year retirement and was coming back to Boston in 1961. Jensen claimed he had been "immature" in making his decision to quit the previous January.

The greatest speculation, however, swirled around the New York Yankees and the uncertain future of both Manager Casey Stengel and GM George Weiss. The seventy-year-old Casey was rumored to be going to Kansas City as general manager, while the 66-year-old Weiss was supposedly being replaced by Assistant GM Roy Hamey. Dan Topping interrupted a vacation in Southhampton, Long Island, to return to the Yankee offices to scotch the rumors. Asked if he would return to the Yankees in 1961, Casey Stengel merely said that he would decide "when the World Series is over."[14]

Chapter Eleven

"The Baseball fates decreed it that way"

When he took over the Pittsburgh Pirates in 1950, Branch Rickey announced the launching of a five-year plan, which he predicted would put the Corsairs in the World Series within five years. The Mahatma miscalculated by another five years — it took a decade. The ascendancy of the Bucs from perennial National League doormats to pennant winners proved to be "inevitable"—but not "imminent." Still, as a result of his labors, along with those of his predecessor Roy Hamey and the current Bucs GM Joe L. Brown, in 1960 the World Series returned to Pittsburgh for the first time since the presidential administration of Calvin Coolidge.

And what a return it was! The city's convention bureau predicted that visitors would spend in excess of $3 million during the four scheduled home games. In fact, the downtown hotels had already sold out. The Pittsburgh Hotel Association sponsored a housing bureau at 2103 Farmers' Bank Building to accommodate those not lucky enough to find rooms. Among the visitors was a Clearfield County man named Jack LeCerf, who had bet his friend Henry McGarry that the Pirates would not win the pennant. LeCerf had to haul McGarry all the way to Pittsburgh in a wheelbarrow to pay off the wager.

Baseball's VIPs began to arrive on Monday, October 3, in more elegant style. Casey Stengel arrived in the back of a limousine, and then held an impromptu press conference at the Hilton Hotel reception desk with his wife Edna's mink coat wrapped under one arm. The Hilton was the headquarters of Commissioner Ford Frick and league presidents Warren Giles and Joe Cronin. Among the many other visitors scattered in various locales in the Golden Triangle were the baseball pitcher-turned author Jim Brosnan and Milwaukee Braves manager Chuck Dressen. Bing Crosby's brother Larry had flown into town with Vern Law's parents in tow. Roberto Clemente's mother and brother came up from Puerto Rico. Dick Groat's brother, an Argentina-based businessman, was also in attendance.

Baseball fever was not confined to the Golden Triangle. Continuing its long tradition, the New York Telephone Company would provide up to the minute scores at ME7-1212. From Western Europe to South Korea, American military personnel were tuning in on Armed Forces Radio. Buck Canel, the popular Spanish language broadcaster, would transmit the play-by-play to fanáticos throughout Latin America. No telecasts of the Fall Classic, however, would be allowed in Cuba. According to the Cuban newspaper *El Mundo*, the Castro regime was angered by Frick's policy prohibiting Major Leaguer players from participating in the Cuban Winter League. Despite their government's stand on "baseball imperialism," Cubans would still be listening on the radio. With no native-born players in the Series, most would root for Puerto Rican Luis Arroyo, a former star of the Havana Sugar Kings.[1]

While Castro railed against Yanqui imperialism, the handicappers picked the baseball Yankees to win the series. Although the Pirates had not played in the post-season since 1927, during that same span New York coach Frank Crosetti had seen service in nineteen classics as player and coach. Yogi Berra was getting set to play in his record-breaking eleventh World Series. By contrast only four Pirates — Gino Cimoli, Don Hoak, Rocky Nelson, and Clem Labine — had post-season experience, all with the Dodgers, and, with the exception of Labine, all negligible time. As much as anything, however, it was New York's World Series record under Casey Stengel — seven pennants in nine years — that had installed the Yankees as 13-to-10 favorites.

Before the creation of the interleague trading period in 1959, relatively few players shifted from league to league. Only three Yankees — pitcher Luis Arroyo, first baseman Dale Long, and skipper Casey Stengel — had formerly donned a Pirate uniform. The Old Perfessor, in fact, was busy regaling the press with stories of his adventures at Forbes Field. Forty-nine years earlier, during Major League Baseball's First Golden Era, he had tied for the club lead in home runs — with four. Although no current Pirate had ever played for New York, catchers Hal Smith and Bob Oldis, and center fielder Bill Virdon, were all former Yankee farmhands.

On Tuesday, October 4, the Pirates and Yankees took turns holding practice sessions at Forbes Field. The visitors familiarized themselves with the field dimensions and playing conditions. It was a venue that favored line-drive hitters, which the Bucs had in abundance. The right field line was 300 feet from the grandstand (compared to 296 feet at the Stadium) but then fell off sharply. A high screen in front of lowest deck of the stands in right field would not make it easier for Mantle, Maris, Skowron, and company to belt one out. The left field line at Forbes Field was 365 feet from the grandstand, running into a twelve-foot brick wall. Dead center field was a whopping 457 feet from home plate. The visitors discovered something else problematic that afternoon: the Forbes Field infield. Bobby Richardson took several ground balls and blinked in amazement at the high hops generated by the rock-hard surface. Tony Kubek, asked about the infield conditions, managed to say that it was "fast, mighty fast."[2]

To knowledgeable observers, the Pirates looked like a "loose" club. Besides having the home-field advantage in four of the seven games, they had other reasons to be confident. Although the experts gave the Yankees an overwhelming edge in power, the Bucs' pitching was judged to be superior. Danny Murtaugh could count on two formidable starters, Vern Law (20–9) and Bob Friend (18–12), as well as one of the best firemen in the game in Elroy Face (10–8, 24 saves). Harvey Haddix (11–10) and Vinegar Bend Mizell (13–5) were judged to be superior to the secondary starters on the Yankee staff. A couple of other factors stood out in the Bucs' favor. The open dates after the second and fifth games would allow Murtaugh the luxury of starting either Law or Friend three times in the Series. Meanwhile, on the Yankees, Whitey Ford (12–9), Bob Turley (10–4), and Jim Coates (13–3) had all been inconsistent. Ford, Stengel's money pitcher, had never won a World Series game on the road. With the Series commencing at Forbes Field, and the Pirates having a primarily right-handed lineup, the Old Perfessor decided to hold back Whitey for Game Three at Yankee Stadium on October 8. Instead, he picked Art Ditmar (15–9), the club leader in victories, to pitch Game One against Law.

To be sure, Murtaugh was not without his worries. The Corsairs had returned from Milwaukee in less than ideal health. Dick Groat was still getting over the effects of the broken wrist suffered at County Stadium on September 6. Vern Law's ankle injury, incurred during the pennant-clinching celebration at Milwaukee, was still bothering him when he warmed up in the bullpen on Tuesday at Forbes Field. In his last start of the season on September 30, he had yielded eight runs and ten hits in losing to the Braves. Meanwhile Don Hoak had suffered a groin injury rounding second base against the Braves the previous week, and was in excruciating pain. Bill Virdon and Rocky Nelson were also nursing leg injuries. Bucs trainer Danny Whalen (the little man who sat next to Red Holtzman during the New York Knicks championship runs in the early 1970s) had his hands full on the eve of the Series.

But this was a team that had defied the experts all year long. The Pirates had overwhelmed Willie Mays' San Francisco Giants and Hank Aaron's Milwaukee Braves, two teams with a preponderance of power. Could they do it once more against a New York club that had finished the season with fifteen victories in a row, and set an AL record for home runs? Dick Groat perhaps put it best: the Pirates-Yankees World Series was a contest between a "boxer and a knock-out puncher."[3]

On the opening game of the Series on Wednesday, October 5, all activity in the Golden Triangle came to a dead halt. Stores shut their doors for the day. The municipal courts closed early. Prosecutor Samuel Strauss petitioned Judge Loran L. Lewis to postpone the trial of Paul Hamilton, a Monroe County man accused of murdering his wife. The schools remained open, but absenteeism, real or in spirit, would naturally be high. Those without tickets could catch the play-by-play on television, courtesy of Bob Prince and Mel Allen. Would-be handymen everywhere had been busy replacing burned out tubes and adjusting rabbit ears on their customers' television sets.

Meanwhile, Pittsburgh Railways made special preparations for those lucky enough to attend the game in person. One hundred and fifty buses and trolley cars rolled from downtown, beginning ninety minutes prior to the game. Driving to Oakland was expressively discouraged. Parking was prohibited on either side of Bouquet St. from Sennet St. to 5th Avenue, and on the east side on O'Hara Street from Sennet to Bates Streets. Outside Forbes Field, ticket scalpers were busy plying their trade. A box seat ticket, which regularly sold for $11, was fetching $50. Over 400 plainclothes police officers, male and female, mingled with the crowds watching for pickpockets. As the old Jewish grocer in Pittsburgh's Hill District used to say, it was "such an excitement."[4]

The 36,676 spectators began twisting through the turnstiles beginning at 10:30 A.M. The Forbes Field ushers, who earned $8.75 a day with $3 for meals, went briskly about their business. Below them on the field, Pirate captain Dick Groat and Yankee coach Ralph Houk covered the ground rules with the umpire crew. Around noon, the University of Pittsburgh and Carnegie Tech bands began to entertain the crowd. Various "nationality groups," a reminder of Pittsburgh's southern and eastern European ethnic mix, performed as well. By the one o'clock starting time, temperatures were comfortably in the 60s. Governor David Lawrence floated the ceremonial first pitch to Smoky Burgess. Jazz stylist Billy Eckstine sang the National Anthem. The last strains of Eckstine's smooth baritone and plate umpire Dusty Boggess' harsh bark of "play ball" were drowned out by the roar of the home crowd. Vern Law then looked in for the sign from Burgess for the first pitch to leadoff hitter Tony Kubek.

It did not take long for Dick Groat's metaphor — the boxer vs. the slugger — to evolve on the playing field. After Vern Law had retired Kubek and Héctor López, Roger Maris homered off the Deacon for a 1–0 New York lead. But the Bucs struck back immediately in the bottom of the first, surprising the Yankees with their speed and cunning. Bill Virdon led off with a walk against Art Ditmar. As soon as the first pitch to Groat landed in Yogi Berra's glove, Virdon broke for second on a delayed steal. Kubek and Bobby Richardson, warned by scouting reports about Groat's hit-and-run prowess, held to their positions. They were slow covering the bag, and watched helplessly as Berra's throw sailed into center field. A double by Groat put Virdon across the plate, tying the score at 1–1. Bob Skinner then followed with another double scoring Groat, breaking the tie. Ditmar induced Dick Stuart to fly out. Roberto Clemente then rapped a single to score Groat for a 3–1 Corsair lead. At this point, Casey Stengel, head hunched between his shoulders, headed to the mound with his customary dog-trot gait. He signaled to the bullpen for Jim Coates. The slim right-hander got the last two outs to end the inning. Afterwards, Virdon explained that the double steal had been his idea, not Murtaugh's: "I figured if I got away with it, it might shake them up a little bit."[5] Indeed, he had.

Many boys dream of patrolling center field for the New York Yankees. Bill Virdon came closer than most. Born June 9, 1931, at Hazel Park, Michigan, a suburb north of Detroit, Virdon grew up in West Plains, Missouri, at the foot of the Ozark Mountains. The Yankees signed the bespectacled youngster out of Drury College in 1950 and assigned him to Independence, Missouri, in the Kansas-Oklahoma-Missouri League —

While Bobby Richardson and Bill Mazeroski are the players most remembered from the 1960 World Series, Pirate center fielder Bill Virdon was the unsung hero.

where Mickey Mantle had also made his professional debut. Like Jackie Jensen, Bob Cerv, Whitey Herzog, and other young Yankee outfield hopefuls, Virdon was unable to crack the big club's lineup. The next year George Weiss dealt him to the St. Louis Cardinals for veteran outfielder Enos Slaughter. He excelled in the Cardinals farm chain, leading the International League in hitting with Rochester in 1954. Up with the big club in 1955, Virdon won the National League Rookie of the Year Award, hitting .281 and swatting a career-high 17 home runs.[6]

In May of the following year Trader Frank Lane, at the time the Cardinal GM, shipped him to the Pittsburgh Pirates. Virdon proceeded to have his best year at the plate, defying the sophomore jinx with a .319 mark. He married the former Shirley Shemwell and started a family. Golfing became his offseason passion. Although his fielding remained exemplary, Virdon's batting average steadily declined, causing Danny Murtaugh to start the 1960 season with Gino Cimoli in center field. In a league with Willie Mays and Cincinnati's Vada Pinson shining in center field, Virdon garnered little attention for his play. The Yankees would soon discover just how good he really was.

In the top of the fourth inning of Game One, with Maris on second and Mickey Mantle on first, and none out, Berra launched a 400-foot rocket toward right-center field. Virdon, running full tilt, flagged down the ball, holding on as he crashed into Roberto Clemente who had dashed over from right. "I thought it was gone," Yogi later said.[7] Virdon claimed to have made better catches in his career, but he had not enjoyed any as much as this one. Rightly so, if Yogi's drive had landed safely, the Yankees would have tied the game with still no one out. Instead, after giving up a single to Bill Skowron to drive in Maris, Law closed the doors on the Yankees. The score: Pirates, 3, Yankees, 2.

In the bottom of the fourth, Bill Mazeroski took the measure of Coates for a two-run homer, and a 5–2 Bucs lead. The Pirates stretched it to 6–2 in the sixth inning, with Maz scoring on a double by Virdon. New York tried to come back in the top of the eighth. López opened with a single against Law. When Maris also singled, Elroy Face came in to get Mantle, Berra, and Skowron in succession. The little forkballer faltered a bit in the ninth, giving up a two-run shot to Elston Howard. But he bore down and got López to hit into a game-ending double play. The Pirates had won their first World Series game since 1925, beating the Yankees, 6–4.

It rained overnight in Pittsburgh, and was still drizzling on Thursday morning, October 6. Although the weather had cleared by game time, the real deluge was about to begin. New York came back in Game Two to pummel the Pirates, 16–3. After being held scoreless by Bob Friend in the first two innings, the Bombers broke through in the top of the third. Bobby Richardson drew a walk. Yankee starter Bob Turley laid down a bunt. In a move he would later regret, Friend passed up a chance to nab Richardson at second and threw to first instead. Richardson came home on a single by Tony Kubek. Gil McDougald then hit a double over third base, scoring Kubek for a 2–0 Yankee lead.

New York got another run in the fourth. Turley (a .073 hitter on the year) helped his own cause by singling in Richardson. The Pirates came back in the bottom half of the inning on singles by Gino Cimoli and Smoky Burgess, and a double by Don Hoak. With the lead cut to 3–1, and two Corsairs on base, Mazeroski hit a hot smash — what Bob Prince liked to call a "blue streaker" — which was caught by McDougald with one knee on the ground. Gene Baker, pinch-hitting for Friend, then popped out to end the inning.

As the Bucs saw it, McDougald's play on Mazeroski was the turning point in the game. If the ball had not been caught, the Irishman would not have pinch-hit for Friend. The righty had good stuff that afternoon (he struck out six Yankees in four innings), and most of the hits tallied against him were seeing-eye jobs. He was "more sinless than sinned against," as Red Smith elegantly put it in the *New York Herald-Tribune*.[8] With Friend gone, the Yankees feasted on the Bucs' middle relief corps. Fred Green came on in the top of the fifth and gave up a two-run homer to Mickey Mantle, a 400-foot rocket into the right center field stands, and a 5–1 Bomber lead.

The cover of the Yankee 1960 World Series program pictured the entire New York squad except for one player. Bobby Richardson, the Yankees' team representative, after exhorting his teammates to be on time, missed the photo shoot. The second sacker, however, was about to make his presence known. After Elston Howard led off the sixth inning with a booming 436-foot triple, Richardson mustered all the strength in his compact 5' 8", 160-pound frame, and doubled him home. Clem Labine relieved Green and gave up singles to McDougald, Yogi Berra, and Bill Skowron for four more Yankee runs. At this point Murtaugh made his third pitching change of the afternoon, sending a hapless Red Witt to the mound.

Howard, up for the second time in the inning, singled to score Berra. Richardson concluded the carnage by singling in Skowron, for his second RBI. The game was now totally out of hand, 12–1 in favor of New York.

There was no let-up of Yankee power, however. In the seventh, Mantle came up against lefty Joe Gibbon and put a ball into the trees past center field, 450 feet away. Murtaugh said after the game that it was the most "impressive" home run he had ever seen.[9] The final Yankee run came in the ninth, Mantle scoring on a wild pitch by the fifth Bucs pitcher, Tom Cheney. All season long the Pirates had been known for their last-inning rallies. But the two runs off Turley in the ninth were far too little to overcome the New York lead. Bobby Shantz came on with one out after Turley had thrown his 141st pitch, and got a game-ending double play. The final score: Yankees 16, Pirates 3. Now it was on to New York, the Series tied at one game apiece.

Friday, October 7, was a travel day. Back in the Pittsburgh area, a Beaver Falls High School quarterback named "Joe Nameth" threw for two touchdowns in leading his team to victory over rival Butler, 26–6. As the future Broadway Joe and teammates were celebrating their win, Murtaugh and company were heading east in their chartered jet to New York. The Irishman took the loss in stride. If you had to get beat, it might as well be a laugher; it was the close ones that hurt. Besides, there was other immediate business to focus on. Bob Skinner had jammed his left hand sliding into third base and would be unavailable for Game Three. It would be up to Gino Cimoli to battle the late afternoon shadows in left field at Yankee Stadium. Meanwhile, the Yankees took a Friday morning train back to New York, arriving at Penn Station in Midtown Manhattan at 11:00 A.M. They soon melted into the crowd of commuters. With the Series tied one game apiece, and the next three games at home, the players were in good spirits as they headed for their suburban New Jersey and Long Island homes.

On Saturday, October 8, the gates opened at 7:30 A.M. at Yankee Stadium to admit the bleacher fans who paid $2.10 a seat. Seating for the more luxurious sections of the "House That Ruth Built" began two hours later. By the 1:30 P.M. game time the crowd had ballooned to 70,001. Red, white, and blue bunting adorned the upper deck of the stadium. Unseen, but nevertheless felt, were the pennants commemorating world championships dating back to 1923. Representatives of two of the Bombers' fiercest rivals were in attendance. In his wheelchair behind the home plate screen was Brooklyn Dodger great Roy Campanella. Sitting next to Ford Frick near the Yankee dugout was Ted Williams. Today, it would be unimaginable to give such a prominent place to a Red Sox. But it was the recently retired Thumper, not Joe DiMaggio or another prominent Yankee, who threw out the ceremonial first pitch.

Casey Stengel was renowned for his unorthodox moves. With southpaw Vinegar Bend Mizell expected to start for the Bucs, the Old Perfessor sent portside-swinging Berra to the bench. Playing left field in his place, and leading off, would be the right-handed-hitting Bob Cerv. Robert Henry Cerv was born at Lincoln, Nebraska, on May 5, 1926, and grew up in Weston, a tiny farming community (population 350) about 30 miles north of Lincoln. Upon graduation in 1943 Cerv enlisted in the U.S. Navy, serving as a radioman on a destroyer in the Pacific Theater during World War II. The war over, he enrolled in the University of Nebraska on the G.I. Bill. Originally a basketball player, he tried his hand at baseball and soon showed he was worth his salt. Signed by the Yankees in 1950, Cerv was one of a cast of youngsters brought up in the wake of Joe DiMaggio's retirement. Casey Stengel looked over the husky outfielder (6'0", 225 pounds) and labeled him a "Lou Gehrig in the making." Unfortunately, unlike the Iron Man, Cerv spent most of his time on the bench, before being traded to the Kansas City A's in 1957.

The Kansas City trade was the "big break" for Cerv. He hit 38 home runs for the Athletics in 1958, still the club record in 1960. Many of those home runs were hit with his jaw wired shut. In May of that year, Cerv was injured in a home plate collision with catcher Red Wilson of the Detroit Tigers. For five weeks he remained in the lineup while taking in processed food through a straw. Despite this handicap, he made the AL All-Star team for the first and only time. By 1960 new A's manager Bob Elliot was on a youth movement, and on May 19 George Weiss pried Cerv loose from Kansas City for little-used infielder Andy Carey. Cerv, the father of eight children, fit in well with the Yankee family, providing additional punch from the bench and giving Stengel more flexibility with his lineup.[10]

On this October afternoon, Bob Cerv made Casey look like genius. He led off the bottom of the first with a single against Mizell. With one out, Mickey Mantle singled Cerv to third. The Nebraskan then scored on a single by Bill Skowron. Gil McDougald drew a walk, filling the bases.

Clem Labine replaced Vinegar Bend and was promptly greeted by an Elston Howard single, scoring Mantle. The usual eruption of Yankee power now emerged from the unlikeliest of sources. Bobby Richardson, after failing to sacrifice, deposited a full-count pitch into the lower left field stands for a grand-slam home run. That gave him six RBIs for the series. After a thirty-six-minute first inning, the Yankees held a formidable 6–0 lead.

The Yankees landed another big punch in the fourth. Yankee starter Whitey Ford singled off the usually dependable reliever Fred Green. Mantle then hit an upper deck job to left-center, making the score 8–0. After the Bombers loaded the bases again, Richardson, batting against Red Witt, singled in the last two runs of the afternoon. For the Sumter, South Carolina, native it was six RBIs in one day — a new World Series record — and eight overall. Meanwhile, Ford faced just 31 batters in spinning a four-hit shutout for a 10–0 Yankee victory. Don Hoak remained unimpressed. His blunt post-mortem assessment: "We made Ford look good."[11] Nevertheless, the Yankees had the Pirates pinned on the ropes, having won two consecutive blowouts for a combined score of 26–3. They led the Series two games to one, with two games left to play on their home territory in the Bronx. Who could have asked for anything better?

Danny Murtaugh decided to start Vern Law in Game Four at Yankee Stadium on Sunday, October 9, so that the Deacon would be available for a possible return in Game Seven on October 13. However, for a while, it didn't look as if the World Series would go that long. Bob Cerv, once again leading off and playing left field, hit Law's first offering to center for a single. Tony Kubek, batting second, fouled off a pitch and then sent a liner to left field, placing runners on second and third with none out. After Roger Maris flied out to Roberto Clemente, Murtaugh called for an intentional pass to Mickey Mantle. With the bases loaded and one out, Yogi Berra came to the plate. Yogi, fooled on a pitch, sent a dribbler toward third base. Don Hoak, still feeling the ill effects of his groin pull, managed to step on the bag and fire across the diamond to Dick Stuart at first. Umpire Dusty Boggess raised his right thumb. Berra was out, completing a rally-ending double play. Yogi and first base coach Ralph Houk hopped up and down, screaming in protest, as did most of the 67,812 fans. But Boggess' decision stood.

Among the spectators for Game Four at the Stadium was the prime minister of India, Jawaharlal Nehru. NBC-TV announcer Joe Garagiola could not help kidding his old friend from the Hill section of St. Louis.

He told Berra that the Indian statesman had asked: "Where is the Yogi?" Incredulous, the Yankee catcher responded: "He's heard of me all the way from India?"[12] Actually, Nehru arrived in the sixth inning, too late to witness what Yogi and the other members of the Yankee squad would later insist was the turning point of the Series. The Yankees had Pittsburgh rubber-legged. A big opening inning could have dealt the visitors the knockout punch. Instead, Murtaugh's men had escaped to last the round.

Moose Skowron homered off Law in the fourth to give the Yankees a 1–0 lead, but that would not be enough to hold off the resurgent Bucs. Once again, the Corsairs capitalized on a Yankee blunder. Gino Cimoli, playing left field in place of the injured Bob Skinner, led off the fifth inning with a single. Skowron fielded Smoky Burgess' slow roller and elected to throw to second in an effort to nab Cimoli. But the throw arrived too late. Instead of a man on second with one out, there were Bucs camped on both first and second with nobody out. Don Hoak and Bill Mazeroski popped out. Again there was a questionable play on the part of the Yankees: had Bobby Richardson trapped Hoak's popup instead of catching it, he would have had an excellent chance for a double play to end the inning. Instead, Law came up and helped his own cause by singling to center, scoring Cimoli. Bill Virdon continued to torment his former organization by singling to center for two more runs. The score was now 3–1 in favor of Pittsburgh.

In the bottom of the seventh, Skowron doubled and went to third on a single by Gil McDougald. Richardson's grounder forced McDougald at second, but Mazeroski's relay throw was late to first. The failed double play allowed Skowron to score. That cut the Pittsburgh lead to 3–2. Johnny Blanchard pinch-hit a single to right, Richardson stopping at second. Elroy Face replaced Law. At this point, Bob Cerv just missed being a World Series hero. He greeted Face by sending a tremendous drive to right-center field. But Bill Virdon broke the hearts of Yankee fans yet again. He went back and leaped high at the 407-foot mark in front of the bleachers to snare the ball. Face then induced Tony Kubek to hit a tapper back to the mound, snuffing out the rally. From here on in, it was the Elroy Face show at Yankee Stadium. He retired the last eight Yankees in a row, helped by a dazzling play at third on the part of Don Hoak in the bottom of the ninth.

The fourth game of the 1960 World Series went into the record books, Pittsburgh 3, New York, 2. It was a bitter defeat for the Yankees. Instead of taking a three games to one lead in the Series, some questionable fielding choices, spectacular plays by Hoak and Virdon, and Face's stellar relief pitching had allowed Pittsburgh to knot things up at two games apiece. Stengel defended Skowron's decision to throw to second and get the lead runner Cimoli. But now, as the Yankees prepared for the fifth game of the Series on Monday, October 10, he had more important things to ponder. Should he start Art Ditmar, the loser of Game One, or should he take his chances with rookie Bill Stafford?

Stengel made the wrong choice. Pittsburgh struck for three runs in the third inning off Ditmar and never looked back. Once again, defensive lapses helped keep a Corsair rally going. Dick Stuart led off the second inning with a single. Gino Cimoli bounced to Bobby Richardson, who tagged Stuart but missed nipping Gino at first. Smoky Burgess smacked Ditmar's first offering for a double, sending Cimoli to third. Don Hoak hit a bouncer to Tony Kubek. With no chance to get Gino at the plate, Kubek threw to third to nab Burgess. But the sliding Burgess managed to jar the ball out of Gil McDougald's glove, with Hoak taking second. Bill Mazeroski then doubled into center field, to score both Hoak and Burgess, for a 3–1 lead. The Yankees would score only twice that afternoon, and land only one solid punch: Roger Maris' home run in the bottom half of the third. Pittsburgh's two "150 pounders," starter Harvey Haddix and fireman Elroy Face, held the Yankees in check for the last six innings. The unlikeliest of events had occurred. Pittsburgh left the Bronx with a three games to two Series lead, with the last two games to be played on their home turf.

A throng of 10,000 well-wishers was waiting at the Greater Pittsburgh Airport to greet the returning heroes. While the Pirates basked in the glow of their adoring fans, the Yankees landed without fanfare on the other side of airport. Meanwhile, other baseball news was making the headlines. The American League owners, it was reported, had met secretly to consider expansion bids by various cities for a 1961 start. A New York bid was expected shortly, along with those of Toronto and Buffalo (Houston had already formally applied for admission to the National League). Los Angeles was also eyeing an AL franchise, but Pirate owner John Galbreath declared that the former Continental League cities should receive priority. The August 2 pact with Branch Rickey and Bill Shea at Chicago's Hilton Hotel had to be honored.

In Pittsburgh that past Sunday, New York Giants quarterback Charley

Conerly connected with halfback Frank Gifford for a 42-yard pass with just one minute remaining to give the New Yorkers a come-from-behind victory over Bobby Layne and the Pittsburgh Steelers, 19–17. The baseball Yankees were now looking for a stunning comeback of their own in Oakland. With his team's back to the wall, Casey Stengel had another crucial decision to make. Who would start on the mound for the New Yorkers in Game Six? Should it be Bob Turley, pitching on five days' rest, or Whitey Ford on three days' rest? The Old Perfessor decided to go with Ford. The left-hander would be opposed by Bob Friend, who was hoping to avenge his defeat at Yankee Stadium and give the Bucs the championship that had eluded them for three decades.

But Wednesday, October 12, was New York's day to celebrate. The Bombers opened the scoring in the second inning on an RBI-single by Ford. The real barrage came in the third. Tony Kubek was hit by a pitch. Roger Maris doubled him to third. Both men scored on a single by Mickey Mantle. A single by Yogi Berra sent Mickey to third and Friend to the showers. Lefty Tom Cheney came on and allowed a sacrifice fly by Bill Skowron, scoring Mantle. This made the score 4–0. Elston Howard had left the game in the second inning, having broken the fifth metacarpal of his left hand after being plunked by Friend. His replacement, John Blanchard, continued the rally by singling against Cheney. The mighty mite Bobby Richardson tripled, bringing in Berra and Blanchard with the last two runs of the inning, and his 10th and 11th RBIs of the Series. When the dust cleared it was New York 6, Pirates 0.

The Stengel men scored two runs each in the seventh, eighth, and ninth frames to complete the 12–0 slaughter. Richardson picked up his 12th RBI in the seventh, to set a World Series record, tripling to drive in Blanchard who had doubled. No one was more disappointed in the results than Bob Friend. The New Yorkers had not hit him hard in Game Two, and he might have righted the ship if not for Murtaugh's decision to pinch-hit for him in the third. But there were no excuses this time; the Bombers had landed nothing but solid punches in Game Six. Ford, meanwhile, had made the best of the opportunity, pitching his first-ever away game victory in a World Series. Despite developing a blister after the fourth inning, Whitey managed to set a couple of World Series records, including most starts (14) and most strikeouts (63). The oddsmakers made New York a 13-to-10 favorite to take Game Seven and the Series.

But the oddsmakers didn't figure with the Pirates. For weeks, the

Pittsburgh faithful had been dreaming of avenging the humiliating sweep by Miller Huggins' New York Yankees in the 1927 World Series. Through the first five innings of the seventh game of the 1960 World Series it looked as if the Murtaugh men were on their way to doing exactly that against Yankees starter Bob Turley. The Corsairs scored four runs in the first two innings. In the bottom of the first, the boxer finally turned puncher. Rocky Nelson settled into his "John L. Sullivan stance," left foot forward, body in a sitting position. In came the pitch from Turley and away it went for a two-run homer. In the following frame, Bill Virdon, the quiet hero of the Series, singled in two more runs for a 4–0 Pirate lead.

But it was too early to count the Bombers out. In the top of the fifth, Moose Skowron measured Bucs starter Vern Law for a home run, cutting the margin to 4–1. The Bombers chased the Deacon off the mound with a four-run onslaught in the sixth. Bobby Richardson singled, and Tony Kubek followed with a walk. At this point Murtaugh summoned Elroy Face, who jumped over the low bullpen fence and headed slowly to the mound. The fork ball, however, did not have its magic on this clear October afternoon. Face got Roger Maris to foul out, but Mantle singled to send Richardson across the plate. Up next was Yogi Berra. Danny Murtaugh regarded Yogi as the most dangerous hitter on the New York squad in the last three innings of a game. The Yankee left fielder was as good as his reputation, launching a ball into the upper right field deck, scoring Kubek and Mantle ahead of him. It was now New York 5, Pirates 4.

Having knocked the Bucs' ace, Vern Law, out of the game, the Yankees proceeded to bloody the nose of the Bullpen Baron. With two outs in the eighth, Berra drew a base on balls from Face. Singles by Skowron and Johnny Blanchard scored Yogi. Clete Boyer, humiliated in Game One when Stengel pinch-hit for him before he even had a chance to bat, doubled to score the Moose. The Yanks were sitting pretty with a 7–4 lead. But the wheel of fortune was to turn yet again, in one of the most bizarre — and for Yankee fans, painful — happenings in World Series history.

Bobby Shantz had held the Pirates to one hit over five innings in relief of Bob Turley. Then, in the bottom of the eighth, Gino Cimoli batted for Face and drew a walk. Bill Virdon, who had stunned the Bombers with his running, fielding, and hitting display, was about to deal them yet one more cruel blow. The bespectacled center fielder took a strike on the inside corner. Shantz delivered once again, on the outside corner this time, and Virdon sent a routine double play grounder in the direction of shortstop

Tony Kubek. The home crowd let out a groan, then held its collective breath. The grounder bounced higher on the cement-like surface than anticipated by Kubek and hit him squarely in the Adam's apple. The Yankee shortstop collapsed backward, clutching his throat in a silent scream. Blood oozed from the corners of his mouth. Bobby Richardson signaled for help. Kubek was helped off the field and escorted to the hospital by the Pirate team physician, Dr. Joseph Feingold. On the field, play continued with Corsairs stationed on first and second with no outs.

The New Yorkers, stunned, began to fall apart. Dick Groat, failing for once to hit to right field, pulled a Shantz pitch to left, scoring Cimoli to make the score 7–5. Casey Stengel dog-trotted his way to the mound and replaced the southpaw Shantz with right-hander Jim Coates. With two outs and Virdon on third, there now came another costly New York blunder. Roberto Clemente fouled off three consecutive pitches, the last one breaking his bat. Armed with a new stick, the Puerto Rican stroked a high bouncer in the direction of Skowron. The Moose fielded the ball and looked to throw to Coates for what should have been an easy out at first. But Coates had turned spectator and failed to cover the bag, allowing the hustling Clemente to beat out a hit and Virdon to score, narrowing the Yankee lead to 7–6. Instead of the Yankees escaping with a 7–5 lead, Groat was now dancing off third, with Clemente ready to fly from second.

Up came Hal Smith, part-time catcher, and along with Face, part of a singing duo in the Pirate clubhouse. Smith was not known as a power hitter, but he could pull the high pitch, as he had done countless times that season against the Los Angeles Coliseum screen. Yankee catcher Johnny Blanchard laid down a sign for Coates. Smith took a called strike, then a pitch high. On Coates' third delivery he swung and missed. The tall right-hander came in high again, and this time Smith barely checked his swing. The scouting reports advised Yankee hurlers to mix up their pitches against the Bucs catcher. Coates did not mix them up enough against the former Yankee farmhand. "Open the window, Aunt Minnie!" as Bob Prince would say. Smith took a low pitch and planted the ball over the 406 sign in left field for a three-run homer and a 9–7 Pirate lead.

The Yankees were the big punchers in the bout, and came up looking for the knockout blow. The luckless Bob Friend, who had failed twice in a starting role, was Danny Murtaugh's choice to replace Elroy Face on the mound. Friend proved to be no more successful as a reliever than as a starter. Bobby Richardson greeted him with a single. The ex-Pirate Dale

Long, batting for Kubek's shortstop replacement Joe DeMaestri, singled to right, with Richardson stopping at second. The Irishman headed for the mound, yanking Friend in favor of another starting pitcher, Harvey Haddix. The Kitten got one out and then yielded a single to Mantle, sending Richardson across the plate. With the score now 9–8, Stengel sent McDougald in to run for Long at third with Mickey holding on first.

Now there came another bizarre play. Yogi Berra was up. Haddix delivered and Berra hit a searing grounder toward the first base line. Rocky Nelson speared the ball, and for what seemed like an eternity, engaged in an eyeball-to-eyeball stare-down with Mantle, who had drifted off first. Suddenly, Mickey darted back, beating Nelson to the bag. Instead of a double play, McDougald scored from third to tie the game, 9–9. Moments later, Skowron forced Mantle at second to send the game into the last of the ninth.

For the Pirates, the 1960 baseball season had been marked by a succession of dramatic last-inning comebacks. They were about to do it one last time. Bill Mazeroski led off in the bottom of the ninth against New York right-hander Ralph Terry. The second baseman had hit the first Pirate home run of the season. Now he would hit the last. The "book" on the Pirate second sacker was that he was a low-ball hitter with "occasional" power to left field. The scouting reports warned the Yankee pitchers to move the ball around on him. Mazersoski, a chaw of tobacco lodged firmly in his jaw, took a ball high from Terry. The rangy Oklahoman then came back with another pitch a tad lower. Mazeroski swung and lifted the ball toward left field. Berra, turned, retreated to the ivy-covered wall — and then stopped short.

"What happened?" Roger Maris asked Yogi as they headed for the clubhouse. The veteran of eleven World Series replied, "We just got beat by the craziest team that ever played baseball." Mickey Mantle, the third Yankee outfielder on this Thursday afternoon, was crying as he departed the dugout for the visitors' dressing room. Someone tried to console him by pointing out the bad break on the Virdon double play ball that hit Kubek in the throat. But the Mick was having none of it. "Yeah," he retorted, "from now on, all they'll know is that we lost."[14]

In the winners' clubhouse, an unsentimental Don Hoak summed up the Series in his typical brash style, observing, "The Yankees weren't able to win with their breaks but we could." The *New York Times* columnist Arthur Daley said the same thing, just more elegantly. The Bombers played "as carelessly as carousing sailors on shore leave, squandering everything." Dick Groat's original prognostication seems equally plausible in explaining the Bucs' surprising victory. The 1960 World Series had indeed been a contest between the slugger and the boxer. The Pirates had played "rope a dope" for the first six games, scoring just 17 runs. Then in the final seconds of the last round they struck the winning knockout blow. It was a bitter loss to swallow for the proud Yankees. They had hit a combined .338, out-hitting the Bucs, 91 to 60, and outscoring them, 55 to 27. It was no consolation to Mickey or his teammates, but there was yet another explanation, this one from the pen of Al Abrams of the *Pittsburgh Post-Gazette*: "The Baseball fates had decreed it that way."[15]

CHAPTER TWELVE

"Perhaps experience doesn't count"

The entire city of Pittsburgh seemed to have gone mad in the seconds it took for Bill Mazeroski to skip around the bases and collapse into the collective embrace of his joyous teammates at home plate. The Golden Triangle became the scene of a raucous celebration, punctuated by the incessant blaring of car horns that carried on all through the night. Nothing like this had been seen before. Not even the V-J Day celebration commemorating the end of World War II in August 1945 had produced such a spontaneous display of civic pride. Meanwhile, the Pirate clubhouse had been transformed into something resembling the famous stateroom scene in the Marx Brothers' 1934 film *A Night at the Opera*. Mayor Joseph Barr led the parade of dignitaries, reporters, and plain citizens straining to get in and congratulate the World Series champions. A path was cleared for fourteen-year-old Andy Jerpo who had been camped outside the left field wall all afternoon, and was rewarded for his vigil with Maz's home run ball.

Ford Frick was not as lucky. Finding the main entrance barred, he finally managed to squeeze in through a side door leading to Danny Murtaugh's office. Before the season began, the commissioner probably imagined himself congratulating the World Series winner in New York, Los Angeles, Chicago, or San Francisco — not in a tiny clubhouse in an antiquated ballpark in the Oakland section of Pittsburgh, Pennsylvania. But change was in the air. John F. Kennedy, the Democratic candidate for president, had been telling Americans for months that we had to get the country "moving again." More than anything else, it was change which would dominate news from the baseball world in the remaining months of 1960.

Four days after the World Series ended, representatives of the eight National League clubs met in executive session in the much more spacious surroundings of the Sheraton Blackstone Hotel in Chicago. After lunch, Warren Giles announced the first structural change in Major League Baseball in fifty-nine years. New York and Houston had been admitted as the ninth and tenth members of the senior circuit, and would begin play in 1962. The proposal for the admission of two new franchises was made by Los Angeles Dodgers owner Walter O'Malley. It was O'Malley who three years earlier had taken the NL out of New York City, saying good-bye to Brooklyn and inducing New York Giants owner Horace Stoneham to vacate the Polo Grounds for San Francisco.

The principal owner of the new Metropolitan Baseball Club was Joan Shipman Payson, sister of John Hay Whitney, former ambassador to Great Britain and publisher of the *New York Herald Tribune*. A familiar figure in New York society, Mrs. Payson attended one of the World Series games at Pittsburgh — and had rooted for Pirates. Holding the reins of the Houston club was Craig Cullinan, Jr., Texas oilman, investor, and charter member of the now defunct Continental Baseball League. Cullinan's group had been wooed by both loops, but had been won over by the NL's more aggressive salesmanship. The Texas metropolis was a real coup for the senior circuit. With a population of 932,680, Houston was the sixth largest city in the United States and one of the most lucrative markets, if not *the* most, available outside of Los Angeles.

The news from Chicago received the jubilant endorsement of New York mayor Robert F. Wagner. Bill Shea chimed in, calling it the city's "brightest day in three years." Wagner said he anticipated no problems regarding the Board of Estimate's approval of the $16,226,250 Flushing Meadows stadium (a total of $687,500 had already been sunk into the project). The Payson group was expected to agree to a rent of $900,000 a year, most of which would go toward defraying the cost of the stadium. Fourteen hundred miles away in Houston, optimism also abounded. Construction on the city's $14.5 million Harris County Stadium was scheduled to begin on February 1, 1961. Its major attraction would be a translucent dome, rising 230 feet above the field. The dome wasn't expected to affect the level of play — research had shown that no baseball had ever been hit that high. Located five miles from the downtown area, the new stadium would have a seating capacity of 43,197 for baseball (50,000 for the AFL's Houston Oilers), and room for 27,000 cars. Completion date was March 1962.

While Texans celebrated their entry into the ranks of the big leagues, New York fans remained somewhat less impressed with the Metropolitan Baseball Club. After all, it wasn't like the Dodgers were coming back to Brooklyn. Asked about the return of the NL to New York, a city cab driver replied: "You nuts pal? I couldn't care less." An attractive young brunette was also dismissive of the new club. She claimed she had given up baseball when Joe DiMaggio retired. Others were perplexed by the Queens location. Gerry Workman, a truck driver, asked, "Why the heck do they have to build a stadium out there? Nobody from New Jersey will attend." Actor William Bendix didn't think "Flushing" was a very good name for a baseball club. A flight attendant was a bit more generous. She hoped the new team wouldn't be as snobbish as the Yankees.[1]

The next day, Tuesday, October 18, at a press conference at the Savoy Hilton Hotel, it was announced that Casey Stengel had been removed as manager of the New York Yankees. Presiding at the public execution were owners Dan Topping and Del Webb. Stengel, looking grim and unsmiling, stood uncomfortably alongside them. In past years, the press would have been treated to a stream of doubletalk from the Old Perfessor. But on this occasion, the doubletalk came from the Yankee owners in the form of a prepared statement. Topping, puffing nervously on a cigar, muttered something about an "age limit program" that, regrettably, made Stengel's departure necessary. The manager would not go empty-handed, he hastened to add. Casey would receive $160,000 from a profit-sharing plan, equivalent to about two years of salary. Asked to respond, Casey did not hide his bitterness at his former employers. Setting aside the usual Stengelese, he told reporters: "I was told that my services were no longer desired ... because they want to put in a youth program as an advance way of keeping their club going."

Mandal Sant Rant, the Broadway astrologer, claimed he had had no advance word of Stengel's dismissal on his astrological chart. He mustn't have been very good at his job. Rumors of Casey's departure had been swirling for months. During the World Series, the Old Perfessor himself had hinted darkly that all was not well between himself and the Yankee management. Sensing a change in the air, at the conclusion of the World

Series the New York metropolitan area sportswriters had presented Casey with a signed petition imploring him not to leave. But the decision was not his to make. After twelve years, ten pennants, and seven World Series titles, and hundreds of gallons in press ink, the Casey Stengel era was over.

The New York fans surveyed by writer Gay Talese did not disguise their bitterness. It was "pretty stupid," declared sixteen-year-old Erasmus High School student Robert Turkel. "Good-by Yankees," said an East 61st St. barber, punctuating his words by snapping his scissors in the air. Meanwhile praise for Stengel poured in from the world of Major League Baseball. The Orioles' Paul Richards, recently voted AL Manager of the Year by the Associated Press, said, "We don't have institutions such as he is." Bill Veeck, himself no slouch at promotion, said Stengel "personifies everything that is colorful and exciting in baseball." The decision was not well received by the chief beneficiaries of Stengelese, the Fourth Estate. Casey, according to *New York Times* sportswriter Arthur Daley, "has imparted warmth to a cold organization, giving it a colorful appeal that it couldn't have bought for millions of dollars."[2]

On Wednesday, October 19, the New York Chapter of the Baseball Writers' Association of America honored Casey with a farewell dinner at the Waldorf-Astoria Hotel. By this time, the Yankee players had scattered to their homes around the United States, or were enjoying a long-deferred vacation (Yogi and his wife Carmen were in Bermuda); the Bombers were represented by just two players. Gil McDougald drove in from Tenafly, New Jersey, and Elston Howard, his arm still in a cast, came over from Teaneck. The chief executioner, Dan Topping, was an incongruous presence among the glitterati of the political, media, and baseball worlds. Ford Frick attended, as did Branch Rickey, who motored all the way from Pittsburgh. The owners of the new Metropolitan Baseball Club, Joan Payson and Donald Grant, were also among the guests. Stengel rose to accept a medallion with the official seal of the city from Mayor Robert Wagner. Eyes welling with tears, the Old Perfessor waxed philosophical. "I've always done all right," he said addressing the audience, "and I think I'll do all right now."[3]

The following night the sixteenth annual Alfred Smith Memorial Foundation Dinner was held at the same Waldorf-Astoria. In attendance were both the Democratic and Republican candidates for president in 1960, John F. Kennedy and Richard M. Nixon, respectively. Addressing the 2,500 guests in the grand ballroom, Kennedy took aim at his Republican opponent. For months now, he said, Nixon had been telling people that JFK was too young and inexperienced to be president of the United States. Kennedy wryly suggested that the worst news for the Republicans that week had been the firing of Casey Stengel. "It goes to show," he quipped, "that perhaps experience doesn't count."[4]

In the days after his firing, Stengel was deluged with job offers of all kinds. A Boise, Idaho, radio station promised him a job as a disc jockey. A Pittsburgh group wanted him to manage the world's largest Ferris wheel. More seriously, would he manage again? The Detroit job was open. Joe Gordon, traded in August to the Tigers for Jimmy Dykes, had absconded for Kansas City and a reunion with Frank Lane, the A's new GM The San Francisco Giants, who had not rehired Tom Sheehan as skipper, was another possibility. Bill Veeck was also interested, some said. Meanwhile the Yankees were busy choosing a manager of their own. A week after losing the World Series to the Pirates, Dan Topping and Del Webb held another press conference to announce the hiring of Ralph Houk, the first base coach and interim manager during Stengel's illness that summer, to pilot the club in 1961.

Houk, forty-one years old, was like John F. Kennedy a decorated World War II veteran. Smiling easily behind pale blue eyes, "the Major" exhibited a crisp, military manner that contrasted sharply with the gnarled looks and meandering phrases of the Old Perfessor. Again as with JFK, Houk was a man in his early forties about to supplant a septuagenarian legend, both Casey Stengel and President Eisenhower being 70 years old. The older generation had been replaced by that of the New Frontiersman. Houk had a limited resume compared to Stengel. But Casey was more popular with the press and the fans than he was with the players. Some of the younger Yankees, such as Tony Kubek, Bobby Richardson, and Johnny Blanchard, had played for Houk at Denver in 1955–56, and spoke highly of him.[5]

Moving quickly to assert his independence, Houk declared that he would brook no interference from the management. He was no "yes man," he said. In the coming weeks the Major indicated the direction the team would take under his leadership. The Yankees would field a set lineup, dispensing with Stengel's intriguing, but often perplexing platoon system, which some players believed undermined their effectiveness — and reduced their bargaining position at contract time.[6] Kubek would no longer be called on to do double duty at shortstop and the outfield. Richardson and Clete Boyer would no longer be humiliated by being removed for pinch-hitters prior to their first time at-bat in a game. The Yankees' biggest problem in 1960, however, had been the state of their pitching. Houk's first official act was to fire pitching coach Eddie Lopat. He was replaced by former Boston Braves ace Johnny Sain.

The changes in Yankee leadership did not end on the field. On November 2, 66-year-old George Weiss, the architect of the Yankee dynasty of the late 1940s and 1950s, stepped down as general manager, replaced by his assistant, the former Pittsburgh Pirates GM Roy Hamey. Houk and Hamey would be operating in an American League much different from that of the Stengel-Weiss era.

At a meeting at the Savoy Hilton in New York on October 26, the AL owners gave Calvin Griffith permission to move his Washington Senators club to Minneapolis-St. Paul in 1961. They also announced the admission of two additional franchises. A new Senators team would replace the old Nats in the nation's capital; another new club would be located at Los Angeles. In a surprise move, the new teams were set to begin play in 1961—a year earlier than the new New York and Houston clubs in the National League. The AL teams would play a 162-game schedule, facing each other 18 times. In Los Angeles, Mayor Norris Poulson called the AL's decision "good news."[7] White Sox GM Hank Greenberg was said to be heading a syndicate interested in purchasing the new club in the City of Angels. Casey Stengel's name immediately popped up as the franchise's new manager.

Maintaining a presence in Washington was politically astute. Given the decade-long congressional scrutiny of Major League Baseball, it was wise not to stir up the Kefauver and Cellar committees once again. However, having quashed one possible controversy by replacing the Nats in Washington, the AL owners created another stir by awarding Los Angeles a franchise. For months it had been rumored that the Kansas City Athletics would move to L.A. with the new ninth and tenth franchises operating in the former Continental League cities of Dallas and Minneapolis. Instead, the AL expansion plans had left the CL team owners out in the cold.

Bill Shea was furious at the AL owners, calling the exclusion of the CL cities "one of the worst things I ever heard of in United States sports history." He threatened to go to Congress with his complaints. Frick was not happy with the 1961 starting date — he called it "hasty and impetuous" — but he supported the AL owners against the charges of unfair play. Having reviewed the matter, the commissioner declared he was "satisfied there had been no irregularities or broken pledges by the majors." The expansion committee had made no promises to Rickey and Shea, he said. Giving first priority to the Continentals had been "strictly a ... recommendation." It soon became obvious that Shea and Rickey would get no assistance from either Senator Kefauver or Congressman Cellar, the latter delighted at the return of baseball to New York. Shea insisted that his defunct league had gotten "shabby treatment from the American League." But, he admitted, "there's nothing we can do about it now."[8]

Given the growing popularity of Major League Baseball it seemed nothing could stand in the way of expansion. In 1960, the majors had set a new attendance record: 10,684,085, a four percent increase over 1959. Season-long pennant fever had helped place Pittsburgh third in attendance in the National League, 1,705,828, behind the Los Angeles Dodgers (who set a new single-season club record of 2,253,015) and the San Francisco Giants (benefiting from the novelty, if not the convenience, of Candlestick Park). In the American League, the New York Yankees placed second in total attendance behind Veeck's Chicago White Sox. There was something to be said for colorful executives, at least as long as their ballclubs remained in contention. Frank Lane's bid for a pennant had backfired on the field and at the gate. The Cleveland Indians lost over half a million customers from the previous year. The "curse of Rocky Colavito" had begun.

Popular as baseball might have been, was it still the National Pastime? On October 30, 1960, CBS-TV opened a window into the future of American professional sports. That Sunday night, millions of viewers around the country tuned in to see a fascinating half-hour documentary narrated by Walter Cronkite titled "The Violent World of Sam Huff." At the center of the story was Huff, the New York Giants' 230-pound middle linebacker. Using the latest technology, Cronkite provided American viewers with a no-holds-barred look into the brutal, kill or get killed environment of one of professional football's fiercest competitors. The last third of the program, filmed at an exhibition game in Toronto, Canada, between the Giants and Chicago Bears was "riveting." Football demonstrated once again what a superior television sport it was compared to Major League Baseball. By placing a small portable microphone and transmitter in Huff's shoulder pads, CBS captured the graphic violence of professional football. "It's a rough game," Sam was quoted as saying. "It's no place for nice guys." (Indeed it wasn't. Three weeks earlier, Howard Glenn, a guard for the New York Titans, died of a concussion suffered in a game against the Houston Oilers.) For this piece of theater, Huff received $500 from CBS. It was the NFL that would reap the benefits in free publicity.

Pirate and Yankee players reaped the year-end baseball awards. Dick Groat, the batting champ at .325, was chosen the NL Most Valuable Player for 1960 by the Associated Press. Teammate Don Hoak came in second with 162 points. Although Groat was the team captain, Hoak was the team's "holler guy," the size of his vote recognizing his leadership skills. The Tiger wondered why Roberto Clemente did not get more recognition for his play. Ernie Banks, the NL MVP the previous two seasons, won the home run crown with 41. Hank Aaron led the league with 126 RBIs. The Red's Frank Robinson paced the league in slugging percentage, at .595; Maury Wills led the league in stolen bases with 50; Richie Ashburn drew the most walks, with 116.

Vern Law was chosen the Cy Young Award winner, beating out Warren Spahn of the Braves and two Cardinals hurlers, Ernie Broglio and Lindy McDaniel. No AL pitcher placed among the top finishers (there was only one trophy awarded at this time). Law's selection as the top pitcher in the majors in 1960 raises questions. The Deacon's record of 20–9 placed him third behind Spahn and Broglio in total wins. His 3.08 ERA was far above Broglio's 2.75. In fact, the Bucs' ace didn't rank at the top of any major pitching category except complete games — a three-way tie with the Braves' Spahn and Burdette. Nor was his WHIP particularly more impressive than that of the others. But, as they say, to the winner belong the spoils.

In the junior circuit, some familiar names dominated the statistical categories. Mantle had led the league in home runs with 40 (Maris finished second with 39). Maris led the league in RBIs with 112 (Mantle was third with 94). Maris had a slight lead in slugging percentage (.583 compared to .558). Mantle's on-base percentage was .399 to Maris' .371. In other statistical categories, Pete Runnels of Boston led the league in hitting with .320; Luis Aparicio was the stolen base king for the fifth straight year with 51; teammate Minnie Minoso led the league in hits with 184; Tito Francona was the pace-setter in doubles with 36; Eddie Yost led the junior circuit in walks with 125.

Roger Maris edged out Mickey Mantle for the AL MVP award by a mere three points. Essentially, the MVP selection was a toss up. Maris had carried the Yankees during the first half of the season. When Maris was felled with a rib injury in August, Mantle had taken up the slack, leading the Bombers to their 15 straight victories at the end of the season. Their diminutive teammate, Bobby Richardson, meanwhile won the coveted *Sport Magazine* award for World Series MVP, based on his record-shattering six RBI in one game and twelve RBIs in an entire series.

But, to this day, it is the Pirates' second sacker, Bill Mazeroski, who is most associated in the popular mind — fondly or otherwise — with the 1960 World Series. William Stanley Mazeroski was born in Wheeling, West Virginia, on September 5, 1935. He was the son of a miner, who had a promising baseball career cut short by a mining accident. The elder Mazeroski had transferred his ambitions onto his son. Sadly, he did not live to see his son's famous home run. Maz was a shy man who profited relatively little from his moment of fame. He attended an all-day ceremony at his childhood home of Tiltonsville, Ohio, and made brief appearances on *The Ed Sullivan Show*, *I've Got a Secret*, and Canadian television. But he stuck close to home for the most part that winter, watching his weight, which had been the cause of his pay cut in 1960. In fact, only Elroy Face and Hal Smith were able to cash in on the Pirate victory to any extent. Guitars in hand, Face and Smith earned approximately $7,500 that fall playing and singing "hillbilly" songs on television and on the nightclub circuit. Maz, tending to his cows on his Ohio farm, quipped, "Guess I should have learned to play the "geetar."[9] Face and Smith were invited to appear on *The Perry Como Show* (Como was a native of Canonsburg, Pennsylvania, a suburb of Pittsburgh). A UPI photo has Face, Smith, and Como gathered around a piano, "played" by no other than the Old Perfessor. The former manager pulled down four figures for his appearance on the Como show, and, in fact, cashed in far more money than any other World Series participant that winter.

The money earned by the Pirates and Yankees (winners' full share was $8,417, the losers got $5,214) was small potatoes in comparison to the millions of dollars at stake in the Major League Baseball expansion drama. Despite the lukewarm support of Commissioner Frick, the American League pressed forward with its plans to field two new teams in 1961. On November 17 AL president Joe Cronin announced that the new Washington franchise had been awarded to a group fronted by General Elwood (Pete) Quesada, a retired Air Force officer and currently administrator of the Federal Aviation Agency. Two days later the new Washington Senators selected Mickey Vernon to be the ballclub's manager. Vernon, who was then a Pirates coach, was a Nats star of the 1940s and 50s and hopefully would draw some fans to the antiquated Griffith Park.

The American League owners, however, now ran up against a much more formidable opponent than either Bill Shea or Branch Rickey—Dodger owner Walter O'Malley. An excess of two million customers had passed through the turnstiles at the Los Angeles Coliseum in 1960 to see the fourth-place Dodgers. O'Malley was not crazy about sharing his lucrative market with an AL club. He was in the midst of building a new ballpark at Chavez Ravine, and wanted to wring as many concessions as possible from Poulson and the Los Angeles city fathers "before the relatives move in."[10] O'Malley pointed out that Rule 1C of the Major League bylaws called for a *unanimous* approval of all sixteen owners in order for a new franchise to establish residency in a territory already occupied by another big league club. His vote would not come cheap.

O'Malley pointed out that he had spent a considerable amount of money moving the Dodgers to Los Angeles: $450,000 in indemnity payments to the Pacific Coast League, and another $250,000 to remodel the Coliseum (much of this to Del Webb's construction company). He was now demanding indemnification payments before allowing the AL to share the lucrative Los Angeles market. Frick, who had earlier announced New York and Los Angeles to be "open cities," now decided to back O'Malley in his bid to collect money from the new AL entry. White Sox GM Hank Greenberg was thought to have the inside track on a Los Angeles franchise, but he balked at paying indemnities to O'Malley. Greenberg soon bowed out of the competition for the new L.A. club, but not before engaging in a heated argument with Frick over O'Malley's demands.[11]

Enter Del Webb. Little known today, the Yankees co-owner had tremendous influence on American culture during the middle decades of the twentieth century. The Del Webb Construction Company, based in Phoenix, Arizona, had made a fortune during World War II soliciting U.S. Army construction contracts. When the war was over, Webb and his associates were one of the principal creators of what would become modern Las Vegas. Sun City, Arizona, one of first senior retirement communities, was also the work of the Del Webb Construction Company. So, of course, was the infamous screen at the Los Angeles Coliseum. Yankees fans coming of age in the George Steinbrenner Era are accustomed to flamboyant, public-seeking ownership. Neither Webb nor his Yankee co-owner Dan Topping craved the spotlight. They left that to Veeck, Frank Lane, and Casey Stengel. By contrast, Webb had the reputation of being a somewhat shadowy string-puller. But now Webb emerged from the shadows to meet with O'Malley in Los Angeles. On behalf of a majority of the owners (Veeck was opposed) he offered the Dodger boss $450,000 as the price for an AL entry in Los Angeles. Judging the amount insufficient, O'Malley turned down the offer.

The American League, as Frank Lane put it, had climbed up a tree and then had sawn off the branches. Having authorized Calvin Griffith's move to Minneapolis-St. Paul and awarded a new franchise in Washington, the AL now found its path to Los Angeles blocked by O'Malley. On November 2, Joe Cronin advanced a new proposal designed to get around the impasse. The new AL entry in Washington and the new NL Houston franchise would begin operation in 1961; the debut of the New York and Los Angeles clubs could wait until 1962. In order to compensate for the odd number of teams in each league under this proposal, the AL trotted out one of Bill Veeck's and Hank Greenberg's favorite ideas: interleague play. According to this plan, the nine clubs in each league would play a 166-game schedule, 54 of them against teams in the opposing league.

Actually, the idea had a great deal of merit. Given the limited ability of the new teams to sign good players, any expansion franchise was destined for the second division. An interlocking schedule would bring big stars like Mays and Mantle into town and help the new teams considerably at the gate. But Frick immediately came out against interleague play, claiming that it would dilute interest in the All-Star Game, and hurt the World Series as well.[12] In any case, what the AL really wanted was not to promote one of Veeck's pet ideas, but rather a quid pro quo with the senior circuit: entry of the American League into Los Angeles in exchange for the National League's return to New York. The Nationals naturally dismissed the idea.

On November 8, 1960, Americans went to the polls, and in one of the narrowest margins in U.S. history, a half of one percent of the vote, elected John F. Kennedy of Massachusetts as the next president of the United States. There was no closure, however, with regard to Major League expansion plans as the Winter Meetings approached. At the center of the storm was Ford Frick. It was not just the National and American Leagues that were keeping the commissioner up at night. Senator Estes Kefauver announced that he was monitoring the situation. Kefauver wanted no backsliding on expansion. With the threat of anti-trust legislation hanging over his head like the Sword of Damocles, one can hardly blame Frick for declaring the situation the "damnest baseball hassle you ever saw."[13]

In 1960, the baseball Winter Meetings were held at St. Louis. Arriving at the Park Plaza Hotel, representatives of the two leagues dispersed to their different encampments. The AL owners barricaded themselves on the mezzanine floor, the Nationals on the 26th floor. Frick was literally stuck between them, on the 22nd floor. One of the NL's first actions was to formally reject interleague play. As the commissioner fretted, the AL owners pressed forward with their expansion plans. With Hank Greenburg out of the picture, they decided to award the new L.A. franchise to a syndicate headed by former western movie and singing star Gene Autry. But the more important question remained: would Walter O'Malley yield on the question of the AL entry into L.A.? At one point, an exasperated Dan Topping exclaimed, "Let's call Branch Rickey and start the CL all over again."[14] If the leagues could not agree on a compromise, Frick would have to make the decision — something he loathed to do.

Fortunately for him, the owners took the decision out of his hands. After much consultation back and forth between floors, a deal was struck on December 8. Rule 1C was amended. The unanimous vote required for approval of any move to a previously occupied city was changed to a three-quarters vote. So much for Bill Veeck's meddling. Proceeding forward, the NL agreed to the AL's entry into Los Angeles. However, O'Malley exacted a heavy price. The new club would have to pay $100,000 plus 50 percent of the original club's moving cost. Furthermore, no new stadium could be built within five miles of the original club's park. The Autry group compliantly went along with the new rules, agreeing to pay O'Malley $100,000 as a reimbursement for the Dodgers' move to Los Angeles. They also agreed to forgo playing in the 100,000-seat Coliseum, settling instead for Wrigley Field, the former home of the Pacific Coast League entry, the Los Angeles Angels. Wrigley Field accommodated just over 20,000 fans.

The situation regarding the ownership of the Kansas City Athletics was also finally resolved. On December 19 the AL approved the sale of the A's to Charles O. Finley, a Chicago-based insurance magnate. Finley had been one of the bidders for the Los Angeles franchise, going so far as try to enlist his own western movie star, Roy Rogers, in the venture. He settled for the A's, and promised to keep the team in Kansas City. The expanded version of the American League would begin play in 1961 and the National League in 1962, as previously planned.

On December 14 the expansion draft to stock the two new franchises took place in the Boston offices of AL president Joe Cronin. The Los Angeles Angels and the new Washington Senators selected twenty-eight men out of a pool of 120 players. The pickings were slim. Each existing club was required to leave just four players unprotected, predictably most of whom were substitutes or rookies. The cost for each player was $75,000, for a total cost of $2.1 million. The Angels won the coin toss, and picked first, plucking pitcher Eli Grba from the New York Yankees. Such was his reward for his clutch pitching against the White Sox in the second game of the doubleheader at the Stadium on July 24, when a Yankee loss might have ended their quest for the pennant. The new Senators' pick was another Yankee pitcher, Bobby Shantz (he would be traded to the Pirates for the hard-luck Benny Daniels). Other Yankees drafted were Dale Long (Senators) and Bob Cerv (Angels), both important contributors in the pennant race, as well as Ken Hunt, and Duke Maas (both by the Angels). The draft had not occurred a moment too soon. Barely two months remained before spring training.

At least one player would not be packing his bags for Florida. A few days before the expansion draft took place, Gil McDougald announced his retirement from baseball. Gilbert James McDougald was born May 19, 1928, at San Francisco. He was a sensation in his first year with the Yankees in 1951, tying a Major League record with six RBIs in one inning. Finishing at .306, he became the third man, and first rookie, to hit a World Series grand-slam home run. He also won the Rookie of the Year Award, beating out Minnie Minoso. A versatile player, McDougald initially alternated between third and second base. With Phil Rizzuto clearly on the decline, he shifted to shortstop in 1956, his fine play at the new position cementing the Yankee defense for yet another World Series victory. Gil McDougald hit .311 in 1956 with .405 on-base percentage, and received some votes in the AL MVP balloting.

In May of the following year a line drive from his bat hit Cleveland Indian ace Herb Score squarely in the face. For a while it was feared that Score would lose an eye. If he did, vowed McDougald, "I'll quit this game." Score came back (although he was never the same pitcher again). Gil didn't

Gil McDougald with his family. The versatile Yankee infielder quit baseball just before the American League expansion draft following the 1960 season. "I won't be so popular in school anymore," moaned daughter Denise, 8 (at top of stairs, having hair combed).

quit, but he wasn't quite the same player afterwards either. He had hit in the .250s for three straight years and by the end of the 1960 season had had enough. The "pressure of business" (McDougald owned a maintenance firm in New Jersey) and the desire to spend more time with his wife Lucille and family weighed heavily in his decision to retire. The McDougalds had four children: Christine (12), Tod (11), Gil, Jr. (10), and Denise (8). The three older children were okay with the decision; the eldest, Chris, felt that "daddy spent too much time on the road." The youngest, Denise, however was disappointed. "I won't be so popular in school anymore," she complained. Lucille, happy to have her husband home fulltime, simply said, "I won't miss baseball and I hope he doesn't."[15]

Branch Rickey was also passing from the scene. Turning 79 on December 21, the Mahatma announced his retirement from baseball. From the comfort of his Fox Hill estate outside of Pittsburgh, Rickey could take a large measure of satisfaction in seeing the Pittsburgh Pirates, a team he had helped build, win the world championship at last. However, he acknowledged that "without the so-called travel days, which Madison Avenue imposed on the World Series, the Pirates would not have won."[16] In fact, whatever satisfaction the Mahatma took from the Bucs' victory was tempered by his unhappiness with the state of Major League Baseball in general. He considered the manner in which the entire expansion enterprise functioned to be illogical. It left, he noted, 180 million Americans in 25 cities without big league ball. It was an "extension," he scoffed, not expansion.

There was a lot of truth to what the Mahatma was saying. The baseball map, as the *Atlanta Daily World* pointed out, was a "curious shape." Placing another AL franchise in Los Angeles made demographic sense. But two cities (New Orleans and Dallas) without big league clubs were, in fact, larger than Pittsburgh in population. With four home dates in Pittsburgh, the World Series shares in 1960 were the smallest cut since 1953.[17] To most contemporaries, Rickey's statements may have seemed merely like the grumblings of a bitter old man. After all, 30 million Americans had attended Major League Baseball games, and 60 million viewers had tuned in daily to see what developed into one of the most exciting World Series ever. Baseball, said NBC sports director Tom Gallery, "still had a bulldog grip on the nation's fans."[18] Just ahead was the glorious 1961 season, featuring the "M&M Boys"—Maris and Mantle—battling for the most hallowed record in sports.

But in retrospective, one can see that the Mahatma was right. Despite the heroics of Mantle and Maris and "61 in 61," the bulldog grip was beginning to slip. On December 26, 1960, the Philadelphia Eagles enthralled Pennsylvanians once more with a 17–13 victory over the Green Bay Packers. Walking off the gridiron at Franklin Field that afternoon were two men who together symbolized the past and future of professional football. One was the Eagles' center and middle linebacker, Chuck Bednarik, the last man to play an entire 60-minute game. The other was Packers coach Vince Lombardi. Lombardi along with Johnny Unitas, Jim Brown, Sam Huff, Joe Namath, and Pete Rozelle constituted the shadow hovering over Major League Baseball. To be sure, future years would see both great plays and great players in Major League Baseball. Curt Flood would ignite a revolution in player-management relations. But the coming decades would also see professional football emerge as the true National Pastime. Whether the Mahatma's third major league or his more comprehensive expansion plans would have made a difference, is anybody's guess. What we do know is that with the 1960 season, Major League Baseball's last two decades of dominance as America's premier sport, its last Golden Era, was coming to an end.

Epilogue

On February 17, 1962, sixteen months after his firing by the New York Yankees, Casey Stengel, decked in a blue suit and brown alligator shoes, ambled into Maas Brothers Department Store in St. Petersburg, Florida. For the next three hours he signed autographs, traded quips with customers, and mugged for cameras — this time, as the manager of the New York Mets. Branch Rickey and Bill Shea had tried to create a rival Continental League team in New York to compete with the Bronx Bombers. The Continental League folded in August 1960, but the residue of Shea and Rickey's design, the expansion Mets, had a decidedly Yankee aura. The Old Perfessor was the field manager and George Weiss had come out of retirement to become the club's GM. The Mets also replaced the Yankees as the tenants at Miller Huggins Field, the Bombers having left St. Petersburg for their new spring training facilities at Ft. Lauderdale.

The change in teams was not all that had occurred, since Casey had last been at St. Petersburg in April 1960. Unlike the Yankees of yesteryear, the Met players (except those accompanied by their families) were living together at a private wing of the Colonial Inn, with access to their own swimming pool and dining room. The days were over when black ballplayers, like the Yankees' Elston Howard or Boston's Pumpsie Green, had been forced to seek living accommodations apart from their teammates. It was now the age of what Yankee owner Dan Topping called "the one roof policy."[1]

"One roof" was also finally the policy at Cooperstown, with Jackie Robinson having been recently inducted into the Baseball Hall of Fame on his first try, along with Bob Feller, Edd Roush, and Bill McKechnie. By this time, according to the *Atlanta Daily World* and many other pundits, professional football had overtaken Major League Baseball as the nation's National Pastime.[2] But it would do well to remember that, at the time of Robinson's election, the NFL's Washington Redskins, under the antediluvian ownership of George Preston Marshall, had yet to place a black player on the field.

The "one roof policy" extended to Major League Baseball itself. Both circuits would have the same number of clubs and play an equal number of games. In Florida, a new Grapefruit League season was getting underway. On March 13, 1962, the Mets traveled to Ft. Myers to meet the team that had hastened Casey's departure as Yankee manager a year and a half earlier. On the this afternoon at Terry Field, the Mets raised their spring training record to 3–1, by defeating Harvey Haddix and the Pittsburgh Pirates, 4–0.

Things had not gone well for the Pirates since Bill Mazeroski had jubilantly rounded the bases on October 13, 1960. The Pirates had slipped deep into the second division in 1961. The Pirates could still muster some hitting. Dick Groat had plunged to .275, but Smoky Burgess and Don Hoak both hit around .300, while Dick Stuart hit 35 home runs and drove in 117. Roberto Clemente replaced Groat as the National League batting champion, with a .351 average, and won the prestigious Dapper Dan Award. Clemente, the *Pittsburgh Courier* proudly noted, was the first "tan player at the head of the table."[3]

It was the pitching staff that bedeviled the Bucs, but with no Law, a bad Friend, a sad Face, and more vinegar than Vinegar Bend. Only Haddix had managed a winning record. It was a real come down for Danny Murtaugh. Sixth-place managers, he ruefully observed, "don't get invited to many banquets.[4]

But he would see happier days. Murtaugh had a history of heart problems, and health considerations forced his retirement at the end of the 1964 season. After a brief stint in 1967, he came back fulltime to managing in 1970 and led the Pirates to their thrilling seven-game victory over the Baltimore Orioles in the 1971 World Series. He retired once again in 1972, but came back for three final seasons in 1974–76. The Irishman died in his home town of Chester, Pennsylvania, at age 59, on December 2, 1976.

The man who many thought would succeed Danny Murtaugh as Pirates manager instead preceded him to the grave. Don Hoak retired in 1966 and became a Pirate broadcaster and then minor league manager. He led the Triple-A Columbus Jets to the finals of the International League championship in 1969. On December 9 of that year, Tiger took off on a chase after his brother-in-law's stolen car. He was found slumped over the wheel, dead of a heart attack at age 41.

Another rescue mission claimed the life of the Bucs' star right fielder. Roberto Clemente, who had garnered his 3,000th (and last) hit at the end of the 1972 season, was a passenger in plane carrying relief supplies to survivors of a Nicaraguan earthquake. On December 31, 1972, the plane crashed shortly after takeoff in San Juan, Puerto Rico, raising Roberto from superstar to legendary figure. Clemente was inducted into the Hall of Fame in a special election in 1973.

The 1990s saw the deaths of four more Pirates from the 1960 championship season. Smoky Burgess died at Asheville, North Carolina, on September 9, 1991, at age 64. He ranks third on the all-time career pinch-hit list with 145. Harvey Haddix was 68 years old when he died at Springfield, Ohio, on January 8, 1994. The Kitten will always be remembered for his 12-inning no-hitter against the Milwaukee Braves. But he liked to remind people that he was the winning pitcher in the fifth and seventh games of the 1960 World Series. Wilmer (Vinegar Bend) Mizell was also 68 when he passed away at Kerville, Texas, on February 21, 1999. Vinegar Bend, who ended his career with the Mets, defied his rube image by serving as a Republican congressman from North Carolina between 1969 and 1975. Gene Baker died at 74 on December 1, 1999, in his native Davenport, Iowa. In 1963 he became the second black coach in the major leagues, under Danny Murtaugh.

The new millennium has claimed the lives of the Bucs' first base platoon from the 1960 championship year. Dick Stuart succumbed to cancer at Redwood City, California, on December 12, 2002, at age 70. Stuart put up some huge numbers after being traded to the Boston Red Sox. But Dr. Strangeglove will always be remembered for his whimsical fielding. The International League legend, Rocky Nelson, who finally found a home with the Pirates, died at age 81 in his native Portsmouth, Ohio, on October 31, 2006.

On July 13, 2010, a reunion was held at the Pittsburgh Pirates' new park commemorating the 50th anniversary of the 1960 championship season. Attending were pitchers Vern Law, Bob Friend, Elroy Face, and Joe Gibbon; catcher Bob Oldis; outfielders Joe Christopher, Bob Skinner, and Bill Virdon; and infielders Dick Groat, Dick Schofield, and Bill Mazeroski.

Also in attendance was 92-year-old former general manager Joe L. Brown (he died on August 22, 2010).

Vern Law, 80, never quite recovered his Cy Young Award winning form. He retired from the Pirates in 1967. His son, Chicago Cub third baseman Vance Law, was selected for the 1988 All-Star team, making the Laws one of the few father-son All-Stars in baseball history. Bob Skinner, 78, also retired in 1967 and managed the Philadelphia Phillies for parts of two seasons. The son that his wife Joan was carrying during the 1960 season, Joel Skinner, was a major league catcher on several teams, in the 1980s, including the Yankees.

Bob Friend, 79, finished his career in 1966 with the Yankees and Mets, in effect, becoming the first major league player to wear both Yankee and Met uniforms. In the late 1960s the Purdue University alumnus was on the search committee (along with Robin Roberts, Harvey Kuenn, and Jim Bunning) that hired Marvin Miller as the executive director of the players union. In the 1980s, Friend's name cropped up again and again as Pete Rose was making his assault on the all-time hit record. Rose's first major league hit had come against Friend on April 13, 1963.

Elroy Face turned to carpentry after his retirement in 1969. Now 82, the Baron still holds the all-time record for wins by a relief pitcher with 96. Elroy Face is not in the Hall of Fame, despite his pioneering role in the development of the relief specialist. Although he's had his supporters, his 193 saves have become less and less impressive over the years. But, to paraphrase Billy Wilder, it's not Face who has gotten small but the game itself, with its mind-numbing parade of pitchers combining to carry the load that the Baron had once borne alone on his stocky 5' 8" frame.

One of the surviving Pirates was missing from the July 2010 celebration. Hal W. Smith, 79, lives in Columbus, Texas. "As soon as I hit it," he recalls regarding his dramatic seventh-inning homer in the final game of the 1960 World Series, "I knew I'd hit it out of the park." Many fans still congratulate Hal Smith on his home run, only it's often the other Hal Smith, the former catcher for the St. Louis Cardinals, who gets the accolades.[5]

Bill Virdon, now 79, lives in Springfield, Missouri. After his retirement in 1968, he went on to manage the Pirates, Yankees, Astros, and Expos between 1972 and 1984. He was the AL Manager of the Year in 1974, and the NL Manager of the Year with the Houston Astros in 1980. Virdon also has the distinction of being the first manager fired by George Steinbrenner.

Dick Groat was traded to the St. Louis Cardinals after the 1962 season. Two years later he was once again in the Fall Classic against the New York Yankees, helping to lead the Redbirds to a seven-game World Series victory over the Bombers team managed by Yogi Berra. Recalling the 1960 series, Groat, now 79, contends that Bill Virdon's delayed steal in Game One had been a happy accident. Groat, it turns out, had given Virdon the hit-and-run sign by mistake.

Bill Mazeroski, 73, was, along with Roberto Clemente, one of only two men from the 1960 team to play with the 1971 World Champion Pittsburgh Pirates. He and Clemente are also the only two players from the team elected to the Baseball Hall of Fame. Mazeroski was inducted in 2001. He recalls sitting in Schenley Park after the seventh game of the 1960 World Series with his wife and "a couple of squirrels," surveying the madness that erupted after his historic home run.[6]

Casey Stengel's public appearance at Maas Brothers on February 17, 1960, was a side show in a much bigger game, that of competing for the entertainment dollar in New York City with the mighty Yankees. On March 22, 1962, when the Bombers arrived at St. Petersburg for a game with the fledgling Mets, Casey was as always the center of attention. His successor, Ralph Houk, bounded from the dugout "as if flung like a catapult" to greet his old boss. Mickey Mantle sidled over sheepishly to say hello to his ex-manager. The Old Perfessor was full of good humor. Looking Yogi up and down, he quipped, "Mr. Berra, you seem to have slimmed down running to the dog track." "Not me," protested Yogi, "I haven't been there once this year." Turning to Héctor López, Casey cried, "Hello, amigo. Got three of them fellers on my team now, which is why I now speak your language."[7] Despite the Cuban Embargo the parade of international players continued.

Under Houk, the Bombers marched to their second straight pennant, vanquishing the Cincinnati Reds in five games in the 1961 World Series. But on this day at Miller Huggins Field, it was the underdog's day to shine. The 6,277 spectators saw the Mets defeat the Yankees in their first ever contest, 4–3. The victory was no doubt sweet. Phil Rizzuto had been quoted as saying that the Yankees would not have won the pennant in 1961 with Stengel as manager.[8] Casey did not win any pennants with the Mets. But he did make them a lovable, and therefore, a profitable commodity in New York City before his retirement in August 1965. The following year he was inducted into the Baseball Hall of Fame. He died at Glendale, California, on September 29, 1975.

Elston Howard, the first black player on the Yankees, died of a heart attack on December 14, 1980, at the age of 51. Howard won the AL Most Valuable Player Award in 1963. Traded to Boston in 1967, he helped the Red Sox win their first AL pennant since 1946. He retired a year later and rejoined the Yankees as the first black coach in the American League.

Exactly five years to the day after Howard's death, on December 14, 1985, Roger Maris died of cancer at Houston, Texas. Maris never came close to duplicating his MVP years of 1960–61. Plagued by injuries, he was traded to St. Louis after the 1966 season. Roger was a member of the pennant-winning Cardinal teams of 1967–68. Long estranged from the Yankees, he returned for Old-Timers Day on July 22, 1984. That day the Yankees retired the number 9 that Maris first wore in 1960 along with Howard's number 32.

Mickey Mantle won his third AL MVP award in 1962. Hobbled by injuries, his career proceeded on a steady decline until his retirement in 1968. Mantle's well publicized addiction to alcohol did nothing to dim the affection of the New York fans, but it did hasten his death at age 63 on August 13, 1995.

The Yankees' double play combination of Bobby Richardson and Tony Kubek remained intact until Kubek's retirement in 1965. Richardson quit a year later. Kubek was a long-time broadcaster for NBC Television's "Game of the Week." Richardson returned to his native South Carolina and entered politics in the 1976. A born-again Christian and lay minister, he conducted the service at Mickey Mantle's funeral.

Mantle's pallbearers included the two then-surviving catchers from the 1960 Yankees team, Yogi Berra and Johnny Blanchard. The super sub Blanchard died March 25, 2009, in Robbinsdale, Minnesota, at age 76. He is buried at Ft. Snelling, the place visited by Dred Scott a century and a half earlier in his short taste of freedom. Berra managed the 1964 Yankees and 1973 Mets to pennants, the only manager to do so. He is still bitter about the 1960 loss to the Pirates, believing that Casey should have pitched Whitey Ford in the seventh game instead of Art Ditmar (he meant Bob Turley).

Bill Skowron was also a pallbearer at Mickey's funeral. After being traded to the Los Angeles Dodgers, Moose helped his new team sweep the Yankees in the 1963 World Series. As for the Moose's keystone mates, Clete

Boyer was traded to the Atlanta Braves, where he had his best power years. He died at Lawrenceville, Georgia, on June 4, 2007. Gil McDougald, whose name is forever linked to Herb Score, eventually went totally deaf as the result of a being hit with a line drive in practice in 1955. A miracle operation restored his hearing in 1995. He died in Wall, New Jersey, on November 28, 2010.

As befits the Steinbrenner "win or else" approach, the 2010 Old-Timers Day at the new Yankee Stadium on July 17 commemorated the sixtieth anniversary of the 1950 championship season. Yogi and Whitey are the sole survivors of the World Series victory over Philadelphia's Whiz Kids. Going unrecognized at the Bronx that afternoon were Bob Turley, Art Ditmar, Jim Coates, Ralph Terry, Bobby Shantz, Luis Arroyo, Héctor López, and other protagonists in one of the most dramatic Fall Classics ever.

Branch Rickey signed on as a special consultant on player personnel with the St. Louis Cardinals in 1962. He retired for good in 1964, but not before seeing his old team win a world championship against his old antagonist, the New York Yankees. On November 14, 1965, while giving a speech at his induction into the Missouri Hall of Fame, the Mahatma collapsed from a heart attack. Hospitalized for a month, he died on December 9, at age 83. The following year he was elected to the Baseball Hall of Fame in Cooperstown. Bill Shea remained active in New York area sports for another three decades. He joked that Shea Stadium would be renamed "fifteen minutes after I die."[9] The name remained, though, for nearly two decades after Shea died on October 3, 1991, in New York City until the facility closed at the end of the 2008 baseball season.

Shea Stadium is gone now, as are Forbes Field and the old Yankee Stadium. Indeed, the afternoon shadows that bedeviled many a left fielder in many a Fall Classic are a thing of the past. World Series games in the Bronx are now played at night, in deference to the higher television ratings polled by pro football.

Notes

Abbreviations of Frequently Used Sources

BD	*Baseball Digest*
NYHT	*New York Herald-Tribune*
NYT	*New York Times*
PP	*Pittsburgh Press*
PPG	*Pittsburgh Post Gazette*
SEP	*Saturday Evening Post*
SI	*Sports Illustrated*
SM	*Sport Magazine*
TSN	*The Sporting News*

Chapter One

1. U.S. Census, 1960.
2. *Miami Herald*, December 7, 1959.
3. *Atlanta Daily World*, December 16, 1959.
4. *NYT*, December 9, 1959.
5. Ibid., October 4, 1991.
6. Joe Garagiola, *Baseball is a Funny Game* (New York: Lippincott, 1960), p. 70.
7. *PPG*, December 11, 1959; *PP*, December 11, 1959.
8. *PPG*, December 15, 29, 1959; *TSN*, January 13, 1960.
9. *SI*, October 10, 1960.
10. *NYT*, December 28, 1960.

Chapter Two

1. *NYT*, January 1, 1960; *TSN*, January 3, 1960.
2. *NYHT*, January 12, 1960.

3. *NYT*, January 12, 30, 1960.
4. *NYHT*, January 12, 1960; *SN*, January 13, 1960.
5. *NYT*, January 30, 1960.
6. *TSN*, March 9, 1960.
7. *Miami Herald*, January 23, 1960.
8. *NYHT*, January 31, 1960.
9. *SM*, April 1960.
10. *NYHT*, January 16, 1960.
11. *NYT*, January 21, 1960; *Newark Evening News*, January 21, 1960.
12. *Chicago Tribune*, July 12, 1957.
13. *NYT*, January 29, 1960; *NYHT*, January 28, 29, 1960.
14. *PPG*, January 7–8, 1960.
15. *TSN*, January 6, 1960.
16. *NYT*, January 31, 1960.

Chapter Three

1. *NYT*, February 4–5, 1960; *BD*, February 1960.
2. Roger Angell, *The Summer Game* (New York: Viking, 1972), p. 1.
3. Danny Murtaugh File, Baseball Hall of Fame, Cooperstown, N.Y.
4. *BD*, April 1960.
5. *NYT*, August 7, 1953.
6. *Los Angeles Sentinel*, March 17, 1960.
7. *Pittsburgh Courier*, December 19, 1960.
8. Kenneth Jackson, *Crabgrass Frontier: The Suburbanization of American Culture* (New York: Oxford University Press, 1985).
9. Robert Caro, *The Power Broker: Robert Moses and the Fall of New York* (New York: Knopf, 1974).
10. *NYT*, February 13, 1960.

Chapter Four

1. *NYT*, October 4, 1957.
2. *TSN*, March 2, 1960.
3. *BD*, February 1960; *SEP*, April 16, 1960.
4. *PPG*, March 1960.
5. *BD*, February 1961.
6. *PPG*, August 17, 1960.
7. *SI*, March 7, 1960.
8. Jim Brosnan, *The Long Season* (Chicago: Harper, 1960), p. 8; *SI*, March 28, 1960.
9. *SI*, March 28, 1960.
10. *Atlanta Daily World*, March 17, 1960.
11. *SEP*, June 16, 1960.
12. *PPG*, March 7, 14, 1960; *PP*, April 2, 1960; *Atlanta Daily World*, March 23, 1960.
13. *PP*, April 10, 1960.

Chapter Five

1. *Cincinnati Post*, April 12, 1960: *TSN*, March 15, 1961.
2. *NYHT*, August 27, 1960.
3. *NYT*, April 13, 1960.
4. Ibid.
5. *Philadelphia Inquirer*, April 15, 25, 1960.
6. *PP*, April 23, 1960.
7. *Boston Herald*, April 20, 1960.
8. *SEP*, May 21, 1960.
9. Ibid., April 4, 1959.
10. *NYT*, April 20, 1960.
11. *PP*, June 30, 1960.
12. *NYT*, May 30, 1960.
13. Whitey Ford File, Baseball Hall of Fame, Cooperstown, N.Y.
14. *NYT*, April 29, 1960.
15. Ibid., May 1, 1960.

Chapter Six

1. *Chicago Tribune*, May 5, 1960.
2. *Los Angeles Times*, February 21, June 10, 1958; *NYT*, April 18, 30, 1958; January 17, 1959.
3. *SEP*, March 12, 1960.
4. *PPG*, January 21, August 24, 1960.
5. *NYT*, May 5, 1960.
6. Ibid., May 6–7, 1960.
7. *SEP*, April 4, 1960.
8. *NYT*, May 13, 1960.
9. *PPG*, May 10, 13, 1960; *NYT*, May 17, 1960.
10. *PPG*, May 25, 1960.
11. *Street and Smith's 1961 Baseball Yearbook.*
12. *NYT*, May 20, 1960.
13. *Chicago Tribune*, May 16, 1959.
14. Ibid., September 10, 1959.
15. Bill Veeck, *Veeck As In Wreck* (Chicago: Putnam's Sons, 1962), pp. 339, 342–43.
16. *PPG*, May 28, 1960.

Chapter Seven

1. *PPG*, June 10, 1960.
2. *PP*, June 8, 1960.
3. *NYT*, June 15, 1960.
4. Ibid., June 21, 1960.
5. *New Amsterdam News*, December 2, 1959; *Atlanta Daily World*, June 6, 1960.
6. *SM*, June 1960.
7. *San Francisco Chronicle*, June 6, 8, 1960.

8. *BD*, February 1960.
9. Brosnan, *Long Season*, p. 224.
10. *San Francisco Chronicle*, June 19, 20, 1960.
11. *SM*, March 1960.
12. *TSN*, January 3, 1960; *BD*, February 1960.
13. *Cleveland Plain Dealer*, June 25, 1960.
14. *New York Journal American*, June 6, 1960.
15. David Nasaw, *Andrew Carnegie* (New York: Penguin, 2006), pp. 514–17.

Chapter Eight

1. *NYT*, July 4, 1960.
2. *Washington Post*, March 13, 1955; April 4, 1956; September 25, 1958.
3. *BD*, March 1960.
4. *PPG*, July 8, 1960.
5. *Philadelphia Inquirer*, July 11, 1960.
6. *Kansas City Star*, July 11, 1960.
7. *NYT*, December 9, 1960.
8. Ibid., July 21–22, 1960.
9. *PPG*, August 1, 1960.
10. *NYT*, July 12, 16, 23, 1960; August 21, 1960.
11. *NYHT*, August 1, 1960.

Chapter Nine

1. *NYT*, August 2, 1960.
2. Ibid., August 3, 1960.
3. Ibid.
4. *PP*, August 8, 1960.
5. *Detroit Free Press*, August 5, 1960.
6. Yogi Berra and Ed Fitzgerald, *Yogi* (Garden City, NY: Doubleday, 1961), pp. 218–19.
7. *PPG*, August 31, 1960.
8. Ibid., August 12, 1960.
9. Don Hoak File, Baseball Hall of Fame, Cooperstown, N.Y.
10. *PP*, October 4, 1960.
11. *PPG*, July 27, 1960.
12. *NYT*, August 28, 1960.
13. *Cincinnati Reds 1960 Yearbook*; *Chicago Tribune*, August 10, 1960.
14. *St. Louis Cardinals 1960 Yearbook*.
15. *Chicago Tribune*, August 24, 1960.
16. *Kansas City Star*, August 31, 1960.
17. *Kansas City Athletics 1960 Yearbook*.
18. David McCullough, *The Path Between the Seas* (New York: Simon and Schuster, 1977), pp. 465–75.

Chapter Ten

1. *Baltimore Sun*, August 15, 1960.
2. *SI*, September 19, 1960.
3. *SM*, August 1960.
4. *Ebony*, August 1960.
5. Dick Groat File, Baseball Hall of Fame, Cooperstown, N.Y.
6. *NYT*, September 16, 1960.
7. Ibid., September 14, 1960; *PPG*, September 17, 1960.
8. *Baltimore Sun*, September 16, 1960.
9. Bobby Richardson File, Baseball Hall of Fame, Cooperstown, N.Y.
10. *SEP*, April 15, 1961.
11. *PPG*, September 24–25, 1960.
12. *TSN*, June 21, 1961.
13. *PPG*, September 26, 27, 1960.
14. *NYT*, September 26, 1960.

Chapter Eleven

1. *NYT*, October 8, 1960.
2. *PP*, October 5, 1960.
3. *PPG*, October 12, 1960.
4. Ibid., October 3, 1960.
5. *NYT*, October 6, 1960.
6. Bill Virdon File, Baseball Hall of Fame, Cooperstown, N.Y.
7. *NYT*, October 6, 1960.
8. *NYHT*, October 7, 1960.
9. *PPG*, October 7, 1960.
10. Bob Cerv File, Baseball Hall of Fame, Cooperstown, N.Y.
11. *PP*, October 9, 1960.
12. Ibid., October 10, 1960.
13. *NYT*, October 6, 1960.
14. *PPG*, October 14, 23, 1960.
15. *NYT*, October 6; *PPG*, October 14, 15, 1960.

Chapter Twelve

1. *NYT*, October 18, 1960.
2. *NYT*, October 19, 1960; *NYHT*, October 19, 1960; *Baltimore Sun*, October 19, 1960; *Chicago Tribune*, October 19, 1960.
3. *NYHT*, October 19–20, 1960; *NYT*, October 19–20, 1960; *Chicago Tribune*, October 19, 1960.
4. Theodore White, *The Making of the President 1960* (New York: Atheneum, 1961), p. 298.
5. *BD*, February 1961.
6. *SEP*, April 16, 1960.
7. *Los Angeles Times*, October 27, 1960.

8. *Washington Post*, October 29, 1960; *NYT*, November 2, 1960.
9. *PPG*, November 9, 1960.
10. *Los Angeles Times*, November 22, 1960.
11. Veeck, *Veeck As In Wreck*, pp. 360–61.
12. Ibid., pp 364–65.
13. *Los Angeles Times*, December 8, 1960.
14. *Newark Evening News*, December 12, 1960.
15. Ibid., December 10, 1960; *NYT*, December 10, 1960.
16. *PPG*, December 11, 1960.
17. *Washington Post*, December 21, 1960; *Atlanta Daily World*, December 14, 1960.
18. *NBC Complete Baseball*, 1961, p. 3.

Epilogue

1. *Chicago Defender*, February 17, 1962.
2. *Atlanta Daily World*, March 2, 1962.
3. *Pittsburgh Courier*, February 2, 1962.
4. *NYT*, March 13, 1962.
5. Norman Macht, "Hal Smith Was Famous For Fifteen Minutes," presentation at SABR meeting of the Rogers Hornsby Chapter, September 14, 2009.
6. *PPG*, July 14, 2010.
7. *NYT*, March 23, 1962.
8. *SI*, March 19, 1962.
9. *NYT*, October 4, 1991.

Bibliography

In this book, I have tried to capture the 1960 baseball season as it evolved, not as a series of reminiscences. I wanted to record and comment on what was said and done at the time, not what was remembered or imagined fifty years later. For this reason I have focused mostly on sources nearer to the times when these events occurred, such as newspapers, contemporary sports magazines, and publicity material provided by the major league teams themselves. To get a more general sense of the times, I have relied on a number of secondary sources. In addition to the ones cited in the footnotes, they include:

Secondary Sources

Branch, Taylor. *Parting the Waters: America in the King Years, 1954–1963*. New York: Simon & Schuster, 1988.

Callahan, Tom. *Johnny U: The Life and Times of John Unitas*. New York: Crown, 2006.

Creamer, Robert W. *Stengel: His Life and Times*. New York: Simon & Schuster, 1984.

Einstein, Charles. *Willie's Time: A Memoir of Another America*. New York: Lippincott, 1979.

Golenbock, Peter. *Dynasty: The New York Yankees, 1949–1964*. Englewood Cliffs, NJ: Prentice-Hall, 1975.

Maraniss, David. *Clemente: The Passion and Grace of Baseball's Last Hero*. New York: Simon & Schuster, 2007.

1960 Photo and Autograph Baseball Album. New York: JKW Sports, 1960.

Reidenbaugh, Lowell. *Take Me Out to the Ball Park*. 2d ed. St. Louis: The Sporting News, 1987.

Schwed, Fred, Jr. *How to Watch a Baseball Game*. New York: Harper, 1957.

Silverman, Al, ed. *Inside Baseball, 1961*. New York: Bartholomew House, 1961.

Singletary, Wes. *Florida's First Big League Baseball Players: A Narrative History*. Charleston, SC: History Press, 2006.

Spink, J.G. Taylor, comp. *Baseball Register*. 1960 ed. St. Louis: The Sporting News, 1960.

Wolff, Rick, et al., eds. *The Baseball Encyclopedia*. 8th ed. New York: Macmillan, 1990.

Index